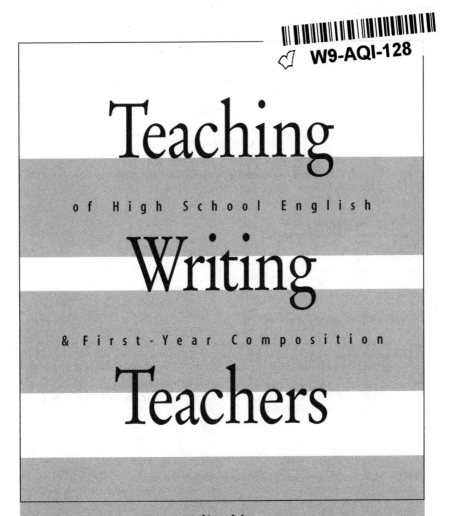

Teaching

of High School English

Writing

& First-Year Composition

Teachers

Edited by
Robert Tremmel & William Broz

Foreword by Richard Gebhardt

Boynton/Cook Publishers
HEINEMANN
Portsmouth, NH

As editors we dedicate this book to
our first teachers of writing pedagogy:
James Britton
Richard Hootman
Richard Lloyd-Jones
Carl Klaus
and
Cleo Martin,
and to our contributors,
without whom there would be no book.

Boynton/Cook Publishers, Inc.
A subsidiary of Reed Elsevier Inc.
361 Hanover Street
Portsmouth, NH 03801–3912
www.boyntoncook.com

Offices and agents throughout the world

© 2002 by Boynton/Cook Publishers, Inc.

An earlier version of the introduction was published in the October 2001 issue of *English Education* under the title, "Seeking a Balanced Discipline: Writing Teacher Education in First-Year Composition and English Education."

Library of Congress Cataloging-in-Publication Data
Teaching writing teachers of high school English and first-year composition / edited by Robert Tremmel and William Broz ; foreword by Richard Gebhardt.
    p.   cm.
Includes bibliographical references.
    ISBN 0-86709-511-3 (pbk. : alk. paper)
    1. English language—Composition and exercises—Study and teaching (Secondary).
2. English language—Rhetoric—Study and teaching.   3. English teachers—Training of.
I. Tremmel, Robert, 1948–   II. Broz, William.
    PE1404. T42 2002
    808'.042'071—dc21

                                                                    2001007471

Editor: James Strickland
Production service: Lisa Garboski/bookworks
Production coordination: Vicki Kasabian
Cover design: Joni Doherty
Typesetter: G&S Typesetters, Inc.
Manufacturing: Steve Bernier

Printed in the United States of America on acid-free paper
06   05   04   03   02   DA   1   2   3   4   5

Contents

Contents

Foreword

During the years he edited *College Composition and Communication,* Edward
P. J. Corbett also served as Advisor on the Executive Committee of the Ohio
Council of Teachers of English Language Arts, an NCTE affiliate that chiefly
serves the state's K–12 language arts and English teachers. When Ed's terms
in both positions ended in 1979, OCTELA honored him by mailing its members *Composition and Its Teaching,* a compact collection of *CCC* articles he
had published — articles which were nominated by a group of composition and
English education faculty at Ohio colleges and then rated by a panel of Ohio
high school and junior high school teachers. OCTELA's officers did this because they "decided that a fitting honor for a man who had worked so hard
to professionalize the teaching of writing should help to strengthen writing instruction in Ohio."

   As the editor of OCTELA's journal, I wrote the introduction and was "especially pleased to develop a collection chosen by secondary as well as college
teachers, because I [was] convinced that *CCC* is a valuable resource for junior
and senior high school teachers facing public pressure to teach writing under
teaching conditions that make writing instruction difficult."

   That story and that editing project from nearly a quarter-century ago came
to mind as I looked through the manuscript of *Teaching Writing Teachers of
High School English and First-Year Composition.* What all of these represent
together is "the common heritage and natural alliance" between English education and college composition, a phrase from Robert Tremmel's introduction
that informs the book as a whole.

   At the same time, they illustrate another of Tremmel's themes: that in spite
of early promises of unity, "writing teacher education in first-year composition
and English education has since developed along separate . . . tracks. . . ." Seeds
of unity seem present in the situation I sketched — a leading figure in rhetoric
playing a role in precollege teaching, and secondary and college teachers sens-
ing that articles by college composition specialists would be useful for secondary teachers. If those seeds — and others Tremmel outlines in his introduction
and a longer essay in October 2001 *English Education* — had grown into full
flower over the past twenty-five years or so, Robert Tremmel and William Broz
wouldn't have needed to develop their book. Such a flowering, of course, hasn't
taken place, which is suggested by a few passages from the book:

Composition studies and English education are just beginning to understand
the reciprocal nature of their fields.

Jonathan Bush, "Common Ground"

English educators and writing program administrators have been engaged in
many of the same disciplinary labors for over half a century, [but] . . . they currently live separate academic lives, fenced off from each other in largely separate bureaucratic compounds.

Robert Tremmel, "Striking a Balance"

[T]here are . . . tensions . . . between compositionists at the university and
teachers in the school. The same, moreover, is true of writing-teacher educators in first-year composition and in English education programs. While compositionists at the university may indulge in such notions as "post-process"
theory . . . , teachers in the schools must continue to generate fresh writing assignments and think of inventive ways to engage students in rhetorical activities. And whereas the first generation of writing theorists thought little of the
distinction between "English Ed" and "Comp/Rhet," it seems unusual today
for the two to meet up.

Dan Royer and Roger Gilles, "Combining History, Theory, and Practice"

Despite what I see as real progress . . . , English teacher educators have yet to
settle on a full commitment to viewing themselves as professional writing
teacher educators. For one thing, some courses and programs fall short of fully
representing the discipline by under-representing theory and over-balancing
toward practice.

Robert Tremmel, "Striking a Balance"

Teaching Writing Teachers seeks to address such blocks—lack of awareness, patterns of university organization, competing scholarly emphases, professional egos—to unity and greater effectiveness in the preparation of writing
teachers. It does this by giving twenty informed writing educators space to present specific course- and program-related ideas about preparing teachers for
first-year composition and secondary English classes. It also reflects on connections (or the lack of them) in the education of these teachers.

In addition, it challenges those of us involved in either kind of teacher education to think of ourselves as working much more closely together. Tremmel
raises the issue, when he says that his reading of our history gives him

a strong sense of the common heritage and natural alliance between English
education and first-year composition, between grades 7–12 and grade 13. All
of us engaged in this work . . . are writing teachers and teachers of writing
teachers. All of us . . . are moving along more-or-less together despite considerable political and bureaucratic forces that conspire to keep our path dissected and obscured.

So Tremmel suggest that we start "discussions about what life would be like if we were to remove some of the impediments that keep us apart." "And while we're at it," he adds, "why shouldn't we start acting as if writing teacher education itself deserves some kind of disciplinary status?"

How we might begin uniting the "two areas of study, forming a single, unified discipline" is a concern of Stephen Wilhoit's "Identifying Common Concerns: A Response to 'Striking a Balance'." Wilhoit writes that "[a]s a discipline, Writing Teacher Education would truly cut across traditional disciplinary lines, uniting faculty in English with faculty in education, closing the gap between secondary school and college instruction, and forging links between English TAs and education majors." And he adds that Tremmel's vision is "compelling but fraught with complications":

> What would such an alliance look like? Where would it find a home on today's campuses? How could it find a common language and speak with a common voice? How could it overcome the barriers of distrust, misunderstanding, arrogance, and neglect that have built up over the years between English education and English?

To those issues, I would add another, one implicit in the suggestion to seek disciplinary status in what Tremmel describes as "the current climate of tribalism and specialization in English studies." Identifying, and identifying with, a separate academic discipline of Writing Teacher Education could mean one more tribe—women and men preparing people to teach writing through grade thirteen—fighting border skirmishes with such groups as people concerned with writing and rhetoric in post-postsecondary and graduate school, those most interested in training K–12 teachers of literature and reading, people committed to the idea of integrated language arts in the schools, and those equally committed to writing across the university curriculum.

I raise this issue not because I disagree about the need for connection, understanding, and mutual support among teachers of writing teachers. Rather I fear that "disciplinary" bickering and competition for resources would undermine those goals. So I put my hope in intensive efforts by concerned professionals to encourage the interdisciplinary connections and mutual efforts that exist, and have long existed, in what Bob Tremmel and Bill Broz's book so clearly shows to be a *de facto* field of writing-teacher education.

I have in mind, here, the spirit behind my opening anecdote: Ed Corbett's sense that there was a role for him, one of the world's foremost rhetoricians and the editor of the leading composition journal, in an organization serving K–12 English teachers in his state. I was there on the executive committee, too— a future editor of *CCC* who at the time was directing first-year writing at Findlay College and also teaching the junior-level Teaching of Writing course whose development during the early 1970s allowed me to write "Balancing Theory with Practice in the Training of Writing Teachers." That article had some influence on writing-teacher education (or at least I've heard, over the years, from quite a few people who used ideas from it in TA preparation programs and in undergraduate courses for future secondary teachers), and so did the little book OCTELA published (I heard from people about it, too). But I would not have written the article—and maybe I wouldn't have gotten so involved in the NCTE affiliate that I was there to edit the book—if my job hadn't called, at once, for teaching in and directing a first-year writing course and helping third- and fourth-year students prepare to teach writing in the schools.

Such dual opportunities (and burdens) come to many faculties across the country. I have in mind, for example, the rhetoric faculty at Bowling Green State University. Members of the group direct the university's first-year writing program, advise Secondary Integrated Language Arts majors, participate in a university professional development program for teachers in area schools, lead seminars and direct dissertations for the Rhetoric & Writing PhD, and teach key courses for the Integrated Language Arts major (Grammar and Writing, Linguistics, Advanced Writing, Teaching of Writing, and English Methods). I'm thinking, as well, of the college and university faculty members—writing specialists and English educators—who provide K–12 teachers with continuing professional education in the teaching of writing through their work with regional and state Writing Projects. And, of course, I have in mind the authors of articles in this collection. Invited to think about their work in the context of broad-based writing-teacher education, they did so, concretely and reflectively. Because they did, *Teaching Writing Teachers* makes it more likely that academics specializing in "composition" and in "English education" can better understand each other's work and cooperate in the important task of preparing writing teachers.

Richard C. Gebhardt
Bowling Green State University

Introduction

Striking a Balance—Seeking a Discipline

Robert Tremmel
Iowa State University

For nearly twenty years I have been teaching courses aimed at preparing secondary English education students to teach writing in the schools. Before that I worked as a TA in first-year composition and as a TA "leader" in a professional development program for beginning TAs. When I add all those years up it seems like a long time to me. However, it has been only a short time since I began thinking about this practice of teaching "writing methods" as an emerging discipline in its own right, with a long history extending across the boundaries of both English education and first-year composition and linking both together in numerous, sometimes surprising, sometimes uncomfortable ways.

This new way of thinking for me rests on the odd fact that even though English educators and writing program administrators (WPAs) have been engaged in many of the same disciplinary labors for over half a century, and even though they have had significant points of contact with each other in the past, they currently live separate academic lives, fenced off from each other in largely separate bureaucratic compounds. "How is it," I have begun—to my extreme discomfort—asking myself lately, "that I can be the coordinator of an English education program in an English department, working daily to prepare beginning writing teachers, yet I never walk down the hall to consult with our department's composition director, who is also working daily to prepare beginning writing teachers whose students are often only three months older than my students' students? How is it that other English educators and writing program administrators around the country generally act this same way, teaching and even writing about their work as if they had no disciplinary connections with each other and no significant shared traditions? More important, given where all of us have come from and where we find ourselves today, why haven't we thought about

1

forming an alliance based on our consillient actions and needs in order to build a broader, more coherent, mutually supportive academic and institutional base for ourselves?"

And behind those admittedly radical questions lies a more radical one: "Why, in the process of ignoring everything else, have we also ignored the potential blessings for both writing teachers and their students in both the schools and the universities that might attend the mindful building of a common discipline?" Despite some notable joint efforts between secondary and postsecondary education, when it comes to the teaching of writing, What do these students need to know when they get to college? and What did these students do in high school? have remained persistent mysteries for as long as I can remember. What would reconfiguring writing teacher education mean for writing instruction in the schools and universities, and what might it contribute to forming cross-institutional writing curriculums, grades 7–13?

In the chapters that follow, the contributors to this book will not answer these questions. However, they will lay the groundwork necessary to begin answering them by discussing their work with beginning teachers and offering, in effect, a working definition of the current state of practice. For this task they are highly qualified. All of them are experienced writing teacher educators in either first-year composition or English education, and most of them have had experience or are currently working in both areas.

My task in this introduction is to create a historical context for the ensuing chapters that, first, renders an accurate account of the development of secondary and postsecondary writing teacher education and, second, offers a rationale for working toward a single discipline based on a union between two areas that are commonly viewed as separate. By examining both the early and recent history of writing teacher education for both English education and first-year composition, I will identify consistently converging trajectories of disciplinary practice in both areas. On that basis, I will propose that all of us, as writing teacher educators, should consider reconfiguring our shared discipline and joining together to occupy the common ground to which we are heir.

Early Histories

First-Year Composition

The familiar historical narrative of how writing teacher education evolved in first-year composition, as it has been written by Berlin (1987), Connors (1986, 1991), Crowley (1998a), North (2000), Stewart (1982, 1985), and others, is a story of marginalization and struggle for recognition. Connors, in fact, might have used the term *devolved* rather than *evolved* to characterize much of first-year composition's early history, including the preparation of teachers.

When the German system of graduate education was grafted onto the undergraduate curriculum in this country in the nineteenth century to form an American university system, what had been the prestigious discipline of rhetoric gradually declined, as Connors (1991) describes it, into what became composition, and increasingly the teaching of writing was consigned to what Connors labels an academic "underclass." The teachers who made up this underclass were not only overworked and underpaid but they also received little or no preparation for classroom practice. From the end of the nineteenth century until well into the twentieth, unprepared, inexperienced new assistant professors were pushed into the "ordeal" of "apprenticeship" (Connors 1991, 72) from the comfort of their studies in literature and were forced to serve several years' duty in composition until they were able to escape its rigors and return to literary study. They were later joined in their misery by graduate students and temporary instructors (Crowley 1998a, 4), many of whom were serving what amounted to a life sentence in composition. Until about the middle of this century, the only form of writing teacher education available to most of these "hapless bottom feeders" (Connors 1991, 72) appears to have been the textbooks they were assigned to use in their classes. "Little wonder," Connors quotes James McCrimmon as saying, "that in such a sea of confusion [the composition teacher] clings to his handbook as a shipwrecked sailor clings to his raft . . ." (1986, 190).

English Education

The early history of writing teacher education in secondary English is also a story of marginalization and neglect. Arthur Applebee's (1974) version of that story begins with how the founders of NCTE worked determinedly to wrest control of their discipline from university English departments and the College Entrance Examination Board (CEEB) and to overthrow what Fred Newton Scott called at the time a "feudal" system in which the "colleges attempted to dictate the content of . . . school programs about which they knew little" (Applebee, 50).

Unfortunately, once this uprising was completed it amounted to little for secondary teachers, for the teaching of writing, and for writing teacher education, since what had previously been secondary to university English departments simply made a lateral shift to become secondary to a new class of university English educators while the curricular focus in the schools, like the focus in the university, ended up staying where it had been since the end of the nineteenth century: on literature. One simple way of illustrating this point is to compare the scant number of references in the index of Applebee's exhaustively detailed *Tradition and Reform* (1974) under the heading "composition" with the numerous and multilayered references under "literature." English education, although not totally ignoring composition, certainly marginalized it, and starting with Applebee's account and looking back in time, the record, or lack thereof, shows that very few people through the first half of the twentieth century, with the major exception of Scott (1908; see also Stewart 1982, 1985; Pytlik 1992), seemed passionately interested in promoting writing teacher education.

Converging Trajectories

It is possible for powerful, well-established entities to marginalize and isolate teachers who have pressing needs and common interests yet little influence, but it is not possible for them to do that forever. And so it was that even as first-year composition and English education separately began to become aware of the need for writing teacher education midway through the twentieth century, ideas for meeting that need emerged jointly and simultaneously from a stubbornly cross-disciplinary matrix of teachers who operated with a working knowledge of both English education and first-year composition.

According to Janet Marting's (1987) "Retrospective on Training Teaching Assistants," some of the very first gestures in the direction of establishing coherent approaches to writing teacher education, outside of a few isolated exceptions, started showing up about seventy years ago in the establishment of rudimentary links between teacher education in secondary and higher education. For example, the proceedings of the Institute for the Administrative Offices of Higher Institutions at the University of Chicago in 1930 proposed that TAs should study not only the "academic side" but the "professional side of the picture," including such familiar basics from secondary education as "understanding the American educational system. . . , the psychology of learning," and, a most important point to which I will return later, "supervised experience in the actual teaching of students" (36). These were apparently not intended as superficial gestures but as serious cross-disciplinary proposals involving academic departments in joint partnership with teacher education programs. Marting writes:

> The other major recommendation of the institute was for prospective teachers to enroll in an education course to learn about the developments in and the current state of education. . . . Hence, the responsibility for training college teachers was shared by the particular department of the prospective teachers and the school of education. (36)

Despite the fact that some universities took such proposals to heart, nationwide there was not much immediate progress in elevating the status of teacher preparation. Nonetheless, as Marting (1987) notes, subsequent conferences in 1949 and 1956 leading up to the joint MLA/NCTE Basic Issues Conferences in 1958 continued to press the need for taking the education of beginning college teachers seriously. An important aspect of the recommendations coming out of these conferences focused on improving the working conditions and preparation of new college teachers by moving in a broad way toward common disciplinary focus for teacher education and "articulation of teaching and teacher training at all levels in English" (Axelrod 1959, 95).

Despite these kinds of efforts, what was lacking from the 1930s through the 1940s was a triggering mechanism to ignite meaningful and widespread action. Consequently, well into the second half of the 20th century many new instructors, TAs, and professors—to say nothing of secondary teachers—were still being issued a textbook and a handbook and expected to teach writing. In the universities this default mechanism worked sufficiently well that it did not attract attention as long as enrollments were low enough to be manageable and students capable enough to get by in a flawed system. However, with the end of World War II, the enactment of the GI Bill, and what North (2000; see also Pytlik 1993) calls the "great expansion," a triggering event finally occurred in the form of rising numbers of underprepared students in first-year writing programs. The pressure those students created made it obvious to composition directors during the entire period of the 1950s that they needed to build courses and programs in teacher education—and fast (Lloyd-Jones 2000).

When these courses and programs started to emerge in the 1960s, they came out informed by a coalescing, but still indistinct, awareness of the disciplinary interrelatedness of writing teacher education for both secondary and university teachers. One example of this process of growing awareness was the National Defense Education Act (NDEA) Institutes in the teaching of writing directed by Carl Klaus at the University of Iowa in the 1960s (Klaus 1999, Lloyd-Jones 2000). These Institutes, which were taught on campus by university faculty in English, linguistics, and first-year writing and were attended by high school teachers and department chairs, were instrumental in establishing a cross-institutional beginning point for writing teacher education that eventually found further expression in the Klaus-led Iowa–NEH Institutes for directors of first-year composition and the development of the State of Iowa Writing Project in the 1970s and 1980s. It was in the Writing Project in particular, under the leadership of James S. Davis and Cleo Martin, where teachers across all levels, from elementary school to the university, began to engage in truly collaborative work.

During this same period at Iowa, writing teacher education courses also began showing up as regular curricular offerings. Following his involvement with the NDEA Institutes, Klaus designed a writing teacher education course that enrolled graduate students in English and English education and particularly served those who were TAs in first-year composition. That course became so popular it later gave rise to another course, also with an English department number, for undergraduate English education students. The first teacher of this course was Richard Hootman, professor in the Rhetoric Program, where first-year composition was and still is taught at Iowa. Hootman, it's worth noting in the context of this book, came to the Rhetoric Program after serving as chair of English at City High School, Iowa City.

Along these same interdisciplinary lines, in 1969 Richard Larson published an article titled "A Course in Advanced Composition for Teachers." Larson, who at the time was director of composition in a university English department, wrote the article for the *Journal of Teacher Education*. The case he makes demonstrates how the common needs in both first-year composition and English education, plus the support of groups with affiliations in both the universities and the schools—the Commission on English, the Basic Issues Conferences, the CEEB, and NCTE's Commission on the English Curriculum—led to courses and programs designed for the joint preparation of writing teachers in the elementary and secondary schools as well as "freshman composition" (172). When Larson outlines the seven features he believes should be included in a course for the education of writing teachers he does not discriminate on the basis of instructional level or institutional identity. Likewise, a later grouping of articles by Donald Nemanich, Joseph J. Comprone, and Maxine Hairston in a "Staffroom Interchange" of a 1974 issue of *College Composition and Communication* sends the same message by applying similar principles in accounts of writing teacher education and "writing methods" courses at the "high school," "junior college," and "freshman English" levels (Nemanich, 46–47).

Richard Gebhardt's 1977 article in *College Composition and Communication,* titled "Balancing Theory with Practice in the Training of Writing Teachers," pulls together the ideas of Larson, Nemanich, Comprone, Hairston, and others and stands as an early benchmark for the design of writing teacher education courses and programs. Gebhardt's inclusive beginning point is that those "who teach writing *in public school or college* (my emphasis) should understand important conceptual underpinnings of composition and the teaching of writing and should test them out in practice" (1977/1981, 153). Gebhardt goes on to identify "four kinds of knowledge [that] are especially important for future teachers of writing" (153) irrespective of instructional level or institutional identity:

> First, writing teachers need to have an understanding of the structure and history of the English Language sound enough to let them apply that knowledge to the teaching of revision, style, dialectical differences, and the like. . . .
> [Second] . . . writing teachers need to have . . . a solid understanding of rhetoric. . . .
> [Third] . . . composition teachers need to master . . . some theoretical framework with which to sort through the ideas, methodologies, and conflicting claims of texts, journal articles, and convention addresses. . . .
> [Fourth] . . . future writing teachers need a broad awareness of reliable, productive, methods to help students learn to write. . . . (154–57)

Recent Histories

English Education

Despite the promise of disciplinary unity in the 1960s and 1970s, writing teacher education in first-year composition and English education has since developed along separate—though similar—tracks, with both still marginalized by the academic establishment on the basis of their commitment to pedagogy.

During and immediately after the period of founding interdisciplinary work, English educators continued to operate on the traditional basis of one methods course in which they attempted to cover the whole discipline from literature to composition but that, in practice, was mostly concerned with literature. It was not long, however, before the active scope of English education broadened toward increasing interest in composition and process pedagogy. By the 1980s rising numbers of programs had developed or were developing courses to meet beginning teachers' newly recognized needs as writing teachers by offering them specific instruction in rhetorical theory and teaching practice.

It is not in identifying such courses but in making sense of their operation that complications arise. Despite the fact that writing methods courses are now common in English education programs, and even though preparing English education students as writing teachers is a formal charge mandated jointly by the National Council for the Accreditation of Teacher Education (NCATE) and NCTE (Small et al. 1996), there has been little effort to study courses or programs in a systematic way or to explore their relationship with other pedagogical and curricular developments and contemporaneous reform efforts like the writing project movement. Most tellingly perhaps, Smagorinsky and Whiting (1995), in their seminal study of English methods, declined even to consider the writing methods course, citing the unpredictable and indeterminate qualities it manifested in their data. They write:

> We decided to focus on the [general English methods class] because other types of classes had a much more specific purpose and so tended to approach the topic and materials differently. A course in the teaching of writing did not necessarily need to be concerned with the relationship between teaching literature and writing, about the uses of drama, about classroom management, and about other aspects of teaching often found in a teaching methods class; several courses in the teaching of writing served more as writing workshops than as courses in how to teach English. (8)

Smagorinsky and Whiting's position here illustrates the diversity of opinion that persists in English education when it comes to preparing writing teachers. Not only do the researchers take a pass on writing teacher education courses because those courses do not feel holistically methodological enough for them, but they do not pursue the idea, formulated in the writers' clubs of the nineteenth century, formalized in the first writers' workshops in the twentieth century (Wilbers 1980), and affirmed in the process pedagogy movement of the 1980s, that practice in writing and workshopping do, in fact, constitute significant methods in "how to teach English." It may even be that the methods associated with workshopping, by virtue of their social and collaborative nature, are among the most significant methods for working in all aspects of English education. (See, for example, Atwell 1998, Beach and Marshall 1991, Daniels 1994.) Thus, as easy as it is to argue that secondary English educators have made significant improvement in their approaches to writing teacher education, it is just as easy to argue that we still have an ambiguous relationship with a pedagogy that may not fit comfortably into the traditional contours of our disciplinary self-concept.

One of the reasons for this ambiguity is the frequently noted fact that attempts to reform traditional views of teaching practice, including the practice of teaching writing (see, for example, Cuban 1993, Hillocks 1999, Pytlik 1991, Shrofel 1991, Vinz 1996), are resisted by beginning and experienced teachers alike, who find themselves locked up in reified public school systems and bogged down by composition curricula rooted in the nineteenth century; the baggage of local, state, and national politics; and, most recently, the pressures of the standards movement. How easy, after all, is it for some of us to fully commit to the teaching of writing while knowing full well the lack of influence we have over the reality into which our students are headed?

Such complications notwithstanding, there is ample evidence in the professional literature that English educators have been active in developing writing teacher education courses and programs starting with the initial surge in the 1970s and 1980s (for example, see Anson et al. 1993; Cherry 1973; Fox 1993; Elliott 1978; Lang 1979, 1982; Ojala 1970; Rose and Finders 1998; Shrofel 1991; Smith 1984; Wollam 1981). It is particularly worth noting how course and program designs in English education, including those represented in this book, have evolved so as to reflect the template constructed by Gebhardt in the 1970s. First of all, most English education programs require courses in "the structure and history of the English language," especially those that hope to be accredited under the rubric of the NCATE/NCTE *Guidelines.* Likewise, English education students study rhetoric and "theoretical frameworks" both in the context of courses required as part of the English major and in methods courses. Students in the program where I teach, for example, take the department's course in rhetorical theory and learn about the parts of a classical oration in the process of discussing the five-paragraph theme. They also learn about Aristotle's *Rhetoric,* as it was reinterpreted by James Kinneavy, in the process of studying epistemic sequencing (Dowst 1980, Harris 1997, Krupa 1982), and they study as well current-traditional rhetoric, expressivism, cognitivism, social construction, process pedagogy as a theoretical construct, language development, and learning theory.

However, it is in the area of "reliable and productive methods" that English educators expend the greatest measure of energy. We are, after all, methodologists who address practice directly in our classes and enact practice with our students during in-class activities, workshops, case-study exercises, and the composition of lesson and unit plans, journals, and portfolios. This commitment to method does not stop at the door of the methods classroom on campus. English educators are strongly interested in establishing programs for field experience, mentoring, and cooperative activity in the schools (for example, Boreen et al. 2000; Graham, Hudson-Ross, McWhorter 1997; Graham et al. 1999; Vinz 1996). Indeed, if I had to cite one area that English educators have strengthened above all others over the last thirty years it would be this one. My own case is not uncommon. When I was an undergraduate and completing a certification program in 1971, my last semester was divided into 2 eight-week segments. The first eight weeks were devoted to *the*—there was only one—methods course. The second eight weeks were devoted to student teaching, which amounted to only two classes a day at the university's lab school. The program in which I teach right now, a program that is developing but still far short of other programs I would call state-of-the-art, ties fifty-hour field experience components to each of two methods courses leading up to what, with the next catalog, will be a full sixteen-week semester of student teaching. In my view, and in the view of my colleagues around the country, field experience, involving guided observation and practice in secondary classrooms with secondary students and experienced teachers, is the most important requirement for teacher education programs.

Despite what I see as real progress, though, English teacher educators have yet to settle on a full commitment to viewing themselves as professional writing teacher educators. For one thing, some courses and programs fall short of fully representing the discipline by underrepresenting theory and overbalancing toward practice. Part of the reason for this is that many of our students, anxious they won't know what to do in the classroom, demand extensive instruction in "how-to." Part of it also is that many of our students, who are after all, undergraduates with "career plans," have not reached the point where they see a need for theory and, hence, resist it with enthusiasm. Unfortunately, on occasion these tendencies are reinforced by the comments of teachers they meet in the schools.

Even in what is arguably our strongest area, field experience, English education programs can be decidedly predisciplinary and ambivalent with regard to both writing teacher preparation and the teaching of writing. The reasons for this include the lack of vertical integration between university and school programs I mentioned earlier as well as unevenness in writing instruction in the schools. Bluntly put, there are still teachers out there who are teaching the five-paragraph essay and the research paper, handing out worksheets, and otherwise not doing much with writing. As a result, it is not uncommon for prospective and beginning teachers—despite their best intentions and the best intentions of their professors—to go through an entire field experience sequence without ever becoming fully involved in the teaching of writing and without ever thinking of themselves as writing teachers. It is in this sense that Smagorinsky and Whiting (1995) are exactly correct: university English educators are still far from the point of establishing with the schools a fully elaborated, coherent, and consistent writing pedagogy. And as far as we are away from that point, we are just as far from realizing a fully elaborated disciplinary commitment to writing teacher education.

First-Year Composition

There is also unevenness, ambivalence, and lack of commitment connected to writing teacher education in first-year composition, but it decidedly does not originate with writing program administrators. Indeed, despite sometimes overwhelming odds, since the 1950s, WPAs have consistently done all they could and more to actively engage the needs of beginning teachers. In this case, the source of ambivalence lies in the English departments and larger bureaucratic entities that house composition programs, and the major issues are economic and political—not pedagogical. As many have argued since at least the adoption of the Wyoming Resolution by the Conference on College Composition and Communication in 1987, and as Crowley (1998a), Joseph Harris (2000), and Michael Murphy (2000) have argued more recently, university administrators and bean counters recognize clearly the manifold advantages that accrue from employing large, poorly paid pools of TAs and temporary instructors who come with low overhead and no political leverage. Not only does maintaining such a powerless labor force make it possible to cut back on costly benefits that might otherwise cut into the bottom line, but it makes it easy to skimp on teacher education and staff development. The term North uses to describe this tradition of academic management is "College English Teaching Inc.," and the name sticks. Faced with these underlying conditions, and subject themselves to such powerful political forces, how can writing program administrators not be involved in an ambivalent enterprise when it comes to writing teacher education?

Carrie Leverenz and Amy Goodburn (1998) have responded to some of the challenges proceeding from the business practices of College English Teaching Inc. by asserting that real staff development, real writing teacher education, and the professionalization of composition teachers must at the very least be focused on the specific practices of teaching composition. They argue against giving in to the special interests of College English Teaching Inc., particularly management's persistent efforts to professionalize and theorize graduate education by shaping the lives of TAs in their own image, which is not necessarily the likeness of a teacher (29). In addition to pointing toward what they see as the problem, Leverenz and Goodburn also point in a wide-ranging way toward a solution in terms that are still very much at home in the framework proposed by Gebhardt nearly a quarter of a century ago:

> The truth is, while we continue to debate how much theory TAs need to read, it's not clear the degree to which undergraduate students benefit when their TAs read this theory. What is clear is that undergraduates would benefit if teachers had more than a few days or even a few weeks of preparation before teaching their first class, and they would also benefit if their teachers had fewer of them to teach. To help our TAs and their students, we need to work for more reasonable teaching loads, better compensation, and a full semester of study, observation, and mentoring before TAs enter the classroom. (28)

The overbalancing of theory that Leverenz and Goodburn refer to here has long been a primary characteristic of writing teacher education programs in first-year composition. Part of the reason for that, in contrast with the theory–practice issue in English education, is that graduate students need and expect to engage in significant study of theory. What they must know about writing and the teaching of writing must also be contextualized in a way that takes in the full range of priorities for members of the professorate. Still, the point I understand Leverenz and Goodburn to be making is that when it comes to preparing teachers, programs have been overly influenced by faculty who are deeply immersed in theorizing their research specialties, apprenticing TAs, and maintaining a market for the products of scholarship.

In a special edition of *Composition Studies* (Bolin et al. 1995), theory easily stands out as the most frequently represented and fully elaborated component in the seventeen syllabi of writing teacher education courses the editors present. Some professors, it seems, deliberately try to minimize issues of teaching practice, communicating a persistent, elitist attitude that the professional development of their graduate students should not be "'tainted' by praxis" (13)— as one contributor, Thomas Recchio (1995), so uncompromisingly puts it.

However, there is also clear evidence in this issue of *Composition Studies* that writing teacher education courses and programs are on the move away from such extremes toward steadier balance. For example, Ruth Mirtz's (1995) course at Florida State University titled "Teaching English in College" has these course goals:

> In this course, you will examine current composition theory and practice, especially cognitive, developmental, and process approaches, within the dynamics of social and expressivist theories of language. Issues in these areas include how post-adolescents learn language and composition skills, the writing process, writers and teachers' roles in the classroom, collaboration, and the relationships among speaking, writing, reading, etc. The goal is to develop a teaching philosophy which synthesizes composition theory, your own teaching style, curricular goals, and student needs. We will ask questions such as, What do we teach and why? Who are first-year writers? What is language and language development? How do I teach and why? (20)

A central way Mirtz's course creates opportunities for new TAs to answer these important questions is through a program of field work in which the beginners observe and intern with experienced TAs. It would surprise no English educator that one of the models Mirtz associates with her approach is the Writing Project, which continues to be an inservice writing teacher education program that is widely attended and taught by English educators, secondary teachers, and compositionists, and that is widely used as a model for writing teacher education courses at the secondary level. Nor would it surprise English educators that Mirtz links the new TAs' field work to classroom research, a leading feature in the curriculum of secondary writing teacher education.

In approaches like these, Mirtz and a handful of other writing program administrators contributing to this issue of *Composition Studies* are, like Leverenz and Goodburn, working to refine the balanced approach to writing teacher education in first-year composition laid out by Gebhardt and sought after by many English educators as well. Despite the ambivalence on both sides, in recent history as in the past, the trajectories of English education and first-year composition are converging ones. In no case is this more true than it is with Kate Ronald, Joy Ritchie, and Robert Brookes' presentation of the program at the University of Nebraska, which is based on "a long tradition of integration [with] K-12 teaching . . . " (1995, 61).

Catherine Latterell's (1996) research on writing teacher education reveals how issues of balance are negotiated in the real world of first-year composition. Latterell surveyed seventy-two doctoral programs in rhetoric and composition, received thirty-six responses, and organized her report around four major components in writing teacher education courses: apprenticeships, practica, methods courses, and theory seminars. The obvious encouraging news in Latterell's findings is that first-year composition is taking writing teacher education seriously and that all these components crucial for balance are present, as I have suggested for English education, in "varying degrees in all programs" (10). There are, however, three pieces of less encouraging news.

The first is that teacher education at some institutions is still thin and unevenly executed. Even though thirty-two of thirty-six responding institutions required an orientation, five of those were one-day affairs (10). (And who knows what was going on in the thirty-six programs Latterell contacted but that did not respond to her request for materials?) Second, even though the components are present to achieve a balanced approach to writing teacher education, apparently the balance has not yet been struck. The theory courses Latterell pulled in for her survey, like the ones Leverenz and Goodburn (1998) warn against, turn out to be primarily conducted as stand-alone seminars separate from serious consideration of teaching practice (Latterell 1996, 16). Also, on the other side of the fulcrum, where some secondary programs rest, according to Latterell the practica are too often established on the basis of a narrow, "skills-based" (19) curriculum that ends up being transferred to composition courses themselves in the form of prescribed practices and a top-down, "antidemocratic" (19), political full-court press.

As far as I am concerned, the worst piece of news in Latterell's (1996) research, though the least surprising, is a continued lack of awareness in first-year composition of another lively venue in English education for preparing writing teachers. Latterell, however, does propose that writing program administrators take the initiative in moving beyond the traditional bureaucratic boundaries that surround their field. Latterell's closing argument proceeds like this:

> More than anything else, and before much else can happen, GTA education programs will need the support and active involvement of many more people than this overview indicates are involved in preparing teaching assistants. Tenured faculty, advanced GTAs, writing center professionals, instructors, and undergraduate students are under-utilized resources in most GTA education programs. Moreover, current administrative structures . . . will need rethinking. (22)

Exactly the case. The same goes for English education.

Where We Are

A recent presentation at the Conference on College Composition and Communication by Stephen Wilhoit (2000) encapsulates the vision for writing teacher education that English educators and writing program administrators first glimpsed in the 1960s, toward which they have been converging, and that they might some day be able to achieve together. The centerpiece of Wilhoit's presentation was what I—and not necessarily he—think of as a compendium of components for a good writing teacher education program. (See Figure I–1.) This compendium, I believe, is much more than the overview of current practices Wilhoit portrays it as; it certainly extends beyond the boundaries of what we usually think of as "training," which is the heading he uses. For me, what Wilhoit has pulled together functions as a contemporary representation of the program Gebhardt formulated a quarter century ago and serves as a template for the kind of program I have been trying to sketch throughout this essay and that I would like writing teacher educators at all levels of instruction to consider as the basis of a design worth striving for.

Wilhoit's template is particularly notable for the emphasis it gives to "preservice" work, "mentoring and observation," "apprenticeships," "teaching portfolios," and "internships." These items define an area of emphasis in recent reforms as well as a long-term main emphasis in English education. In English education, it is on field experience that we have always grounded our work, and it may be through experience in such areas of endeavor that English education derives the expertise to contribute to the development of writing teacher education programs in first-year composition—but first we all need to get together.

Where to from Here?

The distance between school and university may not be so great as our bureaucratic structures make it seem. In my view, Wilhoit's compendium for first-year composition is exactly relevant for programs in English education; and when I put the broader implications of Wilhoit's work alongside my reading of our history and what I hope I have learned from twenty years as a writing teacher educator, I get a strong sense of the common heritage and natural alliance between English education and first-year composition, between grades 7–12 and grade 13. All of us engaged in this work, I am arguing, wherever we are and whatever else our jobs involve, are writing teachers and teachers of writing teachers. All of us, whether we recognize it or not, whether we like it or not, are moving along more or less together despite considerable political and bureaucratic forces that conspire to keep our path dissected and obscured.

I think it makes sense to open negotiations on how we might reroute and regrade this common path, starting with discussions about what life would be like if we were to remove some of the impediments that keep us apart. Writing teacher education for secondary teachers should not be a completely separate enterprise from writing teacher education for first-year composition. The writing

Content	Methodologies
Contextual Information	Preservice workshop
Goal of local writing program	Preservice class
Theory of local writing program	Inservice workshops
TAs' place in department	Faculty mentoring and
Course Information	observation
Goals of course	Peer mentoring and
Structure of course	observation
Texts used in course	Visiting others' classes
Pedagogical Information	Scenarios and role-playing
Designing syllabi	Teaching journals
Designing assignments	Teaching portfolios
Evaluating writing	Videotaping classes
Assessing writing	Apprenticeships
Presenting information	Internships
Collaborative learning	
Conferencing	
Teaching research skills	
Teaching critical thinking skills	
Classroom performance skills	
Theory	
Composition theory	
Rhetorical theory	
Learning theory	
Technology	
Audiovisual equipment	
Computer classrooms	
Internet and WWW use	
Emails, list serves, etc.	
Upper-level courses	
Upper-level writing courses	
Literature courses	
Writing center work	
Student Information	

[Wilhoit (2000)]

Figure I-1. Current Classroom Training Practices: An Overview

curriculum should not be severed between grades 12 and 13. The majority of first-year composition students still have one foot firmly planted in high school, and it makes sense for beginning TAs to learn about the teaching of writing in secondary schools. It makes just as much sense for beginning secondary English teachers to work with TAs and learn about first-year composition. These are not just my ideas (see, for example, North, 245), and they are not new ideas. It is already common for English education students, often in the context of a methods class, to tutor first-year students in the university writing center. Why not go one step beyond that to create practica in which English education students are attached to sections of first-year composition? Further, what if beginning TAs looked into their students' pasts by spending some of their preservice practicum time in a secondary classroom? These are some modest first proposals. The possibilities beyond them are limited only by our inability or unwillingness to administer them—which may turn out to be a serious limitation indeed.

While we're at it, why shouldn't we start acting as if writing teacher education itself deserved some kind of disciplinary status? It is honest work, after all, that creates one of the few genuine opportunities for academics to transact business directly in the social, cultural, and community contact zones that we have been telling ourselves for years are important grounds for critically relevant and valuable work. In addition, it may just turn out that in the process of coming together and occupying a common turf, English education and first-year composition will be able to further their self-interests as well as the interests of students. Neither of our areas has consistently prospered in its associations with English departments, and both have sought out, in various ways, other allies and other constituencies that have variously helped and hurt our causes. Why not seek each other out on the basis of our shared interests and shared efforts and see what we can accomplish together?

Doing this in the current climate of tribalism and specialization in English studies (Tremmel, 2000) is not going to be easy. Teaching, much less teacher education, has never been consistently important to universities, English departments, and the academics who inhabit them. Writing program administrators in particular, many of whom feel a close affiliation with the increasingly professionalized and theorized discipline of composition studies, might not feel that it would be to their best advantage to emphasize their connections with pedagogy by associating with open and unashamed methodologists. Implicit in such complications is also the tension between English education and first-year composition when it comes to structuring programs and balancing instruction in theory and practice.

It follows that English educators may also balk at an alliance with first-year composition. The patriarchal arrogance of some English professors in the past still inhabits the present and is easily generalized to the people who are currently down the hall and across the campus. "Across the campus" is a particular problem. For English educators who are based in colleges of education located in institutions where the relationship between the Department of

Curriculum and Instruction and the Department of English leaves something to be desired, the challenge will be particularly great. Though it might be nice to reconfigure the disciplinary nature of writing teacher education and the teaching of writing, is it worth the trouble? My own actions to this point might be revealing of others: Even though I've obviously done a lot of reading and thinking about this, to date I've only talked in general terms with our department's very congenial composition director. Part of that has to do with the proposed reconfiguration of our university's communications courses, but part also has to do with my own reluctant nature.

My closing thought is that in the midst of all these questions and doubts, the redeeming grace that may just be strong enough to help us all cut through the natural and artificial boundaries that surround us—to say nothing about the boundaries of personal courage—is the commitment to students and teaching practice that we all, as teachers and teachers of teachers, share. What is at stake in our daily work is more important than mere institutional identity and bureaucratic status. The real question is whether making the effort to change will make our teaching lives better and resonate in the lives of our students. That's what this is all about after all, isn't it—living and working well, and helping those we live with and work for also live and work well? We do believe that, don't we? Writing program administrators and English educators, first-year composition and secondary education, and universities and schools not only have much to offer each other, but together they might have much more to offer their students than they have been able to deliver so far. I've come to believe our students and their students deserve one education, not two. Can we offer it to them?

I

Three Commentaries

Two commentaries on the Introduction follow. Stephen Wilhoit, a veteran writing teacher educator and program administrator in first-year composition, wrote the first one after reading an earlier version of the introduction. Jonathan Bush, recently graduated from Purdue University and a new faculty member at Western Michigan University, wrote the second commentary based on yet another version of the introduction that he heard Bob deliver at the 2001 Conference on College Composition and Communication in Denver. At the same conference, but in a different session, Bush delivered an earlier version of his comments here.

A third commentary, in the form of a professional narrative written by Margaret Tomlinson Rustick, closes the book. Rustick is also responding to Bob's CCCC presentation.

Identifying Common Concerns

A Response to "Striking a Balance—Seeking a Discipline"

Stephen Wilhoit
University of Dayton

> I think it makes sense to open negotiations on how we might grade and re-
> route this common path, starting with discussions about what life would be
> like if we were to remove some of the impediments that keep us apart. Writ-
> ing teacher education for secondary teachers should not be a completely sep-
> arate enterprise from writing teacher education for first-year composition.
> —(Tremmel X)

In "Striking a Balance, Seeking a Discipline," Bob Tremmel tells a story and issues a call. The story describes how writing teacher education programs in English and English education evolved along separate but parallel paths. The call
challenges us to reunite these two areas of study, forming a single, unified discipline. His vision is compelling but fraught with complications: What would
such an alliance look like? Where would it find a home on today's campuses?
How could it find a common language and speak with a common voice? How
could it overcome the barriers of distrust, misunderstanding, arrogance, and neglect that have built up over the years between English education and English?

Part of the answer, it seems, can be found in the tone of Tremmel's essay—
personal, reflective, confessional. For this reunion to occur, he suggests, we have
to want it to occur. The revolution begins with a walk across campus, a knock on
a door, and long conversations over cups of coffee. Like Tremmel, I have not
made that walk. For eleven years I ran the English department's TA education
program. During the TAs' two years of required workshops, seminars, and
classes, we covered most if not all of the material I discussed in the conference
presentation Tremmel cites in his essay. One of those classes, composition

theory, is also a required course at our school for any English education student planning to teach high school English. Still, over the years I have had little contact with the English education professors overseeing the preparation of these teachers.

If I answer Tremmel's challenge and take that walk over to the School of Education, what would we talk about? Tremmel has outlined the history of how we got into this situation, but what are our common concerns now? As writing teacher educators, what unites us today? Let me suggest a few good places to start as we pour those first cups of coffee.

Students, Program Goals, and Pedagogies

Preparing new writing teachers is challenging work, whether those teachers will walk into a high school or a college classroom that first day. Those of us working with these students face many of the same questions: What information and skills do our students need to be effective teachers? What are their concerns and apprehensions? How can we lessen them? What gifts, knowledge, and experiences do they bring with them to the classroom? How can we help them recognize and build on their strengths? Our common efforts to understand and meet the needs of our students surely offer abundant opportunity for productive discussion.

The same holds true for our program goals. On the surface, we have the same goal: to prepare our students to be writing teachers. But we must articulate that goal in unique ways, since our students will be teaching in such different environments and contexts. Yet, really, how much does being an effective high school writing teacher differ from being an effective college writing teacher? This is a particularly important question. If we think in terms of a curriculum for grades 9 to 13, how are high school writing teachers learning to define their job, and how are first-year college writing teachers learning to define theirs? Without both groups understanding each others' work, a curriculum for grades 9–13 is bound to fail—there is too much opportunity for teachers to work at cross-purposes. And what about the many other goals we have as writing teacher educators? For example, as we work with our students how do we define and address the need for professional development and for lifelong learning? How do we foster an interest in inservice learning? What role does reflective teaching play in our students' education and development? These are all topics of current interest to anyone educating high school or college writing teachers.

We could also talk about how we attempt to achieve these goals. How do we devise responsible, reasonable curricula? How do we balance classroom learning with field experience? Tremmel, for example, touches on a central concern for all writing teacher educators: balancing theory and practice. Most writing teacher educators are born methodologists—we work in that messy contact zone where theory butts up against practice. We value theory and teach it to our students because without it pedagogy lacks context, depth, and ultimate meaning;

however, we also value pedagogy because without it theory remains abstract, sterile, and ineffectual. We understand that theory must inform practice, but we understand that the reverse is true, too—practice must inform theory. How to balance both in a curriculum is challenging; how to teach our students to find a similar balance in their own teaching is daunting. These curricular and pedagogical issues jointly concern high school and college writing teacher educators.

Assessment Concerns

Increasingly today, high school and college writing teachers are required to document the effectiveness of their instruction, to establish and assess measurable outcomes, and to report on their findings. As writing teacher educators we face a double or perhaps triple burden: we have to teach our students how to design and oversee writing assessment programs, we often have to prepare our students to be assessed themselves, and we have to assess the effectiveness of our own teacher education programs. Additional assessment demands might be placed on high school or college teachers working in writing across the curriculum programs, honors or AP programs, gifted or accelerated learning programs, or basic skills programs.

More now than ever, all writing teacher educators need to discuss these increasing demands for testing, accountability, and assessment and to act collaboratively in our best interests and in the best interests of our students and programs. High school and college concerns here are much the same: how to address calls for assessment in responsible, professional ways; how to prepare our students to assess writing programs; and how to document and assess the work we do in our teacher education programs. Although high school and college teachers face some significantly different assessment and accreditation issues, there is enough common ground here for productive conversation and collaborative action.

Identity and Power

A third area of common concern for secondary and college writing teacher educators arises from the very history Tremmel recounts. The story he tells is one of shared institutional neglect, marginalization, and underclass status. Unfortunately, for many this story continues. They still labor under poor working conditions, confronting chairs and administrators who do not value their work and do not recognize their contributions to the institution or to the wider discipline of English studies.

Tremmel's suggestions are most radical here: establishing disciplinary status for writing teacher education strikes directly at this question of identity and power. As a discipline, writing teacher education would truly cut across traditional disciplinary lines, uniting faculty in English with faculty in education, closing the gap between secondary school and college instruction, and forging links between English TAs and education majors. Describing how this new discipline might take shape is, of course, far beyond the scope of this brief response essay. However, the question is intriguing and certainly offers ample occasion for conversation.

Rewards

Finally, high school and college writing teacher educators can find common ground in the rewards their jobs offer. I've long maintained a secret smugness about my work in TA education—I knew with a certainty that I held the most rewarding position in the department. Like many other faculty working with TAs, my work was barely recognized by my chair and colleagues, unless, of course, a student in a TA-taught class lodged a complaint of some sort! Otherwise, the TAs and I were left alone. As a result, we developed some of the closest, most rewarding professional relationships I've known. Successfully preparing new writing instructors for the classroom requires the students and teacher to work closely with each other and to form a collaborative, supportive relationship. We watch each other teach and critique each others' performance. In class and through reflective journal writing, we share our concerns and apprehensions, our successes and failures. Inside the classroom and out, we swap ideas and material, vent, laugh, and talk shop. This is the great secret of writing teacher educators: we become better teachers by teaching others; we remain enthusiastic because the enthusiasm of our students is infectious; we remain forever on the edge because that's where our students are; we are constantly learners because our students are constantly learning. Certainly the rewards of the job offer common ground for discussion.

As a teacher of teachers I often felt out of place in my department. What I did struck most of my colleagues as rudimentary—get those TAs ready to teach the introductory writing course. In their minds, the job seemed more fitting for the department of teacher education than it did for the department of English, a distinction full of the arrogance and disparagement Tremmel documents in his essay. Over the years, though, I think most of my colleagues have come to realize that writing teacher education is a complex, important, intellectually challenging task. But worthy of disciplinary status? To move the discussion in that direction, I think I need to take that walk I've been putting off, knock on a door or two, put on a pot of coffee, and talk things over with my colleagues in the school of education. It may be about time.

Common Ground

Toward Collaboration

Jonathan Bush
Western Michigan University

> As a director of a first-year college composition program and a teacher in English education we share many of the same responsibilities for the education of writing teachers. Because we both work with novice teachers of writing—Shirley with relatively inexperienced teaching assistants and Margaret with pre-service teachers who are students in English education—we are especially aware that much about teaching is learned from experience.
>
> —(Shirley Rose and Margaret Finders 1998)

Professionals in composition studies and English education are just beginning to understand the reciprocal nature of their fields. A strong example of how these two fields can interact and develop can been seen in the work of Margaret Finders, an English educator, and Shirley Rose, a composition specialist and writing program administrator. Finders and Rose cowrote articles for the journals *English Education* and *WPA: Writing Program Administration.* In these pieces they discuss their common roles in developing writing teachers at the middle/secondary level (Finders) and at the college level (Rose), specifically focusing on how each uses vignettes and situated practices to help develop the complex knowledges that the teaching of writing entails.

Both Finders and Rose found that their partnership was beneficial to their work. Interestingly, their collaboration came as somewhat of a surprise to both. As Finders describes it, they realized their common interests while attending a writing group in the English department. Rose was describing her current writing project, discussing the use of situated performances in her new teaching assistant "mentoring" sessions, and Finders recognized it as being remarkably similar to her own project. At first, Finders was surprised and disappointed that her project was apparently being co-opted by another. However, both quickly came to understand the similarities in their roles and developed a strong partnership that resulted in the publication of their articles for each of their primary audiences.

Rose and Finders show us that a WPA and an English educator have common ground for discussion and collaboration. This is an important and underdeveloped point that can influence the quality of programs and professional identities of English educators and writing program administrators alike. Here I will lay out some key points of connection between these two fields and offer some means of developing mutually beneficial partnerships. These arguments can also be extended, to some degree, to apply to generalist compositionists, to professional writing programs, and to other professionals involved in writing pedagogy.

As Finders and Rose found, English education and writing program administration often serve a similar role for different audiences. The WPA is concerned with the development of new writing teachers at the college level, often teaching composition practica and supervising new teaching assistants and other composition instructors. These courses typically revolve around concepts of composition instruction but are usually pedagogically focused, with assignments and activities developed that include the students' own introductory composition classes. Likewise, English educators teach methods classes for their undergraduate and graduate students, focusing on theory and practice, providing opportunities for students to apply their developing knowledge in field experience environments. In these courses, whether they specifically focus on composition or consider composition within a larger framework of English language arts instruction in the secondary school, the goal, much like the WPA's goal in the teaching practicum, is to help students develop theoretical understanding and create "pedagogical content knowledge" that translates into active and well-reasoned classroom pedagogy in composition.

English educators and WPAs also work to support their students as they develop and practice these pedagogical skills in their classrooms. For the WPA, these practica also serve as a support group for teaching, with emphasis on planning, practice, and discussion of current and ongoing classroom issues. This role also includes the supervision and evaluation of teaching assistants and others through classroom visits and individual conferences, and the development of teaching goals and personal "best practices" for teaching assistants to strive for and develop as their classroom experience continues.

From these and numerous other goals and characteristics common to both fields we can project a potential extension of writing program administration/English education collaborations, creating programmatic elements that build on common characteristics. For example, a common concern in English education is the development of strong field experiences with practicing teachers. It makes sense to develop some partnership programs in which English education students are able to observe and interact with classes, TAs, and writing classrooms at the university level. Likewise, these sorts of interactions can be developed into lab environments in which practicing TAs are able to receive feedback from English education students while the English education students are able to practice their skills by leading short classroom activities and reflecting on their experiences.

Programs can also collaborate in terms of course development. At many institutions with smaller graduate programs, both composition graduate programs and English education graduate programs are hampered by their inability to develop courses to serve the needs of their graduate students. Developing joint classes that discuss issues of writing within both the university and secondary/middle school settings would be appropriate and applicable. Writing program administration, writing across the curriculum, and other elements of composition studies and English pedagogy are also topics that apply at many levels. Similar possibilities exist for partnerships between courses and courses team-taught by English educators and composition specialists.

Finally, English educators and WPAs can navigate departmental politics together. In an era of competitive and diminishing resources in the humanities and education, it is of utmost importance for programs to collaborate and develop proposals that benefit both. It is of even more importance in the case of teacher education and composition, two elements of English studies that have traditionally been marginalized in English departments. It may be difficult for a composition director alone to sell the idea of paying invited speakers to address TAs and composition graduate students about issues in composition pedagogy. However, he or she can be much more persuasive if the speaker is an important element of the English education program as well. Similar positive results can occur through the development of student organizations that are applicable to both English education students and TAs in composition. As Finders and Rose illustrate, two voices are stronger than one.

II

Three Themes

Our instructions for the writing teacher educators who contributed the following thirteen chapters to this volume were very simple: (1) "describe the course or program in which you teach," (2) "focus on one particular aspect of your course or program that strikes you as particularly important or unique," and (3) "say anything else you want about writing teacher education." Even though this was perhaps a dangerous editorial policy that could have led to chaos and an uncollectible collection of essays, we had three reasons for proceeding as we did. First, and most simply, we wanted to make sure each chapter contained concrete information about the nuts and bolts of current courses and programs in writing teacher education—an area in the professional literature that is curiously undeveloped. Second, in the process we wanted to present as clear and unrehearsed a picture of the current state of practice in writing teacher education as we could. Third, we wanted to test our underlying faith that, given the opportunity, writing teacher educators working in a variety of sites and situations around the country would, with a minimum of direction, give readers a reasonably coherent look at a common and reasonably coherent—though far from unified—discipline.

The volume we ended up with, then, was built up out of the materials our contributors gave us and structured around three central sections that introduce and then play variations on the professional practices we all share. Each section is preceded by a short "intersection" that introduces the chapters that follow and indicates, in the manner of mile markers and road signs, what we see as important connections that extend not only across the book but across writing teacher education as well.

Chris Anson has worked as a writing teacher educator and student of writing teacher education across the entire school and university curriculum.

Anson's essay leads off the chapters in this book for two reasons. First, the institute he describes goes a long way toward enacting the balanced, inclusive principles summarized in the Introduction and laid out by Gebhardt and others. Second, Anson's chapter contains three themes that run through and overlap the chapters that follow his: (1) writing teachers must be writers, (2) writing teachers must practice reflection, and (3) writing teachers must work together, an idea we interpret broadly to include the many aspects of both formal and informal, personal and distant mentoring. These three themes, which gradually emerged as centers of gravity in the process of constructing the book, represent, we believe, a set of principles that help define not only the current state of the discipline but the direction further development is likely to take. At the very least, all three fit comfortably with the argument in the Introduction and answering commentaries by Wilhoit and Bush.

Anson's chapter is paired in this section with Gail Stygall's account of two writing methods courses that she teaches, one for English education students and one for beginning TAs in first-year composition. As is the case with Anson, Stygall's teaching practice extends across the secondary/postsecondary gap that has opened up over the last twenty-five years. Also like Anson's, Stygall's approach to designing and teaching writing methods at these two levels emphasizes the disciplinary common ground that we believe underlies writing teacher education.

Unlike Anson's, though, the institutional environment in which Stygall teaches is based on two separate courses that serve two different constituencies. Whereas Anson has set up shop in a place where it is possible for him to broadly replicate the inclusive structure and spirit of the cross-disciplinary writing teacher education course described by Gebhardt, Stygall is in a much different kind of place—similar to where most of us are—that is sometimes "mystifying" to her and that requires her to operate in a much different manner than Anson.

Finally, both Anson and Stygall, in different ways and to differing degrees, address central questions raised by Steve Wilhoit in his commentary. "How much," Wilhoit asks, "does being an effective high school teacher differ from being a college teacher?" and how must writing teacher educators articulate goals for students in ways that acknowledge they "will be teaching in different environments and contexts?" Even though neither Anson nor Stygall offers definitive answers, they do present their teaching practice as writing teacher educators in ways that make these difficult questions seem less daunting and more concrete. In the process they also define a range and field of action on which it seems possible to locate the teachers whose chapters follow theirs.

1

Teaching Writing Creatively

A Summer Institute for Teachers

Chris M. Anson
North Carolina State University

Each summer for seven years I have taught a two-week institute for teachers interested in using writing more effectively in their instruction. I almost hesitate to use the term "teach" because in the institute I am less a teacher than coordinator, facilitator, and participant. Although this is only one of several contexts in which I engage in faculty development (including TA preparation, national writing-across-the-curriculum workshops, and on-campus workshops for faculty), it demonstrates and perhaps amplifies some of the principles I hold to be most rewarding and effective in teacher development—principles of active learning and participation, of experiencing what we teach, of teaching what we experience, and of seeing the development of expertise as an ongoing pursuit.

In this respect my institute locates itself in a genre of writing workshops that stretch back for many years. Breadloaf, Martha's Vineyard, and other well established workshops were founded on the principle that participants would do something more than listen to experts pontificate about the craft of writing or the art of teaching. But every coordinator's style is unique, creating communities of learners in specific ways by using different strategies and activities. Over the years my summer institute has been shaped by my interests in how personal and professional reflection can enhance teachers' success in the classroom. The institute is a place where teachers move between the public and private dimensions of reflection, and the product of their work represents a mix of introspection and display.

Key Features of the Institute

Writing is a powerful tool—for change, for creativity in the classroom, for finding new depths of creativity in ourselves. In the institute, participants practice writing as a way to explore teaching. In the process they actively examine ways they can use writing as a tool for learning and discovery in the classroom, no matter what subject they happen to be teaching. As they experience various writing activities they think about how to translate them into useful strategies for engaging their students at all levels. At the center of our work is the concept of *reflective practice,* a realignment of our focus away from abstract theories or the findings of empirical research and toward personally meaningful, contextually grounded teaching experiences (Schön 1987, 1983). In addition to reflecting on theory, teachers can understand quality and improvement as a function of their own "reflection in action," which privileges narrative accounts, cases, anecdotes, and thoughtfulness in the classroom.

The Teaching Portfolio as a Context for Reflection

To engage in reflective practice each participant works on a teaching portfolio, a recent innovation in teacher education (Anson 1994). While no brief definition can do justice to the potential of the portfolio, it is essentially a place to document and reflect on one's experiences and ideas as a teacher. Participants begin their portfolios by working on several required entries: responses to some case studies about teaching; their own narrative case studies about a teaching experience or a teaching/learning autobiography; a description of an assignment that uses writing in unique ways; and reflective journal entries of various kinds. They also draft and revise additional entries of their own choice. At the end of the institute they will have produced as many as ten entries for their portfolio, to which they can continue to add, ideally teaming up with other teachers to share their reflections.

A Mix of Levels and Subjects

Diversity of both discipline and level is another key feature of the institute. All the institutes have enrolled teachers who work at all grade levels of teaching (first grade through college) and in several different subjects at the higher grade levels (science, math, English, social studies, and so forth). Participants are mainly practicing teachers, some new, some veteran, but the institute includes at least a few preservice teachers pursuing teaching degrees. Although the preservice teachers have little direct experience in the classroom, they benefit in important ways from the mentoring influence of those who have.

Because of this typical diversity of levels, subjects, and expertise, the participants find themselves welcoming and responding fully to all other institute participants, even when their material is not immediately relevant to their own needs or interests. In turn, everyone tries whenever possible to offer implications, suggestions, or direct applications of their work for as many other levels and subjects as possible. Far from impeding progress on instructional principles, the differences in the participants' teaching contexts create a richer and more meaningful experience for the entire group. Although some of the time the participants cluster by teaching level into small groups for workshop activities, there are also occasions when we deliberately intermingle and talk or work across levels. Everyone brings to the sessions a mix of knowledge and (mis)conceptions about what happens instructionally in levels at which they have not taught. College teachers have certain expectations, not always accurate, about what instruction students receive in writing as juniors or seniors in high school. Teachers at each level imagine the context that precedes and follows it, and the picture that forms in their minds often influences the goals and methods of their own classrooms. By sharing perspectives, activities, experiences, and philosophies across levels, the teachers feel enlightened and surprised by what they didn't know and what they thought they knew.

Contract Grading

The institute is designed as a collaborative, hands-on workshop involving lots of writing, revising, talking, and sharing. Because the institute is offered as a for-credit university course at the graduate level, portfolios must contain a certain number of required items. But all participants also have the freedom to conceive their own entries to share with the group. In this way the portfolio is both an outcome of the institute and a personally meaningful tool for teachers' own development and career goals. Philosophically, I want the participants to define their own criteria for success, both collectively and personally. For this reason I opt for a contract grading system that shifts the responsibility for measuring performance back onto the participants. All registered participants receive a grade based on the following system, which is excerpted from the institute's syllabus:

> A: This grade will be granted if you participate fully in the Institute—if you attend all the sessions, participate in the group projects, and turn in a portfolio that contains all the expected documents as well as at least *four* more of your own, self-sponsored entries demonstrating thoughtful reflection about teaching. These additional entries must be new reflections or materials, not ones from your existing files. All materials except journal responses should be of high quality—revised, edited, and polished.
> B: This grade will be granted if you participate in the Institute and turn in a teaching portfolio that contains all the expected documents but no additional documents. Documents should be of high quality.
> C: This grade will be granted if you participate fully in the Institute (and bring in any materials that our daily work will involve) but do not turn in a portfolio.

D/F: These grades are granted if you fail to participate in the Institute, depending on the severity of the problem. Turning in a portfolio without participating will not earn an A, B, or C grade.

An Emphasis on the Social and Collaborative

Although participants do a lot of writing in the institute, much of the time is spent in active paired or small-group work and in large-group discussion. Early on, participants form working teams, usually based on teaching level. These teams work independently to create an innovative, engaging assignment or activity and then decide how to present that assignment or activity to the larger group. Two or three days are set aside at the end of the institute for these thirty-minute presentations. The teams look upon the larger group as a class, and their goal is twofold: to explain their writing assignment or activity to peer teachers who may want to borrow it or adapt it to their own instruction, and to involve everyone as fully as possible in the assignment itself. The class "experiences" the team's assignment or activity from the imagined perspective of middle-schoolers or 10th-graders as well as from the expert perspective of peer teachers.

The Power of Story

From the beginning, the institute engages participants in reading and telling stories about teaching and learning. Regular journal reflections are prompted by published and unpublished cases about teaching (Anson 1998, Anson, Jolliffe, and Shapiro 1995, Anson et al. 1993) that present real(istic) dilemmas and complex situations to be analyzed, discussed, and written about. Having experienced these richly descriptive scenarios of teaching life, participants then craft their own cases, which they share with each other, or write autobiographical accounts of teaching and learning experiences that raise important issues for reflection. In this way, storytelling becomes an important way to encourage critical reflection about teaching, learning, and writing. Although these stories begin personally, tapping into teachers' own experiences, memories, and perceived difficulties, they gradually become more public, both as sites for discussion in the institute and eventually as documents that display teachers' thoughtfulness about their craft. This movement, from private to public, from personal to professional, mirrors the broader textual space—the portfolio—that contains the participants' narratives and serves the twin purposes of development and display.

The process of crafting a good case or story about teaching brings together into one activity some of the most powerful ways that we learn about teaching. The first is writing. To be effective writing coaches, we teachers need to experience what our students experience; we need to struggle to make meaning, we need to feel the pressure of a deadline or that often productive discomfort of imagining our peers experiencing our words; we need to feel that tension between the investment that yielded some bit of our prose and the need, after consultation and consensus, to tear it out of the text with a big circle of crosshatches or the clean and so-final sweep of the black block on the computer screen and the sudden and often irremediable keystroke that deletes it. We need to remember the moments of difficulty, of being twisted up in a tangle of assertions or feeling lost somewhere between two paragraphs that don't make sense together; we need to remember as well the moments of satisfaction or triumph when we're surprised by our own words and their elegance or intelligence.

In crafting stories about teaching, the participants also engage in and reflect on the process of responding to one another, and thus they begin to understand how to respond to students. They experience many of the same things in small response groups that their students experience: social nervousness, insecurity in the face of possible judgment, the tension between ownership and a desire for others' responses and suggestions. Their response focuses both on the craft of their drafts and on their meaning and purpose. As the participants work in teams they find themselves weaving between matters of expression and matters at the heart of the case or story itself, including the articulation of a teaching problem that raises important issues for discussion and reflection. Writing, listening, reading, commenting, revising—as participants experience and reflect on these activities they begin to internalize instructional principles that they can put to use in structuring or restructuring their own classroom activities.

The following outline of the institute shows how some of the methods I have described help shape the individual meetings and activities. The meetings (9:30 A.M.–noon) are short relative to the amount of work in the institute; this is to provide participants with plenty of time to write and reflect in between the usually intensive morning meetings.

General Plan

Day 1

Focus: Introduction(s) and overview. Portfolios. Writing to learn.

9:30–10:15	Brown bags and metaphors: who we are (individual writing and small groups)
10:15–11:00	Introduction to the institute; goal setting (individual writing)
11:00–11:10	Break
11:10–11:30	Writing in teaching and learning: why is there a problem? (individual brainstorming activity and follow-up discussion)
11:30–12:00	The role of informal writing in teaching and learning (presentation); the toolbox as metaphor for teaching and reflective practice

For day 2: (1) Please write a 2–3 page journal entry on the case in the packet titled "Writing Intensity." You may adapt the entry with details from your own experience, try to "solve" the case, or simply reflect on the issues it raises. (2) Please read "Using Informal Writing to Enhance Learning: Some Strategies" in the packet; choose one of the strategies, then write a portfolio entry of about a page describing how you could use the strategy in your present or future teaching, or else reflect on some variations or adaptations of the strategy.

Day 2

Focus: Writing to learn; journals; dialogue journals. Portfolio entries.

9:30–10:00	Response to the case: sharing journal entries (small groups)
10:00–10:30	Informal writing: pros, cons, assessment (discussion); sample strategies (small groups, reports); dialogue journals (swap entries)
10:30–10:40	Break
10:40–11:30	Exploring "artifacts" for the portfolio: envelope strategy (small groups and large-group follow-up for list)
11:30–12:00	Sample entries: the discourse of reflection (presentation)

For day 3: (1) Respond briefly to your dialogue-journal partner's entry by writing directly to him or her. (2) Read the three vignettes titled "Journals: Vignettes for Reflection and Discussion" in the packet, then write a response to the one that is most appropriate for your instructional level. (3) Try some preliminary brainstorming for a significant teaching or learning event that you might decide to turn into a case or an autobiographical account.

Day 3

Focus: Writing as a process. Creative assignments: the heart of school writing.

9:30–10:00	Discussion of journal vignettes
10:00–10:30	Assignment case (reading, writing, small groups)
10:30–10:45	"Working" break
10:45–11:00	Continued work on case; informally rating the drafts (color-dot strategy)
11:00–12:00	Discussion of case; ten principles of effective assignments

For day 4: Please write a draft of an assignment or writing strategy that you have used, adapted, or would like to try out in the classroom. Your goal is to document a creative, principled use of writing. Follow the format described in the packet on page 49. Bring a *rough draft* of the write-up on Friday so we can discuss it.

Day 4

Focus: Writing as process: response and revision

9:30–10:00	Peer groups: theory and practice (presentation); designing revision guides/helping writers revise their writing
10:00–11:00	Group conferences (small groups)
11:00–11:15	Break
11:15–12:00	Discussion of peer groups; designing cases as assignments

For day 5: Please begin drafting your autobiographical narrative or case. *We shall eventually share drafts of these.* Also begin developing additional portfolio entries if you intend to include these in the course.

Day 5

Focus: Group brainstorming and planning for assignment presentation/ activity

| 9:30–10:00 | Prospects and possibilities for team assignments |
| 10:00–12:00 | Team work (see below) |

Note: Please meet with your partner or team members to work on your assignment activity. You may leave and meet anywhere you like, perhaps somewhere more comfortable than our classroom; however, the room is still available for you to use if you wish. If you would rather meet at a different time, you are also free to arrange your own schedule. I will be available in our room for consultation.

Day 6

Focus: Response and evaluation

9:30–10:00	Response: approaches and methods (presentation)
10:00–10:45	Response cases: first grade, fifth grade, junior high
10:45–11:00	Break; mid-institute evaluation
11:00–12:00	Team planning

For day 7: Please prepare a draft of your narrative account of a teaching experience (or a case thereof) for discussion in a small group.

Day 7

Focus: Teaching experience, lore, and narratives in the improvement of teaching

9:30–10:30	Narrative accounts: revision workshop (small groups)
10:30–10:45	Break
10:45–11:00	Follow-up; brief presentation on audience and purpose; ideas for children's purposeful writing
11:00–12:00	Team planning or sharing of additional portfolio entries

For day 8: Please prepare a revision of your autobiographical account to turn in. If your team has assigned any work to you, please follow through. Also be prepared to discuss briefly any additional portfolio entry you are working on or have turned in.

Day 8

Focus: Error and correctness of expression

9:30–10:15	What to do about error and correctness in writing; brief presentation on the social construction of error
10:00–10:50	Project-based writing activities and student portfolios
10:50–11:00	Break
11:00–12:00	Team planning or sharing of additional portfolio entries

For day 9: Please prepare any additional portfolio entries you wish to turn in. Scheduled teams: prepare for your presentation/activity.

Day 9

Focus: Response and evaluation. Using writing creatively: group-led activities.

9:30–10:45	Evaluation: rubrics, holistic assessment
10:45–11:00	Break
11:00–12:00	Groups 1 and 2

Day 10

Focus: Response and evaluation. Using writing creatively: group-led activities.

9:30–11:45	Groups 3–7
11:45–12:00	Wrap-up and evaluation

The Teaching Portfolio

Each participant's portfolio in the institute must contain a certain number of required entries (usually five). These provide common ground for collaboration and small-group revision sessions. In choosing the five required entries, I try to emphasize the process of reflection. Some entries are considered "primary" documents in a teaching portfolio (Anson 1994); they are the direct products of teaching, such as a syllabus, lesson plan, or assignment description. "Secondary" documents are reflections on teaching, and these are not typically required by the act of teaching itself. A secondary document can be created in its own right, such as an exploration of some classroom issue, or it can be created by explaining and rationalizing a primary document. To encourage reflection, any primary documents I ask for in the portfolio or which participants include optionally must be explained, annotated, theorized, or rationalized in some way. The simple description of an assignment therefore becomes an occasion for the writer to reveal his or her goals and explain the methods that she or he uses to structure the assignment.

The following table of contents from the portfolio of Steve, a fifth-grade language arts teacher, shows both the required documents and the documents that Steve chose to develop and include. In this particular institute, participants worked on a philosophy of teaching, a case based on a difficult or complex teaching experience, a fully articulated and theorized writing activity or assignment, a statement of course "outcomes" or objectives and what particular methods are used to measure these, and a series of five reflective journal responses, some of them on published cases discussed collectively.

Table of Contents

Steve also included three documents that show him actively exploring and reflecting on his own teaching from the perspective of parents (letters), a colleague (an observation), and a theorist (Paulo Freire). For his fourth optional entry he decided to develop another innovative writing assignment, which he included along with a reflection on his goals and methods.

Teachers soon learn that they must make critical decisions about every element of the portfolio they create. The required documents offer such freedom of focus and expression that no two entries look alike. Beyond including these required documents, teachers shape their portfolios by selecting entries that show themselves to be "critically reflective teachers" (Brookfield 1995), teachers willing to reexamine difficult moments in the classroom. The best of the portfolios are characterized by self-disclosure, because too glib an attitude toward something as complex as teaching betrays a mechanization of expertise and a belief that good teaching can be acquired once and forgotten about, like riding a bike.

Not all the extra portfolio entries represent a collection of disparate documents like Steve's. Some participants choose to work on an overarching theme. Patti, a third-grade teacher, developed her portfolio around the difficult process of peer observation and review. She chose to reflect extensively on a series of observations her principal conducted over several months. She described in detail each of the classes that he visited, and then analyzed his written evaluation, exploring how his own beliefs about teaching influenced what he saw her doing. Without criticizing her principal, she showed how hard it is to understand teaching just from looking at it, without understanding the broader context of a classroom working over time.

Raoul, a high school teacher of social studies, focused some of his extra portfolio entries on his very creative assignments. He described each assignment in great detail, explaining his rationale for its parts, outlining the processes through which he guided his students, and sharing excerpts from their written work. His final portfolio entry reflected on what happened to his assignments and to his own thinking as he revisited them and tried to explain them to his readers and to himself. His portfolio became a demonstration of how writing and reflection circle back on themselves, creating new ideas and new text.

Because there are no formal criteria set in advance for any of the required portfolio entries, the group must rely on its own collective formulation of standards for each entry. In some cases, notably the required entries, these standards are developed with the collaboration and consensus of all the institute participants. To facilitate this process, I often hand out a rough draft of a previous institute participant's entry in the same genre as that under consideration, used with permission of the author. After a break-out session in which small groups critique the draft, the entire class derives some principles for a successful version of the document. These principles then become a kind of revision guide as all members of the class share and talk about their own drafts of the same type of document. The collectively developed criteria become productive rather than simply evaluative. It doesn't take long for the participants to recognize the value of such a process for their own teaching. Several language arts teachers in the elementary grades have shared with me the results of their experiments in "class-created criteria" for students' writing. Even young children, they remark, "know" what makes a good narrative, description, or letter; they just need practice teasing out this knowledge, recognizing it, and then applying it in turn to their own developing drafts.

As the participants are working on portfolio entries they are also deciding when they think these entries are ready to be turned in to me. I retain the right to return an entry as not yet ready for the portfolio, accompanied by my own comments and suggestions, but in all the institutes this has happened only rarely. When participants leave the institute they carry with them a wealth of new teaching strategies and methods; a fully elaborated new activity or assignment created with their group (along with the assignments presented by all the other groups); and many new insights into the teaching and learning processes. Perhaps most importantly, however, they also carry with them the beginnings of a teaching portfolio. The product of this portfolio—a few well-written entries—is not really the point. The portfolio is emblematic of a new approach to teacher education, an approach that encourages lifelong reflection and development. To stave off complacency, I usually recommend that every participant revisit one of their more speculative entries, such as their teaching philosophy, in five years, and then rewrite it. When I give this invitation I am always hopeful that the portfolio will become the material and conceptual space within which teachers can continually grow, learn, and improve their craft.

The Teaching Portfolio as Tool
for Reflective Practice

As I have taught it, the institute does not represent a high-stakes course in a densely packed education curriculum. Participants take the institute mainly for reasons of personal and professional development. Some teachers earn college credits for "lane changes" in their school systems, for recognition of merit, or to meet recertification standards. Some love their work so much that they are willing to enroll in an intensive course during the summer when many of their colleagues are relaxing (or collapsing) after an exhausting academic year. A few enroll because they recognize they are struggling in their classrooms and want to improve. Almost all are eager to do something new—and something more—with writing.

For this reason the precise "content" or "coverage" of the institute may not be as important as it would be in a course required by an education curriculum or for state teaching licensure. Whether the group debates the merits of personal writing over argument, for example, or reads Dewey or Vygotsky or bell hooks doesn't make or break the course, though the institute covers so much ground that such authors and issues often come up. What matters in the institute are three central outcomes that I believe should enter into every teacher's experience at some point in their preparation and development. In many ways, these outcomes determine everything that happens in the institute.

Teachers of Writing Must
(Learn to) Write—Often

In my work with hundreds of writing teachers, especially those teaching grades K–12, I have been troubled to discover how little the teachers themselves write. Most engage in school-related tasks, such as writing progress reports on students, but very few write the kinds of texts they ask their students to write: descriptions and stories, poems, argumentative essays, summaries of important readings. All the tasks we put before our students have more sophisticated parallels in our own professional and personal worlds. If they don't, perhaps they ought to be removed from our curriculums. Yet, many teachers don't set aside the time to write and to experience the process of writing.

There are many causes of this problem, the most insidious of which is a work life so burdened that there is simply no time to devote to contemplation or to drafting and revising and tinkering with a document that may seem to do little to advance one's professional standing, improve one's teaching, or make a difference to one's supervisors. By providing a rhetorical space where teachers can both improve and document their instruction, the teaching portfolio can bridge the gap between personally meaningful writing and direct connections to one's career goals, advancement, and means of assessment. Students in the institute learn about the goals and nature of the teaching portfolio in a low-stakes environment where they can begin shaping entries that mean something to them and remind them of the processes, in all their complexity, that students also go through in responding to our assignments. If school districts and departments reward teachers for maintaining and building these portfolios, teachers will continue to write avidly and meaningfully for different purposes. They will also find a place where other sorts of writing belong, such as poems and stories about their classrooms, or journal-like reflections on their teaching.

Teachers Should (Learn How to)
Practice Reflection

As Schön (1987, 1983) and others have described and theorized the process of critical reflection, its practice is not always guaranteed in a teacher's daily work. The most successful practitioners in many fields often learn intuitively how to move between doing and reflecting, between the hands-on work of their trade and the speculative process of assessing its progress and results. Many teachers, however, are trained in the science of classroom management, not the art of personal theorizing. They may spend so much of their time looking at and working with particulars that they don't give themselves opportunities to stand back from that work and think about it more philosophically. In teaching writing, for example, instructors may fall into patterns of responding to students' writing that they apply almost mechanically, year after year. Critical reflection means examining those response practices from various perspectives, asking whether the responses are effective, or even trying to assess how students act on or feel about the responses. Predictably, such reflection often leads to changed (and improved) teaching practices and behaviors. More importantly, the process of reflection can move teachers out of instructional complacency and can sometimes reenergize a teacher who has reached a point of career burnout.

Teachers Must (Learn to) Work Together

One of the great ironies of the teaching profession is the way in which we often turn an extensively public activity into an intensely private experience. Students fill the seats in our classrooms and create a community united in a common goal of learning and sharing knowledge; but we symbolically shut out our colleagues, closing the classroom door on our pedagogy and its potential to enrich each other's experiences. We may share anecdotes with our peers, or we may work abstractly on the curriculum we teach, but we rarely show each other our assignments, swap writing samples to compare the way we respond to our students, ask each other for feedback on a teaching activity, or engage in other mentoring activities.

Of course, the teaching portfolio can easily perpetuate this privacy; teachers can write entries alone and place them into a portfolio for possible review, at which time the private becomes public in all the ways that we fear, for purposes of judgment, not development. Perhaps because portfolios beg for public scrutiny, even the most solitary of writers feels compelled to try out a new entry on a supportive reader before the binder rings snap closed on the final draft or it appears on the teacher's website to be viewed by the world.

In any course, program, or school where teaching portfolios may be used as a form of assessment, opportunities for collaboration and mentoring should become the governing philosophy and goal of the portfolio system. Portfolios should never be inert but should remain in a state of constant motion, matching the processes at work when we teach and when we write.

2

Bridging Levels

Composition Theory and Practice for Preservice Teachers and TAs

Gail Stygall
University of Washington

As I prepare to teach new teachers of writing I worry about various students—the student with unrecognized but obvious potential whose class or race doesn't match the school's version of the good student, the student with learning disabilities who is entitled by law to accommodations that the teacher refuses to give, the student impatient with the mindless busywork of his or her English classes. In both my preservice course on teaching writing and the TA seminar I teach, we read about these students and others whose experiences do not resemble the experiences of beginning teachers of writing (see especially Milanés 1998, Dunn 1995). And that is one of the central problems of both courses: how to convince new teachers that they cannot rely on their own educational experiences as a guide for teaching all students.

As I began teaching these two courses several years ago I proceeded as if the previous experiences of students and teachers and the contexts in which each group taught or would be teaching mattered not at all. I was wrong in both cases. Over the years I learned that the teaching context and reflection must be the primary organizing principles of both courses. As a result, the preservice course I teach tempers expressivist theory and pedagogy with the social constructionist perspective on the diverse student populations served by the Puget Sound school districts. In addition, the assessment demands of a statewide assessment program means that my preservice students need deep work in that area, not just on assessment in general but in the specifics of writing assessment. In the TA seminar, on the other hand, my pedagogy turns increasingly to the actual conditions, students, and courses that we offer, fitting theoretical discussions to the questions our teaching assistants are facing as they teach their first quarter. In this essay I concentrate primarily on the preservice course, explaining its student population, the readings, and the assignments. I then make comparisons with the TA course and discuss the major similarities and differences.

Accounts of these kinds of courses in the scholarly literature for either the preservice teachers or beginning teaching assistants are modest at best. Thus initially, when I began teaching the preservice course, I had little to go on other than my graduate school preparation, which had led me to expect to teach beginning TAs at some point in my career. Fortunately, several threads hold writing teacher education courses together at both levels.

The first thread relates to literature. In both courses most of the students have little interest in writing in and of itself, most of them have not had any coursework in the area. Instead, writing is a boring, tedious adjunct to the study of literature, and both groups can be similarly indifferent to the idea that students need to be taught to write. Consequently, the second thread relates to that indifference: most of the students in both courses are fairly effortless writers and have been rewarded for it. They are good at "English," receive high grades, and expect students to be just like they are. Among the TAs a sizable portion have never taken first-year composition, having either attended elite schools that teach a general humanities course in place of writing, or having AP'd out. The lack of understanding of the relations between high school and college is evident in the attitudes of both groups. The preservice teachers know little about first-year composition; the beginning TAs know little about how writing is taught in high schools. Thread number three is the observation, well known in education, that teachers teach the way they were taught. Most of the beginning teachers in both classes have never received direct instruction in writing in their major, not even in writing about literature.

The corrective in all three of these situations is to make reflectivity about both the past and the present, and a focus on the local context in which these teachers are or will be teaching, constant factors in both courses. And both courses, in fact, do present quite similar themes and assignments. Each course begins with a close look at the process classroom and key scholarship. At the same time, in each course I make sure that we enact some of those practices, keeping in mind Mary M. Kennedy's (1998) findings that a reform pedagogy in writing works only if the discussions about pedagogy also include participation in the practices of pedagogy (14). Each course also includes careful attention to the students each group of beginning teachers will be or are teaching. Both courses also provide sustained attention to the critique mounted by social constructionists, especially in relation to diversity. Assessment and grammar are a fourth thread—writing teachers must know something about both classroom evaluation and larger-scale assessment. Both groups need to rethink their attitudes about what standard English represents. In addition, students in both courses write response papers to the readings, do collaborative projects, and engage in serious study of writing itself.

The Preservice Course in Theory and Practice of Teaching Writing

I was not prepared in graduate school for teaching this course for English education students, even though I had completed all but my student teaching for secondary certification before attending graduate school. The course about teaching writing didn't exist when I was in school, or if it did, it was in Education rather than English. Nor did I teach such a course in my first two full-time positions, one as a lecturer, the next as an assistant professor. But when I moved to the University of Washington, however, I discovered that not only was I expected to teach this course, I was expected to teach the English methods course as well. I hadn't been hired as an English Education specialist, so the assignments were mystifying to me, still naive about what literature faculty thought composition and rhetoric people studied. I also was, and remain, puzzled by my department's relative blindness to the fact that anywhere from 25 to 35 percent of the students they taught in literature classes were in fact intending to enter the university's certification program. When explaining what I am teaching, in the context of hiring needs, I am asked again and again why the English department needs to teach this "education" course in preparing to teach writing. I sigh and explain.

The Population

Students enter this course as a part of the education track within the department's available majors. Students in the program are required to take four courses in language and writing and the course in the theory and practice of teaching writing. Some of the students who enroll have come straight through our undergraduate program, nearly always taking these courses very late in their undergraduate careers. Some of the students also come to the program with baccalaureate degrees from other institutions. The students who follow the education track in English are not diverse. Few Asian Americans are enrolled, and the underrepresented minorities—African Americans, Pacific Islanders, and Hispanics—are rarely present.

The Readings

The Writing Classroom

I've divided the readings in the course into four parts. The first part establishes the writing classroom through the work of teacher-scholars such as Nancie Atwell, Lucy Calkins, and Tom Romano. Most students will not have experienced the writing workshop in college, though some may have done so during their K–12 years. In either case, setting out the framework of the "ideal" writing classroom is my first goal.

Atwell's "Building a Dining Room Table" (1987a) and *In the Middle* (1998), along with Romano's "Writing Process in One High School Classroom" and "Literary Warnings" (1987b, c), demonstrate the joy of teaching writing and of seeing what students can create. I also include Burniske's "Creating Dialogue" (1994) summarizing of the uses of journals, and Bruffee's introduction to *A Short Course in Writing* (1985), which presents ideas about writing groups and their function in the classroom. Crowley's "The Emergence of Process Pedagogy" (1998b) provides an overview and history, however critical it may be. Although Lucy Calkins' *The Art of Teaching Writing* (1994) is perhaps the most comprehensive work available, it has only a single chapter, "Teaching Adolescents," devoted to teaching writing in high schools. Finally, I include Mark Wiley's review of four books often found in preservice courses (2000). I, like Wiley, am uncomfortable with the apparent problems matching this text world of process writing classrooms to the realities of urban and suburban schools.

School Profiles/Writing Teachers Teaching Writing

A second reading sequence is formed around two goals. The first is to prepare my students with information they will need to complete the first major assignment, which I'll describe in the next section. The second is to give preservice teachers a good look at the actual schools in which they will be teaching. One reason for my doing so is the astonishing dropout rate for beginning teachers. "As many as 30 percent of our beginning teachers leave the profession by the end of their second year, with up to 50 percent leaving by the end of five years" (McMackin and Boccia 1998, 55). At least part of the problem in my view is new teachers' not knowing what they will be facing. As a response I include all the publicly available reports on three very different high schools in the Seattle School District. Often, my students assume that they will be teaching students just like them; the increasing diversity of the Puget Sound area indicates otherwise. Along with these reports I turn in this section to reports of teachers in action, teaching writing to widely diverse students, in a variety of nonliterary assignments.

The high school reports are drawn from three sources: the public schools themselves, including scores on the statewide mandated assessment; the "School Scout" report produced by a local television station; and the *Seattle Times* newspaper's "Schools Report." The other readings are drawn primarily from *English Journal* and describe writing projects that actual teachers are bringing to the secondary classrooms. Beach and Finders describe "Students as Ethnographers" (1999), and Bomer offers "Writing to Think Critically" (2000) assignments on social action. Cone takes up the issue of "Untracking Advanced Placement English" (1992), while Irby describes "Empowering the Disempowered" (1993), a real-world writing project, for the students deemed worst in English, completed in a Puget Sound area high school. Meyer, in "It's a Lot of Hectic in Middle School (1999), gives the perspective of a teacher-trainer going back to middle school, and Tom Romano makes another appearance with "The Multigenre Research Paper" (1995). I accompany Romano with Grierson's "Circling Through Texts" (1999), which presents multigenre assignments and the resulting student work.

Social Constructionist Critique

Here, my intent is to emphasize and reemphasize that these preservice teachers need to think about teaching all their students, in all their diversity. Attention to language communities, disabilities, gender, and race all play into these readings.

I begin this section with Thomas Miller's historical account of the factors that formed the discipline of English and its teaching (1997) and then turn to James Berlin's (1996) analysis. With the Miller account I am heading into discussions of prescriptivism and the teaching of grammar, supplemented by Patrick Hartwell's classic article on grammar (1985). With Berlin, I want students to begin examining just what it means to study English, as they have been doing. Joseph Harris's "The Idea of Community" (1989) provides a focal point for understanding social constructionism, and Anis Bawarshi's "The Genre Function" (2000) provides an interaction between language communities and the work genres do to "construct" certain writers and writing. Sandra Jamieson's work in "Composition Readers and the Construction of Identity" (1997) offers us an opportunity to talk about how students are constructed in textbooks. Articles by Greg Myers (1986) and me take up the issues of collaboration—it isn't just one happy group of compliant, eagerly collaborating students, but students who bring their identities and their politics to the classroom. Brenda Brueggemann et al. (2001), Arnetha Ball (1992), Lisa Delpit (1998), and Todd DeStigter (2000) help identify three specific language groups that are rendered invisible in the typical classroom. Their learning to write demands a greater commitment from teachers and a reach beyond pure expressivism and process pedagogy.

Assessment

My primary concerns in this section are twofold. First, the statewide performance assessment of writing will become a graduation barrier by 2008. If a student does not pass the tenth-grade set of assessments, he or she will not graduate with a "certificate of mastery." Second, the understanding of what students will be asked to do in either two- or four-year colleges is fairly limited among secondary teachers. In meetings about a possible "benchmark four" (the certificate of mastery is "benchmark three"), I have listened to many high school teachers talk about what colleges expect in writing. The discussion has been nearly uniformly incorrect. The writing program directors at the four-year schools and a number of writing coordinators from the community colleges have explained, sometimes eloquently, what they expect from entering students, and little of it relates to writing about literature. Unfortunately, the weight of tradition is heavy, and reform in the secondary curriculum seems unlikely. The Office of the Superintendent of Public Instruction nixed a recent recommendation by secondary English chairs that all preservice teachers take a course like I am describing.

The holistically scored, performance-oriented Washington Assessment of Student Learning (WASL) requires demonstration of the writing process. As a result, the reading selections here introduce students to discussions about class-room assessment: Daiker's "Learning to Praise" (1989), Camp and Levine's "Portfolios Evolving" (1991), and Connors and Lunsford's "Teachers' Rhetor-ical Comments on Student Papers" (1993). These readings are combined with discussions about larger-scale assessment: Belanoff on portfolios (1994), Vopat on the AP English exam (1989), and Wolcott and Legg (1998) on direct writing assessment and holistic scoring.

Most importantly, I include the materials on the tests their students will be facing. In addition to the WASL materials, I also include a sample from the ASSET "writing" test, a multiple-choice test on punctuation and grammar mas-querading as a placement test for writing in all the community colleges in the state of Washington. Advanced Placement English sample tests and responses, as well as comparison with first-year college writing from the University of Washington, conclude the final reading segment.

The Major Assignments

I use three types of writing assignments in the preservice course as a means of actualizing and instantiating the ideas about teaching writing covered in the course. The first category of assignment is reflective response papers of one and a half to two pages. Each paper includes two aspects: a thorough summary of the article's content and a reflective comment drawn from the students' ex-periences as students in the classroom. I also use these reading responses to en-act the writing process early in the term. On the first day, for example, I ask stu-dents to spend about fifteen minutes reading one of the articles and then ask them to do a free-write responding to what they have read. Afterward, we dis-cuss the responses and how they might begin to form the basis of the paper. Later in the term I ask students to respond to one another through structured peer responses that are based on descriptions rather than evaluations of one an-other's work.

The second major assignment is collaborative and makes use of the read-ing materials in the second segment. In groups of three or four, students create writing unit plans of three to four weeks based on information from the course packet and their research on a particular school. The assignment is structured so that students will have both independent and collective roles in the process. Students can be surprised what the sources tell them about schools they thought they knew. Sometimes they discover segments of the student body they never knew were in the building. Additionally, they discover the public perceptions of various schools, contributing to the information they need as beginning teachers.

The final project asks students to conduct a study of actual writing or the teaching of writing. Students can choose to examine past writing assignments they have received in other classes, conduct a miniethnography of another class, analyze the written commentary they or others have received on their papers, interview someone who writes on the job and examine their writing, analyze a textbook for its positions on writing, or analyze a nonliterary text—perhaps the website of a particular school. One of my past favorites was a study of the machinists' notes from one shift to another, telling their successors on the line about problems with machines and new ideas.

The TA Seminar in Theory and Practice of Composition

In my own department, the "course" for new graduate TAs was initiated in the late 1980s, but it was then a practicum in which there was little introduction to the field. Previous to that time, William Irmscher had prepared TAs without the required course in his repertoire, though to be sure, all writing program directors, course or no course, work as much through persuasion as anything else. Now, in keeping with the idea that change means disengaging old models of teaching, I not only introduce the seminar students to the field of composition pedagogy but invite them to begin thoughtful, reflective pedagogy, applying what we read to actual experiences in the classroom.

The Population

Students enrolled in the TA seminar are already beginning to teach first-year composition, and that provides an immediate, local context for our discussions of theory and practice. The students have quite diverse interests. Most of them are there to study literature, though students who have opted for the Language and Rhetoric track in our graduate program are also enrolled, as well as creative writers and MATESL students. These students have already gone through a two-week preterm orientation, running daily from 9:30–3:30. In that orientation they have already learned the course goals, assignment design, and course construction. In the seminar, I intend to forge a relationship between the course they are teaching and the research and scholarship in composition and rhetoric. In addition, I want students to know something about the important research questions in the field and to begin to engage with those questions.

The Readings

The course readings are divided into nine topics and are directly related to the issues of the course they are teaching. The first week, we take up the Bartholomae–Elbow (Elbow 1995, Bartholomae 1994) debate about academic writing. I follow with materials on reading critically, including Bartholomae's "Introduction" from *Ways of Reading* (Bartholomae and Petroskey 1999), Elizabeth Long's "Textual Interpretation as Collective Action" (1992), and a chapter from Frank Smith's *Understanding Reading* (1994). Collaboration is the next topic, followed by grammar and grading. From this point on we take up more theoretical issues, related to race, class, gender, followed by rhetoric and rhetorical history, genre theory, and multiculturalism. As the students in the seminar are often theoretically inclined and concerned about classroom conflict over ideas, one reading segment includes Linda Brodkey's "On the Subject of Race and Class in 'The Literacy Letters'" (1989), my own attempt to directly address Brodkey's concerns in teacher education in "Resisting Privilege: Basic Writing and Foucault's Author Function" (1994), Richard Miller's discussion of controversial topics in "Fault Lines in the Contact Zone" (1994), and Susan Wells' chapter on the collapse of her feminist classroom and her analysis of what happened in "Giving an Ordered History: Narrative in the Discourse of the Classroom" (1996). These readings address a fairly common clash in the first-year writing classroom: undergraduate students' first contact with materials that challenge their views of the world and TAs' interest in these complex subjects. In addition to the course packet, students also read Richard Miller's *As If Learning Mattered: Reforming Higher Education* (1998) and Martha Kolln's *Rhetorical Grammar: Grammatical Choices, Rhetorical Effects* (1996).

The Major Assignments

As with the preservice course, I ask for reading responses. Although in the TA course I don't use the responses as extensively to teach process approaches, I do ask for the same type of reflectivity. The reflective responses here are more directly tied to the TAs' actual teaching and are useful in working toward the "Teaching Artifact" assignment. That assignment asks students to do the following:

Each student will present an "artifact" drawn from teaching during the quarter or one developed for the next quarter. In developing this assignment, students will need to identify a theoretical position in which the artifact is located as well as ask how the artifact positions students. *This project will be four to six pages of analysis plus an attached copy of the artifact.*

The most important aspect of this assignment is your being able to locate your own work in the readings/positions/theories we've read and discussed this quarter. I also want you to be able to begin to articulate a teaching philosophy through the materials you use in the classroom. In job candidate interviews, the most impressive applicants are those who when asked about teaching are able to move easily into describing what they do and able to draw on a specific practice or approach to teaching for an example.

Your analysis should include the following items:

- Thoroughly describe your artifact (and attach it as an appendix to the assignment).

- Locate it by school, theory, or area of interest in composition/rhetoric, citing and quoting from relevant sources, either from class or from your own research on teaching.

- Explain how students are positioned by the artifact. (How do you speak of them? To them? What sorts of actions can they undertake?)

- Assess the effectiveness of this artifact? Did it work? If not, why not, and what would you change?

Sometimes the papers generated by the artifacts present success, though not always for the reasons the teaching assistant originally thought; sometimes they present failure and an accounting for why something didn't work. Because the assignment asks the students to locate their teaching practice in theories about teaching writing, students move closer to reflecting on and identifying their own emerging teaching philosophies. As with the preservice course activities, the drafting–peer response–revising sequence is built into this assignment, providing the students with an opportunity to do what their own students are doing.

A second major assignment is collaborative, requiring students to work together to present a grammar assignment, drawn from the principles in Martha Kolln's *Rhetorical Grammar* (1996) as well as from the teaching strategies necessary to use the ideas in their own classrooms. My goal here is to help the seminar students make the transition from prescriptive grammar to grammar for rhetorical effect. Very few of our entering students have dramatic problems with prestige written English, but rather than abandoning grammar altogether, I ask that both TAs and their students become aware of and make use of strategic editing for style. Before I included these materials, when seminar students were told that our focus was on writing processes and content revisions, they left the grammar out. As each group presents the assignment to the seminar and makes us actually do the assignment the TAs have an opportunity to construct a mini-lesson on style, making it less intimidating to present in their own classrooms.

The final assignment is quite similar to the final assignment for the preservice course. Students conduct an analysis of writing or materials associated with the teaching of writing. Papers for the graduate course are longer, and the range of topics is less heavily tied to the classroom. Many students have chosen to do historical projects, examining journals or daybooks from settlers in Washington or examining *doxa* or the history of writing instruction at the University of Washington. Other students want to examine ideologies present in their students' writing.

Though I don't have a second term with these students, I do work with most of them for several years. I see them develop as teachers and as scholars of pedagogy. I have some sense of my localized, reflective pedagogy having an impact on their teaching. Some do revert to teaching how they were taught when they move to writing about literature—testimony, I think, to the power of their past experiences. Others apply what they've learned about teaching writing not only to their writing-about-literature courses but to their actual literature courses.

Conclusion

The effects of teacher education are decidedly difficult to observe. With the TAs there is a continuing opportunity for me to observe the positive or ill effects of their preparation in teaching writing. They work together in a cohort for several years beyond the seminar, experimenting with their ideas as they become more experienced in the classroom. They also work with faculty mentors for each new course they teach, and many of them are now choosing to make pedagogy part of their doctoral exams in addition to their areas of specialization. This is quite unlike the experiences of many beginning secondary teachers, who, when detached from their college or university program at graduation, are often isolated and unmentored during their early teaching years, another factor contributing to the high resignation rates among beginning teachers. The fact that they take the course in theory and practice of teaching writing before they actually enter the Teacher Education Program for certification probably decreases the impact of the class on their teaching.

Nevertheless, if Mary Kennedy's (1998) study is correct—that reform efforts can be successful when they are accompanied by both practical experience in the area and a thorough explanation of the theoretical principles—then both of these courses have the potential for affecting the teaching of writing. Attending to the actual contexts of teaching, a kind of "all teaching is local" framing, along with accompanying reflection on theory and practice, makes a small start on reform possible. And maybe, just maybe, my preservice writing teachers will all be thinking about those same students that I fear will be forgotten.

III

Four Essays

The following section is made up of four essays that describe four courses and programs, each highlighting in different ways the three themes for the book, which Chris Anson's chapter brings into focus. In addition, each of these four essays provides additional perspectives for understanding the arguments and complications proposed in the introduction and the ensuing commentaries.

Chris Anson's first imperative for writing teachers is the beginning point and the turning point: *writing teachers must be writers.* This has been a constant since Klaus' NDEA Institutes in the 1960s, through Gebhardt's balanced design in the 1970s, through the proliferation of writing projects in the 1980s, to the present. Catherine Latterell, in the survey of composition programs summarized in the Introduction, found that pedagogy courses in first-year composition, which "often mimic methods courses taught in education departments," include writing and "engage [beginning teachers] in a variety of writing activities designed to model practices they will use in their own classrooms" (1996,15).

In the first essay in this section Tom Romano presents his version of the writing teacher educator as writing teacher—and as writer. For compositionists it may be difficult to connect Romano's passionate presentation of the multi-genre paper with teaching first-year writing. However, it's worthwhile considering that more and more first-year composition teachers (see, for example, Davis and Shadl 2000) around the country are finding "multi-writing" and the multi-genre research paper welcome improvements over the sterile and, with the proliferation of internet term-paper sites, increasingly suspect qualities of the traditional research project. It's also worth noting that genre and genre studies represent a central idea that surfaces often in this collection as a shaping factor for courses and programs at both the secondary and postsecondary levels.

Looking back to the introduction and Smagorinsky and Whiting's well-placed concerns about writing methods courses, Romano and David Smit, author of the second essay in this section, come close to taking on the role of the methods purist's worst nightmare—and they are untroubled by that—(especially Smit. Not only does Smit teach writing in his method's class, but while he's doing it he denies it's even a methods class). We've positioned Smit's chapter after Romano's because Smit provides a theoretical commentary on genre and the importance of genre in writing teacher education. Smit's chapter also describes his use of an epistemic assignment sequence. Not only is sequencing, which Smit originally learned from Carl Klaus, an important teaching practice for the writing classroom (see Dowst 1980, Harris 1997, Krupa 1982, Jenseth and Lotto 1996), but historically it represents one of the few unbroken methodological lineages in writing teacher education that we can trace back to before the 1960s. Dowst and Harris (1997, 34) follow its development back to the 1930s and Theodore Baird's "English 1–2" at Amherst College. Baird, clearly an early mentor in writing teacher education, was successful and influential enough with sequencing that three of his younger colleagues, William E. Coles (1974, 1978), Walker Gibson (1974), and Roger Sale (1970), adopted his approach, refined it, and transported it to other institutions after they left Amherst.

Smit's use of sequencing and his students' use of a "reflection journal" looks ahead to the book's second theme, reflection. Over the last fifteen years writing teacher educators have increasingly felt the need to encourage students to reflect on their own experiences as writers and writing students, especially as a prelude to beginning preparation as teachers. Linda Miller Cleary's adaptation of "in-depth phenomenological interviewing" in the third essay in this section takes up the theme of reflection and shows one way to help beginning writing teachers pay close attention to their experience and apply it to the classroom situations they soon will encounter. In addition, Miller Cleary adds another layer to the usual discussions of reflection by using her and her students' experiences with interviewing as the basis for organizing not only what she knows as writer and writing teacher but what she knows as writing teacher educator as well.

Miller Cleary's focus on reflection also creates a context for Wilhoit's comments about the obstacles that stand in the way of reconfiguring writing teacher education as an interdisciplinary practice:

> If we think in terms of a 9–13 curriculum, how are high school writing teachers learning to define their job, and how are first-year college writing teachers learning to define theirs? Without both groups knowing, a 9–13 curriculum is bound to fail—there is too much opportunity for teachers to work at cross purposes.

Building opportunities for close attention to past writing experience into the fabric of writing teacher education across the gap between the school and university, by means like in-depth phenomenological interviewing, can make it possible for teachers and prospective teachers on both sides to reflect and more deeply understand what they know about themselves and about one another, and about the implications of extending their work together beyond the institutionally imposed boundaries of their classrooms.

Mentoring, our third theme, in the form of supervised observation, practica, and student teaching, has been an important part of secondary teacher education for a much longer time than reflection. In contrast, first-year programs are often perceived to have been slow to adopt these practices, choosing instead to center writing teacher education on theory. Recently, though, especially since the mid-1990s, as Sally Barr Ebest (2000) points out, there is in process what appears to be a decisive shift in emphasis. In the fourth essay in this section, Shirley Rose gives us a close look at a this shift in the form of a first-year program that is no latecomer to mentoring and the principles that underlie it. Mentoring for beginning teachers at Purdue, Rose points out, goes back to the 1960s, and the program they have today is the result of a slow but persistent evolution. The accomplishment this program represents should not be underestimated. The cost of setting up, much less maintaining, such a program in terms of budget resources, political capital, and sweat equity is considerable. In the bottom-line environment of today's university economy, any program that seems to complicate the financing of what might otherwise be attractively inexpensive services like part-time instruction, is always under scrutiny and highly vulnerable when administrators decide to cut costs. More than one of the editors and contributors to this book have firsthand experience with losing programs for mentoring similar to the one that continues to thrive at Purdue.

3

Teaching Writing Through Multigenre Papers

Tom Romano
Miami University

Something had been nagging me. I wondered what Sara would say about it, Sara, my stellar English Education student of two years earlier—and I mean *stellar.* As a junior she turned a multigenre writing assignment into a HyperStudio text that she presented at an NCTE convention; amid a censorship skirmish during her student teaching, she wrote a multigenre essay that was published in *Voices From the Middle* (Boose 1999); and as an art minor she infused visual expression into her teaching, reawakening students to spatial ways of knowing that many had left behind in elementary school.

I emailed her: "Sara, do you think I am too much a writing teacher and not enough a methods teacher?"

"Maybe," she wrote back, "but keep doing what you're doing."

Program Overview

Students at Miami University preparing to become integrated language arts teachers in middle and high school take content area courses in literature, linguistics, writing, journalism, speech, and communication. They also take courses in educational psychology, educational leadership, and teacher education. The year before they student-teach for a semester, they take two courses in methods of teaching English/language arts. The second course concentrates on teaching literature. The first course in the sequence focuses on teaching writing and is part of a block of education courses that students take in the morning. Four weeks during the semester those "methods block" classes do not meet. The students are, as we say, "in the field."

The Eye-Opener

Students find the "field experience" startling. They spend two weeks observing, participating, and teaching in high school classrooms and two weeks doing the same in middle schools. They learn about education and miseducation, the match and mismatch between theory and practice. They see educational philosophies and teaching methods in action that excite them. They see others that appall them. They see how subject matter they love (or are frightened of, in the case of grammar) has been translated/enhanced/ignored. Students leave campus before sunup, and return early in the afternoon. Such a schedule is a shocker for most of them:

> The alarm clock rings—5:45 A.M. flashes at my face. "Jesus Christ!" I think to myself. I should've NEVER decided to be a teacher. I take a quick shower, get dressed in my "teacher clothes" that I have been acquiring over the past four years, and put on makeup so that I can look at least twenty years old. I begin to think that Miami should require that all education majors take a "how to get up, take a shower, and get primped at 5:45 A.M." class the very first semester that you declare yourself an education major.
>
> *Casey Brown*

The first time I taught the writing methods course I asked students to interview high school and middle school writers during the field experience—writers who were successful and ones who were not. I gave students a list of questions to start with and asked them to branch off from there as the interview developed. The assignment didn't work. We discovered that in more classrooms than I realized not much writing was going on. Infrequent essays. Few narratives. Little poetry. Sometimes nothing, not even journal or response writing. If writing occurred in such classrooms, it was because the university student initiated it.

Since I couldn't count on students finding writing cultures in the classrooms they visited, I changed the assignment. Now I ask students to become miniethnographers during the field experiences, immersing themselves in the culture of a classroom, learning its customs of teaching, learning, and behaving. I want students to become insiders. I want them to participate and observe as they listen in on conversations, tend to housekeeping duties, plan and present lessons (if the teacher makes room for them), and confer with students about their work—*whatever* that work may be. I ask them to capture their experience in a research notebook, where they take notes, write expressively, describe thickly, draw pictures, and reflect.

The "Old Saw" That Still Sees

Good writing teachers write. Writing teachers ought to know the exhilaration and humility that come from working to get written words right. I believe that, even though in thirty years I've seen exceptions. Some of my students already see themselves as writers. Some were hooked on writing by the time they got to me. Many of my students, however, are not. They've learned to write tightly structured, thesis-driven argumentative essays. But they don't look at writing as a vital part of their lives. They don't see themselves as writers. They don't love to write. And they haven't given much thought to *teaching* writing either, although they are concerned about teaching usage, grammar, and punctuation, so often have those matters been marked on their papers.

If students come to my class already hooked on writing, I set the barb deeper. If they are not hooked, I'm angling to do that. I want students to discover the pleasure, challenge, and satisfaction of exploring their own minds with language, of seeing their experience through a variety of genres. As students move closer to teaching writing I want them to think of themselves as writers.

Multigenre

Sara's "maybe" in answer to my query made me cringe for a millisecond until I got to her counsel: "keep doing what you're doing."

What I do in that methods class is to teach students how to teach writing by demonstrating it through teaching them to write what I've come to call multigenre papers (Romano 1995a, 2000). I want students to experience the big world mural of writing. I want them to create genres they haven't had much experience with before. I want them to break the habit, for a little while, of writing only exposition. A paper composed of multiple genres will accomplish that.

The multigenre idea came to me as I read Michael Ondaatje's first book, *The Collected Works of Billy the Kid* (1996, 1970), a work of fact and imagination, a postmodern blend of genres, a puzzling and rewarding collage of poetry, character sketches, songs, newspaper interviews, fiction, quotations from secondary sources, even photographs . . . all unified into one cohesive book, yet each piece standing alone in its own right. Ondaatje employs many compositional strategies within these genres, too. He varies point of view and sometimes writes impressionistic passages, stream of consciousness, multiple voices, figurative language, repetition, and repetend. The mode of writing that doesn't show up often in the book is exposition.

And that's all right. My students have been expositioned to rhetorical death. Some have learned to write so well for college that they have forgotten story, poetry, metaphor, image. They produce a voice no one wants to listen to for long. They sometimes write sentences like this:

> It is a proven theory that technology is an integral and undeniable constituent
> of the modern constructivist classroom.

Makes me shiver. I see in that voice my own more than thirty years ago, a Johnny-One-Genre who cultivated a detached, third-person, thesaurisized voice. *Demise* was one of my favorite words. I used it indiscriminately without regard to tone or context. Fruit flies met their demise in biology lab; soldiers about my age met their demise in Vietnam half a world away. I was long-winded and loved adverbs. My motto: Tell don't show. Better yet, tell with lengthy sentences, verbose prose, and plenty of abstraction.

Metaphor, dialog, imagery, and story—elements of writing so many of us find essential to living and understanding—found no place in my writing as I sought to sound educated and profound. I didn't really learn to write with a voice close to my personality until I met my first writing mentor, Milton White, the author of three slim, elegantly written novels. Milton moved us to write with detail, drama, and simplicity. I loved the world of writing that opened to me. And my writing got better.

Many of my students have not met their Milton Whites. Their experience writing in the university has steered them away from story, metaphor, and poetry. So disdainful of such writing was one professor that he named it "narrative sickness." We have to beware when others name what we care about, especially when their naming makes us doubt our worth, our identity, our core beliefs. I was more than "Dago" when my family celebrated Christmas Eve with a dinner of baccala, calamari, and spaghetti with anchovies, garlic, and oil. I was more than "politically correct" when I sought to be sensitive to women's ways of knowing and refused to use only masculine pronouns for singular, indefinite references. I was more than "just a teacher" when I wrote letters to the editor that argued against larger class sizes.

Some who name, though, empower us by articulating what we feel. Jerome Bruner named the use of story and metaphor something very different from "narrative sickness." He named such writing "narrative thinking" and made a strong case for it as a valid way of knowing and communicating, just as essential as "paradigmatic knowing" that emphasizes logic, order, tight analysis, and argumentation (Bruner 1986). In fact, I would argue that narrative thinking is essential for many of us to learn to see clearly, to understand life on the lived level of actions, feelings, and sensory awareness. Narrative thinking helps us *experience* writing, not merely understand it, and the multigenre writing assignment helps students gain or regain experience in the use of narrative thinking.

A Multigenre Dabble

Each day of the field experience in the schools students are surrounded by voices and scenes, personalities and conflict, characters and intrigue—a rich milieu for writing that calls for detail, voices, and dramatization. From the data they've gathered in their research notebooks, students write four- to six-page multigenre papers, a new kind of writing experience for them. They need a lot of support and guidance. Although we don't read *The Collected Works of Billy the Kid,* we do read multigenre papers from past students and a chapter I've written about multigenre writing (Romano 1995a). On the syllabus I provide this definition:

A multigenre paper arises from research, experience, and imagination. It is not an uninterrupted, expository monolog nor a seamless narrative nor a collection of poems. A multigenre paper is composed of many genres and subgenres, each piece self-contained, making a point of its own, yet connected by theme or topic and sometimes by language, images, and specific actions. In addition to many genres, a multigenre paper may also contain many voices, not just the author's. The trick is to make such a paper hang together.

Multigenre papers move writers away from abstract language and generalizations. Instead of explaining what they mean, I ask students to be "implicitly emphatic," to render experience with such detail, imagination, and drama that their subject is revealed. In one piece of her high-energy multigenre paper Jenn crafts comments she has gathered from interviews with middle school students who had three weeks to read a sixty-page biography of Amelia Earhart. Jenn reveals the chasm between teacher expectations and student reality, between curriculum materials and student ideas of relevance, between attendance and academic accomplishment.

"This book is dumb. I didn't even read it. No one did."

"Who care about some stupid woman plane-flyer. Ain't no one here give a damn who she is."

"These questions are too hard. This test is too long. This room is too cold. This pencil is too short.

This desk is too tall. This . . . "

"I hate reading. Why we got to take a test over this dumb book anyway? No one care that we know about this b———."

"Why ya'll gotta be so loud? Some people's tryin' to take a test in here!"

Note: Only five of twenty students were available for questioning.

Jenn Reid

This first multigenre foray of just a few pages allows students to experiment with the form and create with story and imagination. Students bring the dramatic material of their field experience to life through narrative knowing. Although I want my students during the field experience to pay attention to their mentor's pedagogical strategies and try their hands at teaching, they are invariably drawn to their students' lives. These aren't characters in novels they come to care about. These are flesh-and-blood people with obstacles to overcome and possibilities to realize. Tina imagines herself into the voice of a high school student who reveals a story alien to Tina's middle-class, Christian sensibility:

I lie in my bed,
asleep, yet still conscious of my surroundings.
The front door creaks open,
the bedside clock reads 2:36 A.M.
I hear her toss her keys to the table,

her coat follows to the chair.
Footsteps creak noisily and unsteadily
down the hallway.

I hope she'll go on by my door this time,
leave me to sleep without disruptions.
I hope I won't have to smell her drunken breath,
her smoky clothes,
or hear her tired complaining.
Tonight I don't feel like cleaning up a mess.
I don't want to care for her like a child.
Perhaps tonight she'll take care of herself
and act as she ought to act.

My bedroom door opens nonetheless,
without regard for my peace.
I see a silhouette against my wall
and my mom comes stumbling in.

                                        Tina Smith

Students have been forming their educational philosophies and ideals for some time now, but during the field experience that formation is accelerated as they experience school from the point of view of a teacher-to-be. Donnie, a nontraditional student who spent twenty years in the Air Force before coming to Miami, brooked little nonsense, jargon, or red tape. He was outraged at the professional neglect, bureaucratic incompetence, and student apathy he observed. He expressed his criticisms in a brief newspaper item:

HOPE FOUND DEAD
By Donnie Becker
Romano News Service

Becky's prospects for a future as a learner and possible lover of knowledge were found dead today in a classroom at _____ High School.

The anonymous discoverer of the putrid carcass of what was once a glorious bucket of endless possibilities stated, "It was too late by the time I got there. If Becky could have been shown that books allow us to learn truths about ourselves, she might have held on to her prospects. I am ashamed at what I saw."

Becky herself remains blissfully unaware.

The hopes were last seen in the care of Mr. X, but a conspiracy is suspected. The investigation was closed without comment from school administrators or parents.

Writer and Teacher:
The Major Multigenre Project

After their appetites have been whetted by the brief multigenre paper over their field experience, I engage students in a major multigenre project the last month of the semester. It's the difference between playing in the backyard for an hour and spending an entire day at the beach. If the assignment works right, students blissfully lose themselves in the writing, engage in optimal psychological experience (Csikszentmihalyi 1990). While students develop this paper, I bear down hard to teach both writing and teaching.

Topic Choice

"What I produced went beyond my expectation."

Students may write the final multigenre paper on anything they are passionate about. I want them to experience love, immersion, dedication, and fidelity toward something they pursue with language on paper (and graphic images, too, if they choose). Students take this opportunity to explore big topics in their lives. They realize it is a time to go full bore. In the past, students have written about gender, historical figures or time periods, bulimia, anorexia, relatives, religious faith, the suicide of a friend, rape on campus, multicultural issues in the writing class, attending college full time while raising a daughter and tending bar twenty-five hours each week. Passions run the gamut, sometimes academic, often personal.

I help students identify topics to write about. I want them to realize there is plenty of subject matter available. I show them how to make lists, to cluster, and to map out their passions, their interests, the imperatives that consume their thinking, that emotionally and intellectually pull them. Once they have an abundance of these possibilities down on paper, I get students talking with classmates about one or two topics. I want the classroom abuzz with talk—with writers' unfolding stories, listeners asking questions, and writers elaborating. I want language to swirl in the air above facial expressions, gestures, and little epiphanies. After they've talked, I give students a week more to mull over the topic(s) they identified before we get down to writing particular genres in class.

Kristina wrote a multigenre paper (turning it into a HyperStudio production with music, voices, and pictures) about the life-changing summer she spent living in Puebla, Mexico. In assessing her project, she wrote,

> I was really surprised how emotionally involved I got in my paper. I was also surprised how easily one piece led to another and how natural it seemed to portray different aspects of my topic in different genres. At first I was scared about the whole concept of multigenre but now I would love to try another.
>
> *Kristina Ristev*

Walking the Walk Through Demonstration

Beginnings are difficult: the first class, the first date, the first swim. To overcome the inertia and fear that sometimes accompanies beginning, I lead students into quick-writes, so they commit language to paper fast. Most end up launching their multigenre work before they know it. I ask students to identify indelible moments in their topics, instants that have stuck in their minds (Romano 2000). Indelible moments are powerful. They are usually connected to images and laden with emotion. That's why they're indelible. A brainstormed list of such moments serves as the genesis for many later pieces.

I get students to talk about the indelible moments just as I asked them to talk about topic possibilities. Through easily spent oral language students flesh out detail, move beyond code words, explain to a disinterested listener what they mean, imagine, see, hear. After students have spent sufficient time talking, I have them choose one indelible moment and begin writing. Here Andrea writes about the indelible image of her Italian grandmother at work in the kitchen:

> Up to her elbows in flour, hair flying every which way, spaghetti sauce simmering spitting red droplets over the white enamel of the stove, steam carrying the sweet basil scent to my nostrils, homemade spaghetti covers the counter, pale off-white and starting to harden but Gram doesn't notice because she's slicing carrots into the sauce "plop . . . plop." She has my old apron on, primary colors splattered every which way, still, it only reaches to her mid-thigh because she's only five feet tall. A soft blanket of flour covers the sleeves of her green sweatshirt and black stretch pants. "Too cute," my mom always says and I think I agree because there is more food on Gram than in the pots or on the counter and when she looks at me I look away, quickly, pretending that I wasn't watching.
>
> *Andrea Bailey*

Other significant material that students might write about are meaningful places, important things, crucial scenes, big decisions—subtopics that might live at the heart of their material. Samantha's topic was a brave one that broke my heart. Four years of sexual abuse had caused her to withdraw into two years of self-imposed silence as a child. Here she writes about a significant place, her grandfather's farm, where she began to heal and recover:

Grandfather's Farm

He would already be in the barn moving among the cattle when the sun crept through my windows, urging me to my chores. He never told me to do this work, but in my watching I began to discover my role in the rhythm of my new home. When I arrived, my parents at their wits end, he greeted my silence with a comfortable muteness of his own, sometimes grunting in satisfaction or distaste, at home with the language of animals.

On these mornings, I crept into the chicken coop, its musty dryness warming my skin, and eased my hands under their feathers and into their nests to steal away their eggs.

On these mornings, I took the pure whiteness or speckled brown and found solace in pressing their smoothness to my cheeks. I learned that if you squeezed the fragile shells they wouldn't crack. If you dropped them, however, they shattered and oozed, your breakfast smeared in the dust. So I stepped carefully as I made my way to the house. Once in the kitchen we, he and I, regarded each other with unspoken warmth—as the eggs and bacon added to the rich manure and milk air the scent and sputter of home.

Samantha Taylor

Demonstration and Deconstruction

I introduce students to more writing possibilities through minilessons followed by workshops in which they try writing poems for two voices, photograph poems, prose poems, haiku, dialog, stream of consciousness passages, and dramatic scenes. In these brief workshops students begin pieces that might end up in their papers. But because of the nature of the class—a teaching methods class—of equal importance to students' writing is their experiencing my demonstration of teaching. They participate in my pedagogical world.

After I've conducted one of my lessons, I engage students in talk about it: What worked and what didn't? What part did direct instruction play in my lesson? Talking? Visual representation? Student movement? Variety and pacing of activities? How did my language and quality of voice affect my teaching? What part did my physical presence play? I show students my lesson plan, point out the objective I hoped to achieve, note how I allotted time, identify where my plan went astray when I followed something spontaneous that happened because of the dynamics of the classroom. Nancie Atwell (1998) talks about "taking off the top of your head" as a writer so students see processes of composing, not just its products but so they see the actual decisions and reasoning that a writer makes. I want to do the same thing as a teacher.

As students continue to develop their multigenre papers I turn over to them the role of teacher, strategist, presenter, inspirer. Each student teams with one or two others to cooperatively plan and teach a lesson to the class, one that engages their fellow students in writing of some sort, writing that everyone can turn toward their multigenre papers. Students have gotten their peers to write about characters, setting, color, the senses. They have experimented with dialog, drawing, and lead writing. They have enacted the dictum that Ralph Fletcher (1993) learned from novelist/screenwriter Richard Price: "The bigger the issue, the smaller you write." Each lesson lasts about twenty-five minutes. The groups make plans that they distribute to everyone, and we talk about the lesson after it is enacted, discussing some of the same aspects of teaching we did after my lesson.

"The presentations helped me write my multigenre paper," wrote one student. "Just when I thought all my ideas had run dry, we'd have a presentation that opened an entirely new way of looking at things or approaching my subject and I could write again."

The lessons they conduct might be the most valuable pedagogical part of the course for students. They plan and imagine and negotiate, then they enact their teaching ideas, give them flesh and breath. Classroom activity goes into motion because of their initiative.

The Heart of Teaching Writing

> The most helpful part of the multigenre process was having conferences with the professor and talking with my classmates about experiences that dealt with my multigenre theme. I learned that talking through my memories and free writing on them helped stir up details.
>
> *Katy Clark*

As much as I enjoy showing writers a strategy for writing or revising and then launching them into trying it, I know that the heart of my own teaching lies in the writing conferences I have with students. It is there I model attentiveness, focus, and absolute fidelity to students and their work. I demonstrate a no praise–no blame stance toward working with another human being and her writing (Stafford 1986). I demonstrate how I seek to move beyond dog yummies of positive reinforcement—*good, great, excellent, fine, beautiful, perfect*—to pay the greatest respect I can to writers through complete intellectual and emotional engagement with their language and ideas. During conferences I ignore the telephone's ringing, the computer's announcing the arrival of email, the pull of appointments and classes later in the day. I wave off colleagues who come to my door. For the time of my writing conferences with students I am theirs and no one else's.

Before I begin holding fifteen-minute conferences with each student in my office, I demonstrate one or two conferences in class with volunteers so I can show students both toe stubbing and success—invariably a little of both takes place as I listen to students read pieces aloud, then say back what I heard, telling what I understood or where I was confused, asking questions, occasionally making suggestions. Mainly, however, I try to get writers to talk, to say something they hadn't thought before, to discover what they might do next to move their writing forward. After a demonstration conference, the students talk about it. What did they notice about my body language, where were my eyes focused as the writer read (at the writer), how did I first say back things to the writer that I understood from the writing, where did I become too directive, where should I have been more directive? I ask the writer to tell what she felt during our conference. I tell what I felt, what I noticed as a teacher and tried to move on or what I noticed and decided not to say anything about at that point (no title, for instance, or an unsatisfying ending). Then I set students to conferring with one another in groups of three or four to practice their conferencing skills and to help their peers develop their writing.

I conference three or four times with each student during the four or five weeks they write their multigenre papers. This last semester I had it easy. Only thirty-four students spread over two sections. That meant eight and a half hours for each round of conferences. It is labor intensive, but it's the only way I know how to teach if I'm going to have the impact I want to have both on students' writing and teaching.

One More Lesson

I model one more lesson two or three weeks before the papers are due — a lesson about cohesion and unity, about helping readers see pattern and purpose. Here is a piece from Andrea's paper about her grandmother that follows eight pages after we see Gram making spaghetti sauce at the stove:

> The sweatshirt was a dark forest green. I remember it because she wore it all the time in the winter and the appliquéd Christmas tree was starting to fall off and the lace collar was wearing out and starting to fray. The green sweatshirt embarrassed me so much when we were out in public because *nobody* wore holiday sweatshirts. There were old stains and fuzzies, and the elbows were thin. I HATED it, but now I'd give anything just to hold that sweatshirt to my cheek and remember.
>
> *Andrea Bailey*

When I read this piece, I felt a familiar, satisfying echo, a fulfilling recurrence, the completion of something. I flipped back through Andrea's paper to that first description of her grandmother. There it was: "A soft blanket of flour covers the sleeves of her green sweatshirt . . . ." That sweatshirt had been tucked away in my subconscious, and then later Andrea took time to devote a loving description to the significant piece of tattered clothing she so often saw her grandmother wear. As a reader I am rewarded with meaning and memory and pleasing repetition. Andrea's grandmother was real with idiosyncrasies of dress. The image so indelible to Andrea becomes meaningful to me. My understanding of Andrea's grandmother deepens.

I don't merely encourage students to add unity to their multigenre papers. It's not mandatory but I still press hard to get them to develop recurring images, repeated ideas, identical language, and extended scenes that are broken apart into separate pieces to reveal the story a little at a time. I want to experience that little shock of recognition as I read, to be fulfilled by the unity I perceive in their papers.

Where Poetry Lives

Samantha's multigenre paper traced her journey from being a victim of sexual abuse, through slow healing, and on to becoming a young woman ready to face and make sense of her experience. She ended her paper with this poem.

And I was four years old. And my uncle touched me. And I bled.
And I was five years old and he hit me. And they believed his excuses.
And I was six years old. And now he owned me.
And I was seven years old. And I stopped speaking.
And I was eight years old. And we moved.
      And I spoke
        And Mama cried.
          And Daddy said he'd kill him.
And I was nine years old. And it stayed a secret, this time ours instead
      of just mine.
And I was ten years old. And I blamed them.
And I was eleven years old. And there was still silence, only a
      different kind.
And I was twelve years old. And I was ashamed.
And I was thirteen years old. And I had nightmares.
And I was fourteen years old. And I wanted to forget.
And I was fifteen years old. And I wanted to be normal.
And I was sixteen years old. And I was angry.
And I was seventeen years old. And I still had nightmares.
And I was eighteen years old. And I asked God why.
And I was nineteen years old. And there was still a silence.
And I was twenty years old. And I began to write.

                                            Samantha Taylor

Contemporary free verse is the soul and spirit of my teaching. Poetry is a form of narrative knowing and communicating I want my students to get into their bones. It is a genre I didn't write until I was twenty-nine years old, and I tried writing free verse only after I began reading it, only after going beyond traditionally anthologized, classic poetry.

Few people read contemporary, free-verse poetry. Most magazines don't publish it, and most readers don't buy or borrow the books of contemporary poets that are often published by small presses. I want future teachers of writing to come to know the voices and word ways of modern poets. In addition to helping my students enjoy poetry, I encourage them to experience the language and rhythms, imagery and metaphors, insights and condensed expression of contemporary voices like Mary Oliver, Lucille Clifton, Marge Piercy, Alden Nowlan, Peter Meinke, and Ken Brewer.

I read my students a modern free-verse poem at the beginning of each class period. I give the oral interpretation everything I've got. I use my voice, my body, my face. I pause. I emphasize words. I turn written symbols on paper into emotion and perception. I seek to express in one reading all I've come to feel and understand about the poem. After I've read, we don't dissect or analyze it. We usually don't even discuss it, unless someone says something or asks me to read it again. A smile or raised eyebrow is about all the reaction I get. That's enough. For a minute or more on a daily basis, we perform a ritual of language and listening, perception and expression, interpretation and meaning making. I want students to absorb modern poetry, to come to know its accessibility, and to understand it as a possibility for writing. I do this against the days ahead when students will gamely lead adolescents through literature anthologies, beginning with *The Pilgrims* or *Beowulf* and never hear a modern poetic voice in the classroom. Samantha's modern contemporary voice is one I've begun sharing with my students.

Gaps

There is so much I don't teach my students about teaching writing: an effective way to teach the use of thesis statements, for instance, or how to write prescriptive essays, how to formally assess writing by 150 students, how to reduce the big world of writing to four modes of discourse that someday their students will be asked to produce in single drafts in a set time on a state proficiency test of writing. The list of what I don't teach is lengthy.

I do teach students that good-faith participation counts, both in learning to write and in learning to teach. I show them how I value approximation when they write their first wobbly-legged poem or use the overhead projector for the first time. I show them how I look for growth and development and how I celebrate when I detect them. I teach students that when they teach they are essentially creating a *draft* just as they do when they write. They can shape and tinker with this teaching draft, just as they do with a writing draft. They can delete, enhance, change the lead, rethink and revise the whole lesson, or replace it with another draft. I teach them the crucial step of choosing a topic they are passionate about. I teach them to cut loose with their writing and their teaching, to dive in, to go for the jugular, to write with faith and fearlessness. I teach them the great gift of listening that I hope they will give their own students one day.

Revisions

Something else has been nagging me, too, and here is what I'll do about it. Next year I'll add another piece to that first multigenre paper students write about their field experience—a final reflection. I'll ask students to write a bit of exposition when they are done with their genre explorations. I'll ask students to make sense of the voices and dramatic scenes they have rendered. I'll ask them to name what it all adds up to. The making sense, the naming, the striving to generalize out of the implicitly emphatic narrative thinking of their multigenre papers will help our understanding of teaching and students and classroom cultures. Expository writing is, after all, an integral and undeniable constituent of the modern constructivist classroom. It is an important part of the big world mural of writing.

4

Practice, Reflection, and Genre

David Smit
Kansas State University

Course and Structure

ENGL 400: "Advanced Expository Writing for Prospective Teachers" at Kansas State University is taught in the English department but required of secondary education majors. Occasionally, however, English majors or others interested in writing take the course.

ENGL 400 is not a methods course. It is intended to complement EDSEC 476: "Content Area Methods in the Secondary School," which is offered in the College of Education and is the only other course that secondary education majors take that is in any way connected to the teaching of writing. The course description in the *KSU Undergraduate Catalog* (1998–2000) for "Content Area Methods in the Secondary School" is this: "Principles of teaching applied to content area instruction in the secondary school; motivation; organization of subject matter; lesson planning; evaluation and reporting; challenging the levels of ability; organization and management of the classroom; methodology and materials of the secondary schools" (174). Clearly, EDSEC 476 covers such a wide range of language instruction that relatively little time is devoted to methods of teaching writing per se. As a result, ENGL 400 is designed to focus exclusively on writing, both as an upper-level course in writing and as an undergraduate introduction to composition theory. The *KSU Undergraduate Catalog* describes ENGL 400 this way: "Expository writing and a brief introduction to the history and theory of teaching writing, primarily for candidates for secondary certification in English" (108).

ENGL 400 is taught by a number of different instructors, all of whom conceive of the course in different ways. I have always structured the writing in the course along the lines suggested by James Moffett. I offer students the opportunity to write a range of discourse for a variety of purposes, in a variety of genres,

66

for a variety of audiences, and to reflect on what it means to be able to write, what it means to be a writer, and what it means to teach writing. As a result, I bring up "the history and theory of teaching writing" only as these topics relate to our reflections on the writing we have actually done, although over the years I have experimented with various theoretical and methods texts, such as Moffett's *Teaching the Universe of Discourse* (1983). None of these experiments in theory and method were very successful at integrating writing and theory. In general, the students respond well to the writing assignments and appreciate reflecting on the implications of what they have done. However, they have difficulty dealing with the "abstractions" of theory. For example, I have always thought of Moffett's work as a model of clarity, and so I was shocked to discover that students in ENGL 400 found him difficult to read and understand.

Purpose and Style

The last time I taught ENGL 400 I listed the following as my goals:

1. You should be able to write appropriately for a variety of purposes in a variety of genres to a variety of audiences.

2. You should be able to use simple, balanced, series, periodic, and cumulative sentences effectively, and you should be able to explain why you used these patterns as opposed to others in specific contexts.

3. You should be able to explain in detail the ways in which language helps and hinders communication.

4. You should be able to explain the role of "rhetorical stance" in communication and in your own personal notion of "truth."

5. You should be able to define and provide examples of the following terms: ethos, pathos, logos; expressive, referential, persuasive, and literary discourse; loose and periodic sentences; primary and secondary focus; syntactic focus and rhetorical focus.

6. You should be able to explain your own personal theory of "what makes writing good."

Students in this version of ENGL 400 wrote a major piece approximately every two or three weeks, a total of seven for the course. I borrowed the overall framework for thinking about writing from the text by William Coles and James Vopat (1985), *What Makes Writing Good*. That is, for each assignment I invited students to write for a particular purpose in a particular social context, and after the students had produced a piece each and we had read one another's papers, the focus of the discussion was on this question: How can you tell whether this writing is any good? What makes writing good, anyway? As we wrestled with this question over the course of the semester, I brought up other related questions about how certain kinds of writing were similar and different, how certain methods of composing were similar and different. And when the moment seemed right, I would sneak in the big question: What is writing anyway, and how do people learn to go about doing it?

In this last version of ENGL 400 students also frequently did exercises in style or in sentence combining, using my own idiosyncratic taxonomy of syntactic patterns (simple, balanced, series, periodic, and cumulative sentences), and they practiced various kinds of rhetorical strategies, such as using longer and more complex sentences to set up a short and simple climactic sentence. For each of these exercises we discussed the possible effects of particular kinds of sentences or particular rhetorical strategies; we discussed how certain ways of saying things might have implications for how readers understood the truthfulness of what was being said, the persona of the writer, and the emotional impact of the writing.

The students' final grades were based on portfolios of their work, which they submitted at the end of the semester. The ultimate purpose of the course was simply to complicate a prevailing notion among students—and the culture at large, I might add—that writing is just writing, that to learn to write one genre or to compose in one way is tantamount to learning to write any genre or to compose in any way. By the end of the course, students tended to see that teaching writing is not as simple and straightforward as they might have previously thought.

Theory and Sequence

As I have already indicated, my primary theoretical orientation is from James Moffett (1983). Moffett conceptualizes learning to write as a developmental process of learning to master a variety of textual conventions in order to accomplish a series of increasingly abstract and complex social tasks. In his own curriculum Moffett moves his students from the early elementary grades through high school by inviting them to write what he calls "reporting" (personal narratives, autobiographies, and memoirs; biographies and chronicles), then what he calls "generalizing" (histories, essays, and scientific reports), and finally what he calls "theorizing" (argumentative essays). In this sequence Moffett also moves his students from writing to familiar, known, sympathetic audiences to more distant, unfamiliar, and potentially hostile audiences.

Although I do not use Moffett's genre categories, I do keep his overall conceptual scheme in mind when I am designing assignments. I also rely on James Kinneavy's (1971) classification of purposes for writing: expressive, referential, persuasive, and literary. I design a series of related assignments around a common theme or experience, and the sequence is generally from expressive to referential to persuasive; from personal audiences to more distant and hostile ones.

Usually, I start with our practices as writers: drafting, reading, and responding to one another's work; reflecting on what we have written; understanding the differences among the various genres of writing we do; and becoming competent in these genres. I introduce "theory," broadly construed, only well into the course. I do this because I strongly believe that before students can make sense of the more abstract issues of composition theory, they need a sense of themselves as writers and of how writing works. Only if they think of themselves as writers and only if they begin to think and act like writers will they be able to assimilate much of what they read in composition theory. Only if they are self-conscious about their own writing processes; only if they confront themselves with the difficulties of writing for different purposes, in different contexts, using different styles, formats, and conventions; and only if they are exposed to the writing processes of others will they become sufficiently sensitive to the many ways writing gets done and the many variables that go into writing in any particular rhetorical situation.

Here is an assignment sequence I often start with. These assignments and sequences are modeled after those in Gene Krupa's *Situational Writing* (1982).

Writing # 1: An Experience of a Place or an Event

Describe your experience of a public place—any place from McDonald's to the Colosseum—or a public event—a concert, a lecture, a movie. Your purpose should be to put us inside your skin and make us experience as much as possible what you experienced. To do this assignment you will probably have to establish your own feeling for the place or activity by describing as specifically and as concretely as you can what happened to you, what you heard, saw, thought, and felt, using the first person. Reconstruct dialogue as exactly as you can. Put your sensations, your thoughts and feelings, into a clearly recognizable order, and indicate the order with cues such as "first" and "then" or "to the left" and "overhead." Write informally, as if you were telling us a story directly.

Writing #2: A Newspaper Account of a Place or Event

In a previous writing you tried to capture a personal experience in words, on paper. You tried to make us feel what you felt in that situation, primarily by using specific and concrete imagery. Now let's see what happens to your experience when you remove it one step from your immediate sensations, your own thoughts and feelings, and report just the facts.

Rewrite your experience of a public event or a public place as a newspaper account. Be sure to incorporate these aspects of newspaper style into your writing: Begin with a lead paragraph that tells us who, what, when, where, and possibly why and how. Limit yourself exclusively to third-person point of view. Provide just the facts, no opinions, and use an anticlimactic structure.

When you are finished with your article, think about the contrast between this kind of writing and your earlier piece, which tried to capture your own private experience. In your reflection journal, ponder which kind of writing was more truthful to your experience. Which kind of writing seems more constrained by formulas or conventions? How would we judge the goodness or badness of each kind of writing? Is there any way to compare the two kinds of writing by a single criterion or group of criteria and choose one as being superior to the other, or is comparing the two kinds of writing similar to comparing apples and oranges?

Writing #3: A Review of a Place or Event

Write a review (a recommendation or a criticism) of a public event or a public place, preferably the event or place featured in your two previous writings. You should address a general audience such as the readers of *The Collegian* or a *KSU Guidebook for New Students* or a local publication suitable for the event or place you are reviewing. Your ultimate purpose should be to convince your readers that your opinion is the correct one, that the event or place you are writing about is to be experienced at the first opportunity or avoided at all costs.

Once again, in your reflection journal, think about how or in what sense this review captures your experience and is "truthful," the degree to which it is shaped by formulas or conventions, and how we should go about deciding whether the writing is any good.

How and What

I have long felt that there is something wrong with the way writing is taught in our high schools and first-year college writing programs, but I have been hard pressed to articulate just what the problem is. Recently, I have come to think of the problem in two ways: the first has to do with how we learn to write, and the second has to do with what we learn when we learn to write. To put it in more theoretical language, the problem has something to do with the fact that people largely acquire the ability to write; they are not taught it. And the problem also has something to do with the fact that beyond the sentence level, writing always involves the use of genre conventions, which are largely determined by the social contexts in which people use writing. If, in fact, people do learn to write by acquisition, and if, in fact, learning to write beyond the sentence level is a matter of internalizing an infinite number of conventions and being able to adapt them to the demands of particular rhetorical circumstances, then how can we design a single course—or even a curriculum—to help young writers acquire the knowledge and skills they need in order to write for a wide variety of purposes in a wide variety of genres in a wide variety of social circumstances? And more to the point of this book, how can we prepare teachers to help novice writers accomplish all this?

How We Learn to Write

Writing is developmental and takes a very long time to learn. If young children are exposed to reading and writing, and if they recognize that reading and writing have a purpose or function that will serve their needs, they will spontaneously begin to develop their own approximations of these tasks without formal instruction, and their approximations will gradually evolve into what we label "literacy." These approximations are what Thomas Newkirk calls "intermediate forms" (1989, 72), analogous to the early stages of oral speech, or what Eleanor Kutz, borrowing from the literature on second-language learning, calls an "interlanguage," a form of discourse containing features that occur in the target language (1986, 392–93).

Once they sense what writing can accomplish, once they grasp how it can function in their lives, children begin to use writing for a variety of purposes. Often before they go to school, children begin to write in a variety of genres, such as stories, lists, notes, plans, and thank-you cards in order to accomplish various tasks. These genres seem to represent much of the range of later adult discourse (Newkirk and Atwell 1985, Gundlach 1982, Jacobs 1985, Sowers 1979). Gradually, with the help of schooling, young writers expand their ways of writing various genres and begin to make them more cohesive and more hierarchical, thereby increasing the ways that their writing approximates adult discourse. (Newkirk 1989, Graves 1979, Loban 1976, Taylor and Dorsey-Gaines 1988).

Thus, the ability to write involves an array of knowledge and skills that young writers master over time, in different degrees, and at very different rates. Young writers of the same age may have very different writing abilities. In addition, they may be good in some things and not in others. They may be competent in the format of a certain genre but not as competent at spelling or punctuation. They may be competent in a few genres and not in others. They may be able to get words on paper in a relatively "correct" manner, but this aspect of writing may so preoccupy them that they don't have the ability to also monitor their writing in terms of their purposes and audiences. The picture we have, then, of novice writers is of many kinds of knowledge and ability in various stages of development. This is a messy picture with few neat lines.

But if writing ability is developmental and takes so much time to learn, if writing ability is largely acquired through immersion in many different literate environments or discourse communities, most of which are outside the classroom, how can we design a curriculum for any particular grade level or for a college-level course? How do we go about deciding what young writers need to know at any particular point in their development? I have no answer to this question, except to say that I think secondary and college-level writing curricula are going to have to be more wide-ranging than they currently are, they are going to have to introduce students to a wider range of discourse than current school genres, and they are going to have to introduce students to a wider range of rhetorical situations and discourse communities than they currently do. My introducing ENGL 400 students to a range of discourse is a very small first step in that direction.

What We Learn When We Learn to Write

Much of the skill involved in writing involves using particular genre conventions, and to write well means having the ability to adapt a flexible set of conventions in new circumstances. Genres are not collections of rigid rules and formats. Rather, they are, in the formulation of Carol Berkenkotter and Thomas

Huckin "inherently dynamic rhetorical structures that can be manipulated according to the conditions of use" (1995, 3) or, in the words of Carolyn Miller, "typified rhetorical actions based in recurrent situations" (1984, 159). Like simple sentences in a natural language, genres can be described and codified, but these descriptions are always reductive. It might be more useful to understand genres as part of the patterning of all language, as part of the way human beings develop recurring strategies to use in recurring situations. For example, the most studied genre in the history of language study is the story—fictional or nonfictional narrative. Psycholinguists have demonstrated convincingly that despite a basic "grammar" of narrative, stories come in so many variations that teaching abstract principles about the structure of stories seems beside the point (Johnson and Mandler 1980, Rumelhart 1975, Labov 1972, Peterson and McCabe 1983, Freedman and Pringle1984). Even less open and more seemingly conventional genres involve a great deal of variation. For instance, Janet Giltrow (1994) found that the opening paragraphs of news stories varied so widely that even this genre seems too rich and complex to be formally taught.

Now, if writing varies so much from genre to genre, and if the conventions that define a genre are so various from situation to situation, from context to context, just what genres should we be teaching in school and just what defining characteristics of each genre would it be most helpful for students to learn? As far as I can tell, most secondary and college composition curricula require only school genres—personal essays, critiques, research papers, and arguments. Frankly, this is not much. For us to do a better job, we need to expose students more thoroughly to the range of writing within genres, to in effect immerse them in discourses and discourse communities, and we need to find ways of integrating writing into other disciplines and arranging for students to have extensive experience in rhetorical situations outside of traditional academic disciplines.

Educating Writing Teachers

Consider this anecdote:

> My daughter has a wonderful assignment: she has to write a story to entertain the rest of her middle school class. Since she is in her Nancy Drew period, she begins to write a Nancy Drew mystery. She does a nice job of setting up the crime and introducing the main characters, but after five pages, she stops because that is the page limit for the assignment. The following week her story is returned with a few minor editorial corrections and a word of praise. However, the teacher never says a word about the fact that my daughter has not done the assignment. She has not written a story; she has written a beginning to a story. The pattern is repeated throughout the year. My daughter is invited to write many stories, but none of them ever gets past an introductory episode and a few brief character descriptions.

This sequence of events, or some variation of it, has often been repeated in my daughter's education. It is also replicated in the university writing program

I administer and in the assignments I see from my colleagues at the university. I see writing teachers providing little useful information about how various genres are actually written; I see a great deal of instruction in how to write using rules, formats, and formulas and little practice in actually writing.

Now, I realize it is dangerous to generalize from particular incidents, but it is my sense that these episodes are not unique, that a great deal, if not most, of what passes for writing instruction at the secondary and college levels in this country is rule-ridden and formulaic and unrelated to writing as it is actually done by people who write. Would a teacher who actually wrote stories herself respond to my daughter's story in such a limited way? Perhaps. But isn't it more likely that a writer of stories would recognize how little my daughter had demonstrated the ability to write a story and try to work with her to improve her ability to develop character and plot? A number of recent surveys of the profession indicate that although English teachers may very well have been taught to teach writing in more flexible and open-ended ways, when push comes to shove, they resort to the same old rigid rules and conventions that have been the bane of the profession since the nineteenth century (Hillocks 1999, Kennedy 1998).

Why is that? I believe it is for this reason: When teachers at both the secondary and college levels are instructed in how to teach writing in college classes, inservice workshops, or TA apprenticeship programs; when they are taught a little theory about how people learn to write; when they are asked to read a few articles about composing; or when they are given texts that pretend to offer techniques in how to teach "the writing process," many teachers tend to interpret what they are taught and what they read in bizarre and impractical ways because they are not writers themselves.

Nowhere in the secondary and postsecondary English curriculum are there any requirements that teachers be able to write a wide range of discourse themselves or even the kinds of discourse they will be expected to teach their students. Certification to teach secondary English in Kansas requires at least some upper-level writing experience, but the nature of that experience is not specified. At Kansas State the only writing requirement is ENGL 400 and one other composition course. Students most often fulfill the second requirement by taking creative writing. I suspect that most other states are equally lax about requiring experience in writing. Moreover, a recent collection of syllabi from secondary English methods courses across the country indicates that students in these courses write primarily journals and lesson plans, although the larger programs may have requirements similar to Kansas State's (Smagorinsky and Whiting 1995).

In addition, there is little evidence that graduate students in English have any more experience in writing a range of discourse than secondary education majors with B.A.'s. All the evidence is that M.A. and Ph.D. programs in composition and rhetoric, and the programs designed to prepare graduate teaching assistants to teach introductory writing courses, assume that their students are adequate writers, primarily because they write graduate papers in their disciplines. Graduate programs in English, both in literature and in composition and rhetoric, do not require any evidence that future writing teachers can write the genres they will be teaching, or that they are particularly insightful about the ways these genres are actually written (Haring-Smith 1985, Latterell 1996, Brown, Meyer, and Enos 1994, Sullivan 1991).

As a result, secondary English teachers and college TAs have very little personal experience and knowledge with which to understand and evaluate the information they do get from their coursework, their inservice training, or their apprenticeship programs. In the jargon of learning theory, both secondary English teachers and graduate TAs in college English departments lack a mental script or schema for how writing is actually learned and how writing is actually done. And it seems to me that the only way to improve their ability to adequately absorb and evaluate everything they are told about writing and writing processes is to make them writers themselves, especially writers of the kinds of discourse they have to teach. The question, of course, is how to make prospective teachers at all levels writers of the genres they will be teaching. This question may be the most important one facing the discipline today.

5

An Interviewing Project for Writing Teachers

Reflection, Research, Action

Linda Miller Cleary
University of Minnesota—Duluth

Our students have a history with writing that will affect the way they teach. Prospective writing teachers come to our classes with years of developed assumptions about writing and the teaching of writing, and they have had years of what we might consider good and less-than-good models of teachers before them. If, as the phenomenologists would have it, the meaning we make of what we do affects the way we do it, then I believe that prospective teachers and teachers already in the field ought to reflect deeply on their histories with writing so they can understand how those histories might affect their writing and their teaching of writing. In this way they can make informed decisions about how they want to teach writing without the manacles of the past or without unreasoned rebellion against that past. They can, as the current lingo goes, deconstruct and reconstruct their beliefs about writing instruction. I orchestrate this reflective experience through in-depth phenomenological interviewing, a research technique that I reconstrued as a pedagogical strategy. I will begin by describing this process and then talk about how it fits into a course which includes English education students, practicing secondary teachers, and graduate TAs who teach college composition.

The Classroom Scene

Twenty prospective secondary English teachers, two practicing secondary teachers, and four current graduate TAs sit in a circle during week three of the semester course "Composition for Teachers." Each has interviewed a partner about his or her experience with writing, and the partner has reciprocated. These aren't simple one-time interviews but a series of interviews that provide an in-depth exploration of the participants' past experiences with writing, their current experience with writing, and, finally, the sense that they make of these writing experiences and of their present or future teaching. They gather in class after generating profiles of their partners as writers, using interwoven selections of actual interview material. And in the circle, while Dawn looks down at her hands, Joe reads the following profile that he has developed of her as a writer, using her own words. Dawn knows what will be read because she has had a hand in its editing.

Dawn's Profile

I don't remember learning to write, but as far back as I can remember, I was writing. Most of the time then I wrote scary stories and showed them to my parents. I know now I was lucky to have parents who encouraged me. As long as my parents gave me a proud smile, my fragile esteem became stronger. In elementary school, we would write our own plays and then act them out, but my passion was always with what I was writing and not the audience.

In seventh grade I wrote a scary story entitled, "Doomsday," and I love to read it now and see how much I have improved. In eighth grade, I started writing plays and poems, but there was a change in writing. It was not my parents' lack of support, nor was it my own dwindling passion. It was the research paper. Don't get me wrong, I did enjoy researching, but my writing was getting criticized, and I no longer could express my creativity in assignments. I was no longer writing for myself. I would write for my teachers. I didn't stand a chance of enjoying what I was writing. I was in a slump. Writing had been a way of expressing my thoughts and feelings. Without that I had to look elsewhere. I found acting: I could still expound my passion, but now it would be on stage. I stayed in drama all through high school.

My passion for writing didn't really come back until college. I found myself writing a letter to a friend once when I was so mad at her that the words just flowed from my heart to the page. In no time I had four pages of angry prose. I realized that I still had the ability to write my emotions on paper; I recalled the creativity I once had in elementary school. Now in college, I am writing again. I write poetry, and I write in my journal. I am self-motivated and enjoying it. I write for me. Now when I write a paper, I make sure that I am interested in the topic. I let it linger in my mind while I look for articles; each concept gets a separate sheet of paper. I love quotes, and I use the best one as a subtitle of sorts. I know my paper is a success when I answer the question my topic asks of me. Time tells me when or what I can write. My writing is a self-exploration; it helps me be more the person I wish to become.

In-Depth Phenomenological Interviewing
as Pedagogy

In-depth phenomenological interviewing as a research process is best described in Irving Seidman's book *Interviewing as Qualitiative Research* (1998). The theoretical underpinnings of this method stem from the phenomenologists in general and Alfred Schutz (Schutz, Walsh, and Lehnert 1967) in particular. In this model the researcher considers the experience of the participant with regard to the subject being studied as important, and the interviewing strives to maximize the participant's rendering of that experience. A three-interview sequence provides enough time, privacy, and trust so that both of the people involved can relate and reflect on the experience and, with each successive interview, deepen their understandings. Years ago, mentored by Irving Seidman, I adapted this method for a study of eleventh-grade writers (Cleary 1991) and subsequently began using it with prospective and practicing teachers of writing, not as a research method but as a pedagogical tool. This interviewing process has evolved into an early and important part of my "Language, Cognition, and Writing" course, a beginning to the class's inquiry into writing pedagogy.

When Dawn and Joe and others gathered for their first class, I asked them to find a partner whom they didn't know well and one with whom they could find common time for interviews. They began the process during the very first class of the semester. Those who were new to the group thus found an instant companion with whom to share their expectations and anxieties about the class. The pairings always seem to work, and mutual understanding often builds ongoing relationships (and has even led to one marriage). The students often think it's chemistry, but I believe it to be a natural human reaction to listening and being listened to. As they interview they try to capture as many of the words of their partners as possible because they know these words will be used to build the profile. It is remarkable how they can take full notes without impeding the pace of the interview; the interviewer is too busy listening and writing to be tempted to interrupt with his or her own parallel experiences. Some students want to tape the interviews until I tell them of the four to six hours that transcription takes for every hour of taped interviewing.

I urge the interviewers to ask open-ended questions such as those below and to use follow-up questions when they (1) want to know more, (2) have questions, or (3) sense that there is more to be said. I encourage those being interviewed to tell stories whenever possible in response to questions because stories, by their nature, already contain a sense of meaning.

The first interview asks students to reconstruct their histories with writing. The second asks them to explore their current experiences with writing. These two interviews ask for the concrete. The third asks them to reflect again on their reconstructed past and present writing experiences and to make meaning of them in relation to the students' future teaching of writing.

Interview I

What has writing been like for you from the time you first remember until the present? What do you remember of writing before you began school? in elementary school? junior high school/middle school? high school? college? Who helped you with writing and what was that like? What kind of writing did you see your parents/siblings/other family members doing? Tell me about a time(s) when writing was really good/bad for you? Can you recreate that experience for me? You haven't said much about that _____ (insert some aspect of your experience).

Interview II

What is writing like for you right now? Can you tell me stories about the kinds of writing that you do in and outside of school? How does writing fit into a typical day? How do you go about a writing project from the beginning until you feel it is finished? What is the process like for you? When is it exciting or hard? What do you worry about? How do other people help or hinder the process? If I had a picture of you at home writing, what would it look like? Where do you write, when, how, with what? If you are teaching writing, what is that like for you? What do you like/dislike about it?

Interview III

Now that you have described what writing was like for you in the past and what it is like for you in the present, what meaning do you make of your experience with writing? What sense do you make of it? (Asking this question in several different ways helps.) What things are important to you in your life? How does writing or the teaching of writing connect with things that are important? How has the past experience made current experience good/bad/exciting/distressing/frustrating? How do you understand that? What is there that seems important to you that we haven't covered? Are you realizing anything through these interviews that might shape your way of being (or not being) with future students?

Constructing Profiles

Students take the building of their partners' profiles very seriously. In a way, it provides a first writing assignment that has both real audience (the class) and real purpose (many choose to use the profile that their partners construct as the frontispiece of their portfolio). As a first assignment, this Studs Terkel–type piece in the first person also eliminates the students' self-consciousness about the content, for they are using their partners' words. Their job is to look for the center of what their partners have said and to weave words from the three interviews in a way that is true to the entirety of the interviews. Interviewers ask me how exactly they must quote their partners, and I often tell them the rules I myself use when constructing profiles from research interviews. I caution them that to change words is to reinterpret the data they have gathered from their partners, but that for syntactic and transitional purposes, some words may need to be added in brackets and some tenses changed. I let them know that they can delete as long as what they end up with is true to the interviews as a whole. I suggest that they begin by using highlighters to underline what they see as important lines in the interview notes. I tell them that they will begin to see a theme or interrelated themes that are its center. When they finish a draft they check out what they have written with their partners and revise based on the partner's advice. This prevents the interviewees from being embarrassed in a public forum by something they said to their partners. When I first started doing this process I had several students who were disappointed with the profile constructed of them, and so I emphasize that both partners need to be active in the editing process. Though I have experimented with alternatives (returning the notes to the interviewees, who then build their own profiles; having the students write from the three interview questions and build their own profiles), having the interviewers build the profiles works best. Several years ago a student said, "My partner's memories helped to trigger my own memories, and so I was able to dig deeper into my brain than if I was to "talk to myself" via a journal." Since then, I have abandoned journal writing as a sole form of reflecting on the writing experience. Furthermore, there is something validating about the interviewer's constructing and then reading the profile. Students seem to feel understood, and the compelling nature of the first-person voices helps make the ensuing discussion engaging.

For years I participated in the interviewing if there were an uneven number of students, and I certainly would encourage instructors to experience this process for several years. A few years ago I heard myself come out with the same pat phrases when I was interviewed, and I realized that the process wasn't genuine any more. Some years I read a profile done of me in the past, but in other years I'm content to let the students research their own experience, leaving me out.

The Matter of Inquiry:
Students Research Their Own Experience

Before the profile reading begins in class I ask my students to engage not only as colleagues but also as researchers, listening for common themes that arise from their collective writing experiences. We listen to the profiles read in the circle (when the class is large, I split it in two for this process), but we don't discuss each profile individually; the cumulative stories seem to make a profound impression on the students. I ask students to take notes about what they are hearing during the profile reading. I can almost hear the insights zing around the room as I give them several time-outs to consider emerging themes. Following the reading, students often express the realization that they are not alone in some important formative experiences. In reflective writing one student said, "Everyone who participated in this process knows that there are other individuals who are struggling and doubting about the same things concerning writing and teaching writing. There are some common threads of experience which we all need to realize." The discussion helps them delineate those common threads of experience.

In preparation for writing this chapter I collected the notes from two class sections, notes that students had taken on the common themes they found in their classmates' profiles. From these notes I did an analysis of their analyses. I then checked these notes with those that I myself had taken for about ten years. The themes that I have listed below are consistent, and they look remarkably familiar. As we prepare teachers we depend on a body of research filled with similar assertions. The difference is that students generated these realizations themselves, and their assertions become grounding for their future reading of research and practice. Along with each theme I have included quotes from reflective writing or from my students' profiles:

1. Unless the writer has strong confidence, teacher/peer criticism can be counterproductive. Student with less confidence: "I remember my writing in junior high with red marks; it was always rejection in red and white. I began to act stupid, swallowing my viewpoints." Student with strong confidence: "He was an American with a British affectation in his speech, and he also had venom in his comments and utter contempt for misuse of the language. He was so pompous that I still intend years later to prove that I have a glimmer of style in my writing."

2. Teacher interest in the particulars of our writing can be stronger than praise. "When that thin-lipped teacher . . . took interest in a quirky view I had on the bombing of Hiroshima, I became really excited about my essay entry. He sent it off to a writing contest, and though it didn't win, [I did feel] like I had something to say."

3. Family involvement (audience, models, cheerers-on) is a powerful presence in writing. "My mother would let family and friends know what extraordinary accomplishments my compositions were. I believed my mother."

4. Writing events that give students real audience and purpose increase motivation, even events that precipitate nothing more sophisticated than letters or surreptitiously passed notes. "We had to make up inventions in writing that we would later pose to a manufacturer. We were so excited. Mine was a breathalyzer that would prevent a car from being started."

5. Confronting writing demons gives them less power. "I always said, 'I'm a good writer,' and got mad at teachers. I still think I'm a good writer, but I think I refused to acknowledge that the dumb little problems with punctu-

ation and grammar were holding me back. My rebelliousness has been counterproductive. It is time to just put the time I need into getting correct."

6. When students don't have room for choice in topic/format, they are forced to write for a grade, for what they think the teacher wants from them, and don't find writing to be a voicing experience. "I realize that I was a writer for a time, and now I'm not. It made me see how school has really sucked the soul out of my writing, turned me into a robot, or should I say I let it. But now that I see it, I can do something about it for my future students."

7. Writers vary in the genres that they prefer and are often anxious about writing in those with which they have had little success. "My partner is a writer; he loves writing poetry. I would rather eat worms than write it, but I'm coming around to thinking about trying it again based on his and other classmates' enthusiasm. I've been the practical writer, utilitarian."

8. Procrastination is a serious writing problem, perhaps a habit brought about because the writer too often had no wish to do assignments in the first place or feared the hypercritical teacher. "We were both procrastinators, and we could see the pattern in the other when we couldn't see it in ourselves. We laughed at our elaborate strategies to delay the beginning of writing and depended on deadline pressure to get started."

9. Writers have very different conditions that facilitate their concentration: loud music, no music, music with lyrics and without, TV in the background, hustle bustle in the background, severe isolation, friends in proximity to try things out on. "I need absolute silence—a disturbance devours a good idea, but my partner writes in front of the television!"

10. Writers have developed different processes that work for them, often very different from one another. "When we talked about writers writing in different ways, it made more sense to me than it would have if I hadn't heard the profiles. The interviews made it very clear that what works for one person may not work for another." Another student said, "We understood the need for flexibility in our classrooms, the need to look at the students' individual approaches and foster them, strengthen them."

11. Writing is much more fun/creative in elementary school and becomes a chore in secondary school; students seemed to regain voice sometime during college. "I discovered that writing teachers need to give students enough freedom to discover their own process and voice. Most high school teachers dwell on the five-paragraph stricture; my writing became stifled. Freshman composition didn't help, but now my writing has changed for the better."

12. Students all liked to write in some circumstances but realized that they were the survivors in the school systems if they wanted to be teachers of writing. "We all were successful and listen to our horror stories; I can only imagine what writing was like for those who were always wrong."

Course Components

I would guess that the other class components in Language, Cognition, and Writing are not so different from what is going on in similar classes around the country: reading and responding to texts on the teaching of writing; journal entries on the individual's writing process and about life in general; practicing in real classrooms; writing pieces with real audience and purpose; working on the development of writing curriculum; and responding to writing—that of peers and that of prospective students, either secondary students or first-year college students. My class is graded by contract, which may be a quick way to show the different course components. I use a contract because I feel much more comfortable in the role of responder than grader. Students grade themselves; I turn back work if it is not correct or complete, or if I sense that the student is not satisfied with it. Although a "C" option is included, only teachers already in the secondary classrooms have ever taken this option. Unfortunately, there are always a number of students who decline the "A" option as the end of the semester looms, heavily.

Grade Contract

C Option

- Interviews and a profile of your partner
- Multiple drafts of one piece of individual writing done for a real purpose and/or audience; conferences with the instructor about this piece
- Goodwilled effort in your journal
- Complete and thoughtful response to the class reading in the journal
- Evidence of quality and growth in written expression on either an individual I-Search, Multigenre, or Cultural Journalism research paper
- Participation in an adopt-a-class project for prospective teachers; curriculum work for practicing teachers
- A final take-home exam discussing progress on personal goals
- A portfolio of your work for the term and a reflective guided tour of that portfolio

B Option

Completion of C contract work and

- Evidence of constructive response to peer and student writing
- A portfolio including multiple drafts of two individual pieces, grammar and spelling logs, and a personal usage booklet
- An additional piece of writing for real audience or purpose

A Option

Completion of C and B contract work and

- A fifteen-minute presentation to the class accompanied by a handout about composition theory or practice gleaned from the reading of one additional book, which must be approved by the instructor. For practicing teachers, this may be replaced by a presentation about changes or plans for change that they have made or will make in their classrooms.

Reemergence of the Interview Research

Although the interview process is completed in the first weeks of the course, it is remarkable how often the interviews and the themes that arise in the analysis of the interviews reemerge in later classes (or staff meetings when used with TAs). For instance, in discussion of different writing class structures, one class member said, "I strongly agree that the basic skills approach is deficient because of thinking over the interview profiles. I know it didn't help me, and it didn't help many of the others." Questions of "basic skill" versus "grammar in context" approaches arise as a sort of surprise to many students, something they had never thought about as they accepted the way writing instruction had been dished up to them in the past. Although many of the preceding themes resurfaced and intertwined with other class content, several seemed omnipresent and worth the following special discussion. They are indicative of the kinds of action that come out of the interview research.

Action #1: Getting Control over Writing Weaknesses

Even though the more seasoned teachers tell them, "Don't worry; you'll get it when you teach it," prospective teachers are often quite concerned about the surface weaknesses that they have in writing. "How can I teach when I still haven't got commas straight?" The metacognitive nature of the interview reflection and research clears a place for identifying personal goals and weaknesses to work on, most of which have been divulged in interviews and witnessed in profiles. The interviews seem also to shake students loose into an honesty with themselves and their peers about their particular shortcomings. "I realized that everyone has problems with writing and that helped me to acknowledge my weaknesses and gave me inspiration to work on them. Defensiveness disappeared." As an instructor, I do it too. This year I told about my propensity for narrative exposition, my perhaps gendered predilection for telling stories, and the difficulties that causes me in trying to please many reviewers and editors who want me to get on with decontextualized analysis. Students pick a surface-level mistake they make and teach minilessons to the class, shoring up their own weaknesses and strengthening those of other class members in the process. We log our own spelling and grammar errors as a way of gaining some control over surface correctness, using peer and instructor responses to spot them. In an atmosphere of trust, students become somewhat desensitized to criticism, even actively seek it from peers and the instructor.

Action #2: "What's with the Friggin Wolf?" Students Circle Around Respect

This year students were struck with a comment made by Yolanda about her fifth-grade teacher's marginal comment on a story and the source of humiliation it held for her. "What's with the Friggin Wolf?" the teacher had written. And the students kept coming back to that phrase and incident in our discussion, circling around the need for teacher respect of student work. It seems that each year students return again and again to a similar phrase that someone has used in a profile that exemplifies the pain attached to teacher disrespect in student writing. They take this lesson to heart, thinking hard about the need for respect interwoven with honest feedback as they struggle to respond to students' writing in their "adopt-a-class" setting. In these borrowed classrooms, mentor teachers assist them in designing an assignment and doing multiple conferences with the same students over a series of drafts, grading the papers, and conferencing about the graded papers. Writing groups are another setting into which the students carry their reflective work.

Action #3: Putting into Practice Parallels Between Interviewing and Teaching Writing

So much of writing, the class members often realize after reading an article by Sondra Perl (1980), is based on having a "felt sense" to express oneself (retrospective structuring), on the subsequent articulation of ideas, followed by interested, curious response from others who listen/read carefully and respectfully, all with the hope of being heard by an audience (projective structuring) and affecting the outside world in some way. The interviewing process contains all these elements intact. For those who do well with oral rehearsal or who come from oral cultures, the interviewing process is particularly powerful. Indeed, the basic skill of interviewing is active listening, and all the skills of interviewing, taken together, are closely related to skills of good teaching and conferring with students. I remind students of suggestions I have made to them in interviewing, about trying to keep as quiet as possible, letting their partners articulate what is on their minds in response to the topic at hand, asking questions that lead to deeper reflection, and asking questions when they don't understand something or when they want more information. In many classes the students come to see the parallels between teaching and interviewing on their own; when they don't and when we are talking about conferencing, I bring them back to the intersections of these skills.

Conclusion

Year after year I am aware of the potent effect of this interviewing process on the course. The initial interviewer/interviewee partnerships break down cliques that might have previously existed amongst the members of the class (prospective teachers often take three semesters of courses together; TAs have been in graduate classes together; practicing teachers often come in isolated from one another). The profile reading itself provides insights that promote a group spirit that follows them through to graduation and beyond. In addition, students come to understand more deeply what they are about in their chosen profession: "After these interviews, I have realized that part of the reason I'm going to be a teacher is that I don't want anyone to feel as desperate as I did at times when I was learning to write." This exploration of their experiences can solidify their intentions. The interviewing process gives teachers insights that they might not otherwise achieve as they begin to teach, and it nudges seasoned teachers to rethink their role as teachers and writers. "In the process of reflection, I have called up memories that have been long-buried. I needed a dredge to get those memories to come clear with so much silt in the way. I have realized that writing has always been a center for me, forming a kind of thread of my life. In a way, it was a relief to sort through those memories and make some sense of writing and its place in my life."

6

Mentoring for Teaching Assistants in the Introductory Writing Program at Purdue University

Shirley K Rose
Purdue University

Preparation and support for graduate teaching assistants assigned to first-year composition at Purdue is provided by a mentoring program organized around a required three-credit teaching practicum. This chapter describes this mentoring program, focusing on the ways in which it reflects its institutional context.

Purdue is a public Research I university originally founded as a land grant institution in 1869. The student body is about seventy-three percent Indiana residents (many from relatively isolated rural areas in the state), sixteen percent students from other states (many of whom are attracted to Purdue's nationally ranked engineering programs), and eleven percent international students. Enrollment reached a record high of 37,762 in the fall of 1999.

First-year composition courses, which all Purdue schools require of their students, are offered by the Introductory Writing Program in the English department. In the 1999–2000 academic year, first-year composition courses accounted for about fifty percent of the total eight hundred sections offered by the department and about fifty percent of the total student enrollment in department course offerings. These composition courses were taught by a staff of one hundred TAs and twenty-some continuing or limited-term lecturers. The department also offers one hundred fifty sections of other courses that are considered "service" courses enrolling students from other majors in the School of Liberal Arts as well as students from other Purdue schools. These service courses, which include introductory literature courses, advanced composition, technical writing and business writing, are staffed primarily by senior TAs and limited-term lecturers. Because the department's service courses enroll such a large number of students in comparatively small classes (from sixteen to thirty-five students), a correspondingly large staff is needed. This need is met by appointing a large cadre of graduate TAs. These TAs, in turn, enroll in graduate courses, thus creating a demand for a comprehensive program of graduate English studies, which is staffed by professorial-rank faculty.

In addition, the department offers four undergraduate majors—a literature major identified as the "English" major, an English Education major, a Creative Writing major, and a Professional Writing major. Courses for English majors are staffed almost exclusively by professorial-rank faculty. Several courses for each of the other majors are frequently staffed by senior TAs—usually students who have passed preliminary exams and been advanced to candidacy for the Ph.D.

For most incoming students at Purdue, the required composition curriculum consists of two sequenced, three-credit courses completed in their first year. Students whose standardized college entrance test scores, high school grades, and class standing are high may complete a one-semester accelerated composition course. Students who need additional preparation for college-level writing complete a developmental writing course prior to the standard two-course sequence.

Because such a large number of students enroll in the relatively low enrollment sections of first-year composition, it is necessary to ensure that all instructional staff in the department—TAs, lecturers, and full-time faculty—are prepared to teach composition, in order to maximize staffing flexibility. For this reason, all TAs are assigned to first-year composition in their first year of appointment and required to participate in the Introductory Writing Program's mentoring program.

The foundation of the mentoring program is English 505, a required three-credit teaching practicum in which first-year TAs enroll in their first two semesters of appointment. In the fall semester they are mentored in teaching English 101, the first course in the introductory writing sequence; in the spring semester they are mentored in teaching English 102, the second course. Every summer, the Director of Composition assigns newly appointed teaching assistants to one of several mentor groups. The number of groups varies from five to eight, depending on the number of new TA appointments made. Each mentor group is made up of six to eight "mentees" and one mentor.

To the extent possible in making assignments to mentoring groups, the Director of Composition considers gender, cultural background, educational background (size, type, and location of B.A.- or M.A.-granting institution), range of previous teaching experience (tutoring experience, high school teaching experience, TA experience as an M.A. student elsewhere), and emphasis for graduate programs of study (creative writing, theory and cultural studies, linguistics, literary studies, and English education). These factors—together with a consideration of mentors' interests, expertise, and pedagogical approaches—inform the director's creation of groups that are likely to form cohesive communities and provide strong support for the individual members. In some cases, for example, all members of a group may be inexperienced teachers but be pursuing very different programs of graduate study. In other cases, a majority of members may be international TAs but differ widely in their previous teaching experience. Students entering Purdue's well-known graduate program in rhetoric and composition are all assigned to the same group in order to support their long-term scholarly and professional development in composition studies as a specialization.

The mentors themselves are appointed by the Director of Composition, drawing from professorial-rank faculty and senior TAs with a strong background and expertise in composition theory and pedagogy. TAs are eligible for appointment as mentors only after they have passed preliminary exams and been advanced to candidacy for the Ph.D. The requirement that mentors be specialists in composition studies usually limits eligible faculty appointments to rhetoric and composition specialists and typically limits senior TA appointments to advanced students in the graduate program in rhetoric and composition. Occasionally, however, there are exceptions, such as students who have studied rhetoric and composition as a secondary Ph.D. area or have chosen English Education as a focus for graduate study. In determining teaching loads for faculty and TAs, assignment as a mentor teaching English 505 is equivalent to assignment to any other course.

The mentoring program formally begins with a week of orientation activities for the new TAs. These activities include a plenary meeting in which the Introductory Writing Program curriculum and design is explained, six three-hour meetings in individual mentoring groups, introductions to campus resources such as Purdue's Writing Lab, and a staff meeting for all instructors in the program. During the mentoring group meetings in this week of orientation, mentors introduce their mentees to their shared curriculum for English 101 in the coming semester. This curriculum is consistent with the Introductory Writing Program's "Statement of Shared Goals" and is typically organized around the textbook or coursepack of readings the mentor has selected for the mentees to use in their classes and ordered for their students in advance. Though mentors make these choices independently, they are consistent with the program-wide set of shared goals for the first-year composition sequence; frequently, several mentors will choose the same textbooks for their mentees to use with their students. Most mentors provide their mentees with a sample or model syllabus for English 101. Some mentors provide no more than an outline at the beginning; others provide a highly detailed calendar of assignments including detailed suggested agenda for class sessions. Most mentors try to achieve a balance by making highly specified and detailed guidance available yet allowing the individual TAs they mentor to make alternative decisions and try variations where appropriate.

During the orientation week, mentors also introduce TAs to the theoretical underpinnings of the curriculum and pedagogical approaches they will be using in their composition courses in the semester ahead. Typically, mentees read key articles on the composition theory and research that has guided the mentor's curriculum choices. Mentors also often choose the same textbooks and other resources for the practicum itself, introducing their mentees to the theo-retical foundations for their own approaches to teaching the practicum. In men-toring meetings during orientation week, new teaching assistants often engage in the same classroom activities they will be using with their students, such as discussions of readings, small-group invention and planning exercises, peer editing groups, and one-on-one writing conferences. Participants also learn program and university policies and develop their own statements of course policies on issues such as attendance, late assignments, and plagiarism.

This week of orientation meetings is supplemented by several hour-long "extended orientation" meetings for all IWP staff throughout the academic year. Extended orientation programs focus on shared teaching concerns such as work-ing with ESL writers, teaching students with disabilities, using the resources of Counseling and Psychological Services, and preparing teaching portfolios.[1]

Once the semester is underway, mentor groups meet at least once a week for seventy-five minutes. Two seventy-five-minute class periods are reserved in their weekly schedules to allow for supplemental group meetings when neces-sary, one-on-one meetings with the mentor, or attendance at all-staff extended orientation meetings. For a typical weekly meeting, the agenda might begin with a review of the mentees' teaching experiences during the previous week, with TAs telling stories about problems or successes with particular assign-ments and exercises. The group might then move to a discussion of their own reading assignment for the week, one that typically developed a theoretical ar-gument for a particular classroom practice, such as peer editing groups. Next, the mentor might ask mentees what questions they encountered in their prepar-ing for classes in the week ahead and might preview assignments and activities still several weeks ahead. If a major writing assignment is due soon, the group might discuss what their expectations and criteria for evaluation will be. If a writing assignment has recently been collected from students, the group might discuss problem papers or develop a rubric for evaluation. Depending on group members' previous teaching experience, the mentor might ask mentees to work individually or in teams to prepare detailed suggestions for ways to use class time, such as in-class exercises or discussion questions.

In addition to leading these weekly group meetings, mentors visit each mentee's class at least twice each semester. (Sometimes an observation of an individual student writing conference is substituted for a visit to a regular class session.) Each visit is followed by a one-to-one consultation in which mentor and mentee problem-solve and plan ways to draw on the mentee's teaching strengths and develop in weaker areas. Twice each semester, TAs submit for the mentor's review a sample set of student papers to which they have provided written responses.

Throughout the practicum, individual mentors have the same responsibili-ties for evaluating TAs' work that any instructor would have for evaluating stu-dent work. At the end of the semester, mentors report an English 505 grade (sat-isfactory or nonsatisfactory) for each group member and write a detailed letter of evaluation for each. These evaluations address the mentee's teaching effectiveness—in planning a class period, leading a class, working individually with students, and responding to student writing—as well as his or her participation in and contribution to the mentoring group meetings. This letter is copied to the Director of Composition and filed in the Introductory Writing Program office.

Though each mentor is fully responsible for his or her section of English 505, mentors meet frequently to share expertise with and provide support for one another. These meetings are usually organized around an informal lunchtime meeting with the Director of Composition (also a mentor).

Thus far I have described a typical mentoring group's activities. There are, however, some variations from this pattern. As I mentioned previously, TAs who are students in the graduate rhetoric and composition program are all in the same mentoring group and are mentored by a professorial-rank faculty member who is a specialist in rhetoric and composition. For two years, one of the mentoring groups focused on feminist pedagogical approaches to teaching composition (mentees elected to participate in this group). In 1998–1999, for the first time, incoming TAs were offered the option of teaching composition in a computer classroom; those who chose this option were placed in the same group and were mentored by a senior TA with experience and scholarly expertise in computers and writing.

After their first year of teaching in the Introductory Writing Program, TAs do not participate in a mentoring group unless they take on a special assignment in the program. Two special assignments of long standing are ESL sections of first-year composition and the developmental writing program, English 100. TAs who are assigned to ESL sections of composition are mentored by a faculty member or senior TA who is a specialist in ESL writing. TAs who teach in the developmental writing program are mentored by a senior TA with expertise in issues in basic writing curricula and pedagogies.

Two recently developed special assignments are composition courses taught in computer classrooms and a cohort-enrollment project with Purdue's School of Science. For the past four years, continuing TAs (those who have completed their first year or appointment) who are teaching in computer classrooms for the first time have participated in a mentor group focused on computer-mediated instructional approaches and issues in teaching electronic discourse. Beginning with the 1998–99 academic year, TAs who teach sections of first-year composition enrolling cohort groups of students with majors in the School of Science—e.g., biology, mathematics, or chemistry—have participated in a mentor group focused on developing composition curricula appropriate to students who are interested in science. This mentor group has been led by a senior TA with special expertise in writing across the curriculum. Mentoring in these special programs also involves presemester orientation workshops, weekly group meetings, class visits, consultations, and discussions of shared readings in related composition theory and research.

After their first year of teaching in the department, TAs have a number of options for teaching assignments in undergraduate classes other than first-year composition, such as professional writing, the Writing Lab, introduction to creative writing, introduction to linguistics, and introduction to literature. Each time a teaching assistant teaches a course for the first time, he or she participates in some kind of mentoring program, though the programs have a variety of structures. For example, TAs who are assigned to Purdue's well-known Writing Lab for the first time participate in weekly meetings of all lab staff in addition to observing a number of tutorial sessions led by senior TAs and being observed and critiqued in several of their own tutorials. TAs assigned to the professional writing courses for nonmajors attend weekly all-staff meetings, and their classes are visited several times each semester. TAs who are students in Purdue's M.F.A. in Creative Writing program prepare to teach introductory writing courses by regularly observing and occasionally assisting a professorial-rank faculty member teaching such a course for a semester. A TA who is teaching a particular literature course for nonmajors, such as "Great Narrative Works," is mentored individually by a faculty member who regularly teaches that same course. Instead of weekly group meetings, mentor and mentee are likely to plan a syllabus together, exchange class visits, design exams and writing assignments together, and exchange a set of student papers.

The description of our mentoring program that I've provided here represents its current structure and practices. A mentoring program of some kind has been in place since the 1960s, when Purdue first established its Ph.D. program in English. The first-year composition mentoring program has provided the standard model from which other programs have diverged to greater or lesser degree, depending on the perceived difficulties of teaching the courses to which TAs are assigned. Because the Introductory Writing Program offers a strong, thorough, yearlong support system, the other mentoring programs can build on it.

Our mentoring program reflects several special features of its institutional context. Because we are an M.A.- and Ph.D.-granting institution, we staff most of our first-year composition courses and a significant number of our other service courses with TAs, who require a systematic and extensive program of preparation for teaching. Because we have a strong graduate rhetoric and composition program, we have well-qualified senior TAs upon whom we can rely to supplement faculty assignments to mentor positions, allowing us to keep the mentoring groups to a relatively small size even when increases in new student enrollments lead to awarding larger numbers of teaching assistantships. The involvement of a large number of composition specialists—faculty and doctoral-level graduate students—in mentoring for the Introductory Writing Program makes it possible to allow mentors to develop curricula for their mentees independently, rather than prescribing the same textbook and syllabus for all teachers and students in the program.

In his history of Purdue's mentoring program, "When Teaching Assistants Teach Teaching Assistants to Teach," Irwin Weiser (forthcoming) explores the reasons for the way in which the program has evolved since it was begun in the 1960s. As his study shows, the mentoring program has enjoyed a relatively large investment of the department's resources, especially the resources of faculty time and talent, since its inception. The department, the School of Liberal Arts, and the university have continued in their willingness to commit these resources because they have viewed the mentoring program as a way to meet two equally important responsibilities that constitute the role of a research university. The mentoring program allows us both to support the professional development of future higher education faculty and to provide quality instruction for our undergraduates.

Note

1. The Introductory Writing Program offers an award for "The Best Teaching Portfolio" each year. Preparation and submission of a portfolio is voluntary.

IV

Where All Roads Lead to the Writing Classroom

The seven courses and programs that follow develop seven different perspectives on instructional priorities and design and present seven further variations on the book's three themes.

In Chapter 7 Steve VanderStaay places his English education students in an edgy quandary by first enticing them to embrace writing process pedagogy and then asking them to bite down hard critiquing it. In pursuing his goal of situating preservice writing teachers in the midst of the current debates about writing pedagogy, VanderStaay's students write and reflect critically as they explore our professional discourse. By implication, Chapter 7 argues that experiencing the dialectic of immersion in "best practices" and serious critique of those practices is as valuable for new teachers of first-year composition as it is for new secondary teachers.

In Chapter 8 Dan Royer and Roger Gilles also lead students into critiques of writing process pedagogy but with a different twist than VanderStaay's. Students at Grand Valley State get a significant discussion of recent disciplinary history and how it applies to the development and critique of classroom practice. Students also, if they choose, can consider Moffett as a kind of terra firma on which to stand during the position-taking and debates. In addition, Royer and Gilles' course displays a bent toward reflection and active considerations of theory, demonstrating that English education as well as first-year composition can be a site for the study of theory.

Doug Hesse and Kirsti Sandy's picture of TA education in Chapter 9 shows a multilayered effort at mentoring within a composition studies program that takes seriously not only traditional research and theory but the English educator's commitment to "teaching apprenticeship" as well. These authors do not spare the messy reality of "practical concerns" disrupting discussions of theory. Here we see a "lived-in" program complete with personality conflicts and hallway politics demanding a special kind of management from the WPA. So much writing teacher preparation for teaching college composition goes on at Illinois State, in fact, that the program leaders are considering cutting back.

The picture of mentoring Melissa Whiting presents in Chapter 10 is unique and personal. Viewing first-year composition from the vantage point of a writing center for college athletes, Whiting reveals that mentoring college writing instructors is not always about composition theory or pedagogical technique. Sometimes the barriers to student writing success are located in the teacher's personal attitudes and cultural prejudices. Most writing teachers at every level know a colleague who damages students through academic arrogance or lack of cultural understanding and respect. This chapter asks the question, Are we willing to try to mentor them?

In Chapter 11 William Broz admits to being a true believer in writing-process pedagogy. As a teacher of high school writing and first-year composition, he asserts "You cannot teach well what you don't believe." His goal is to give future writing teachers student writing experiences that amount to new "apprenticeships of observation" that help create professional belief, belief that "teacher knowledge" theory shows is the basis for both effective practice and teacher change. He also structures reflective experiences that lead beginning writing teachers to adopt distant mentors among the authors of the literature of writing pedagogy, mentors whose support can help sustain those beliefs.

Greg Hamilton's metaphor of mapping fits the metaphor of the Intersections in this book—guideposts on the way in which we think writing teacher education as a discipline is moving. Likewise, Hamilton's students identify, a, b, and c pattern map and reflect on important stops along their personal routes to becoming writers. Chapter 12 also shows preservice teachers in the roles of student, writer, *and* beginning writing teacher, since they take Hamilton's course in the evening during their student teaching semester.

In Chapter 13 Michelle Tremmel presents an economical way to configure a mentoring exchange between English education students and seventh-grade writers. Tremmel shows that the dynamic nature of mentoring allows seventh-graders to teach college mentors a few things about writing and a lot about seventh-grade writers. In the spirit of cross-institutional collaboration, this essay underscores the benefits of looking at teaching writing and at preparing writing teachers as a joint school and university endeavor.

7

Critiquing Process

Teaching Writing Methods as Problem Solving

Steven L. VanderStaay
Western Washington University

I. Why

Let us start with what is at stake.

School failure predicts delinquency for children of all socioeconomic classes and races, as does a lack of "school bonding" and weak attachments to teachers. Conversely, high grades and a positive attitude toward schooling appear to lower risk factors and foster resilience in children and juveniles.

The benefits of education accrue to both the individual and the society. A high school graduate earns more than twice what the average high school drop out makes; college graduates earn twice the salary of high school graduates. Raising educational achievement within a community reduces crime, strengthens social cohesion, improves public health, and raises productivity. Educational failure, on the other hand, is costly. According to a recent economic analysis, each high school dropout costs a community $243,000 to $388,000. Conversely, "Saving a high risk youth" from drug abuse, criminal behavior and/or school failure returns up to 2.3 million dollars to his community.

A community honors those who undertake to shape the educational destiny of its children by calling them teachers. Because school success depends chiefly upon success in reading, writing, and mathematics, teachers of these subjects perform work of particular significance. At the secondary level we have a special designation for those willing to bear responsibility for two of these three subjects, calling such individuals the "language arts teachers."

So begins my two-quarter sequence, "Teaching Composition and Literature in the Secondary School." If this introduction seems heavy-handed, I mean it to be. As a literacy scholar who specializes in the relation among schooling, crime, and delinquency, I know that educational success or failure may quite literally be a life sentence. The heavy-handedness has a second advantage, one stemming from the peculiar nature of the present moment within composition and literacy. Acquainting oneself with the fields and disciplines that pertain to this pedagogy demands an ability to shift perspectives, to trace practices to assumptions, and to consider readers and writers very different from oneself. These features make pedagogy exciting but also foster a fascination with abstractions that can detach such tasks from their importance. By beginning my course with what's at stake in teaching reading and writing I ground it there, establishing the great significance of literacy as our central fixed point.

II. How

With the *why* of studying methods of teaching composition and literature established, I move next to the *how*—a question I answer with a teaching method rooted in problem solving. This is a three-part effort, pertaining to the nature of learning, our limited understanding of literacy learning, and the key task I set for students in my class. My first-day lecture notes continue:

> *The gulf between ability and understanding is strikingly large where our language abilities are concerned. Consider learning to talk. Acquiring a first language may be the greatest intellectual feat of our lives. Yet we typically achieve it before we are four, and without effort or instruction. When held up against this achievement our efforts to teach language skills are comparative failures. To put it simply, our powers as language learners are vast; our record of marshalling this power—say in the teaching of vocabulary, grammar, or fluency—is dismal. Indeed, I would be lying to say that I can teach you how best to teach these skills.*
>
> *Fortunately, that is not my task. Teachers are professionals in the sense that they are not so much told how to do their job as appointed to decide for themselves how best to do it. Regardless of what you may have heard about district philosophies or curriculum guides, the gritty reality is that there is no higher authority than the teacher. People will, of course, tell you how to do things. But the advice you'll hear will be contradictory and it will vary from year to year. Ultimately, you have little choice but to become subject-area experts, professionals capable of deciding how best to assist the students in your care.*
>
> *The course, in this sense, is a quest of sorts. We are all searching for solutions to the problem of how best to teach adolescents the language arts. Your final project is your set of solutions to this problem, your description of the tools, approaches, and practices you'll use in teaching writing and literature in secondary schools. Working behind-the-scenes, I've organized course-work in terms of the smaller problems one encounters en route to reaching a workable solution to the larger one. For our purposes, these problems concern*

criticism and debate over aspects of the current, most recommended approach to the teaching of composition, which we will over-simplify by calling the process approach. Many of these problems can be rendered as binary oppositions comprising the distinctions shown in Figure 7–1.

The consistency of experience I used to be able to count on in such classes simply does not exist anymore. My students certainly have bad memories of their writing teachers, but they are now more apt to complain about journaling than sentence diagrams. Reflecting on their best teachers, they are as likely to praise a grammarian as an expressivist. Consequently, the "wasn't it terrible" (i.e., oppressive), "wouldn't this be better" (i.e., liberating) structure writing methods courses I used to depend on no longer work. This changes things— and for the better.

Because my students have all had at least some experience with process approaches, our discussion of such methods no longer occurs in a vacuum. And it is no longer so one-sided. My own introduction to process methods occurred during the early 1980s. Enthusiasm for expressivism was at fever pitch, and composition was compelling as well as exciting. Riding the tsunami of enthusiasm for the changes in thinking about writing, which Maxine Hairston (1982) first called a "paradigm shift," my professors swept us up with them and we rode the current, spreading the gospel in writing projects and, later, our own methods courses. Within secondary schools the key assumption of the process movement—that language skills are acquired, not learned—was rendered more explicit by association with "whole language" methods of reading, and opposition to current-traditionalist practices meant a closing of ranks among process proponents. As Joseph Harris (1997) has put it, "so far as teaching went there were really only "process people" and "current-traditionalists," and no one wanted to be counted among the latter" (55). Within this context, studying writing methods as a preservice teacher looked rather more like conversion than critical thinking.

Learning	Versus	Teaching
Inductive, acquisition models of learning	versus	Deductive, direct instruction models
Student-based instruction	versus	Curriculum or standards-based instruction
Support-centered models of motivation and climate	versus	Academic-press models of motivation

Figure 7-1.

Fortunately, the present moment in composition is not so tidy. Debate and disagreement leave more room for problem solving. And, because they can be found in the establishment as well as in the insurrection, process methods now inspire the very kinds of challenges that foster critical thinking. The same conditions cloud things a bit. A student pushed through free writing, collaborative essays, and grammar exercises during her own high school years will sometimes have trouble recognizing sharp differences in the theoretical camps to which each practice can be traced — especially if she disliked them all. Consequently, I look for readings that take strong, clear positions. And I begin by asking students to concretize their experiences in writing and literature classes and then to reflect on those experiences in terms of the debates we'll enter. Braiding experience and reflection to analysis in this manner, the course begins with a diverse footing of perspectives that fosters reflection and an appreciation for perspectives and experiences different from one's own. Thus, the stage is set for the kind of perspective taking and critical problem solving I seek to encourage. Typically, the nuts and bolts look like this:

III. Nuts and Bolts

Writing

The course opens with the students writing. Assigning a biographical essay, I ask my students to

> *Tell stories from your life of literacy, accounting for some of the books, people, and experiences that have been most important to your development as a reader and writer.*

Hoping to break old habits and assumptions, I tell my students their essays must be written in a creative or nontypical form. To help with the confusion and fear this instruction usually occasions, I lead students through free-writing and drafting exercises while providing class time for students to share ideas and drafts. I draw freely from a wide range of instructional strategies as we do this, such as describing Peter Elbow's (1981) advice for separating the "mentalities" of creating and criticizing in one moment, or assuring the class that since writers of the King James Bible used that and which interchangeably, so can we.

Students print four copies of their essays; I bind these into eight anthologies, each of which holds half the papers. For their next assignment, each student reads one of these anthologies, taking notes along the way regarding what these stories have to teach about learning to write and to read. Questions I pose for this purpose include: What is the combination of acquisition and direct learning described in these stories? What aspects of literacy learning seem most often to occur in and outside of school? Working from these notes, students write their second essay — a reflective commentary describing what these stories taught them about learning and teaching composition and literature.

The results of these efforts provide a map of the great range of moments, experiences, and people that may shape a student's literate life. Some students taught themselves to write, putting thoughts to paper in diaries and letters; others learned mainly at school. Many learned chiefly on their own but needed the resources—the books, school newspaper, poetic forms, and so on—the school provided to do so. Describing the people most important to them as literacy learners, my students suggest a cast of significant characters equally as diverse. Reflecting on this diversity of experience, students see schooling and literacy within the larger context of a student's life. They connect school and home experiences, recognizing the roles literacy may play in matters both personal and professional. They see, too, that students differ in their needs and in the approaches that work best for them at different moments in their lives. Some are awed by this, others frightened. But whether awed or frightened they move on in the course with a greater appreciation for the complexity of literacy learning, and a well-earned skepticism about accounts claiming that a single approach or style will work for all learners.

Recognizing Claims and Opinions

Working from the momentum generated by these first essays, we move next to defining our terms, asking, What is it we teach when we teach composition and literature? I assign readings from William Bennet (1987), E. D. Hirsch Jr. (1987, 1977), and Ravitch and Finn (1988) asking students to describe how these writers answer that question. For all their excesses, these writers are clear about where they stand, and we work hard both to understand their positions and to trace their conclusions back to their assumptions. Wanting students to experience as well as to examine the "current-traditionalist" approaches recommended by these writers, I present plot summaries of Shakespearean plays for them to memorize and assign a formal essay that I grade "for clarity, accuracy, and usage" with a red pen. We practice grammar exercises, and I push students particularly hard on Hirsch's most persuasive point: that his is the truly democratic approach, the one that aims to bring the texts and methods heretofore reserved for our wealthiest and most privileged classes to all children. Reviewing these experiences in a second, reflective essay, students ponder what they have felt, thought, and learned and how their experience might compare with that of the students they are apt to teach.

This close attention to the tenets of these current-traditionalists provides the contrasts I draw from in introducing process approaches. I begin with Nancie Atwell's *In the Middle* (1998, 1987b), which we approach in the same way we studied Hirsch, Bennet, and Ravitch and Finn: by working to solve the problem of how she defines writing and literature and how she believes they should be taught. The sharp differences between her approach and those of the current-traditionalists bring substance to the binary distinctions outlined in my introduction to the class; suddenly the difference between acquiring an ability and learning it through direct instruction becomes very clear. The book, moreover, is both theoretically and historically useful, providing clear examples of how process theories were applied while acquainting students with the period that first generated the methodologies we now find most recommended. Additionally, for students like mine, who were schooled over those years, reading the book creates audible markers of realization ("My 8th grade teacher did this!") as they fit their own experience as students into Atwell's portrait of the methods and manners she advocates.

Of course, *In the Middle* (the first edition, in particular) is a shamelessly persuasive book. The narrative is first a romance and then, in the signature move of the process movement, a conversion story as Atwell and her teaching are "saved" by the new process methods she embraces. Cautioned by the more complicated portrait of literacy learning they created in their own literary biographies, my students are less seduced by these narratives than I was. They think harder about them, too, tracing Atwell's workshops and assignments to the assumptions at their roots. They find Rousseau in her insistence that adolescent interests and instincts are essentially good and to be trusted; they find Dewey in her student-centered stance; they find the assumptions of modernity in her expressivist emphasis on the writer's self; they find constructivism in her insistence that writing and reading skills are rather more acquired than learned.

This tracing leads to questioning as well as criticism. While convinced that leading students to enjoy reading and writing is better than forcing them through such activities, my students wonder what to do with students who can't be led to find such pleasure. While uncomfortable with Bennet's declaration that it is the teacher's job to decide what students should be reading and writing about, my students are uncomfortable with the lack of authority Atwell seems to recommend over such issues. And they begin to see similarities instead of binaries: is Atwell's notion of clarity in writing really that different from Hirsch's standard of readability, for instance?

Seeking to experience as well as to study the methodologies Atwell recommends, we turn our class into a writing workshop. Borrowing from a strategy common in M.F.A. programs in writing, I divide my class into groups of five students, each of which is responsible for publishing a literary journal. The students create a name and format for their journal, issuing a "call for submissions" describing the writing they would like to publish and the criteria they will use for choosing submissions. Each journal publishes ten pieces; each student in the class must get two pieces of his or her own published (something longish— such as an essay or a short story—and something shortish, such as a poem or microstory). For two weeks we write, draft, edit, submit, accept, and reject creative writing—reserving a few minutes each day for parallel activities in a reading workshop. I interrupt the workshopping on occasion, asking students to note what they are learning about the "natural" process of writing for real editors and responding to real writers.

The published magazines and journals are shared and read over a long class period inevitably marked by my students' laughter, praise, and respect for their accomplishments. We conclude this class with small-group discussions of what they learned about reading and writing through this process. We discuss the benefits, including motivation, of student writers' being able to leave the class with "published" work to be proud of. Completing this circle, I ask the class to reflect on my work, as the teacher, over the three weeks it took to write and publish the journals. This surprises them—they become so involved in their own editing and writing that they momentarily forget that we are studying how to teach. Then, the lights go on as they realize the pleasure and fun that can accrue to the *teacher* who uses process and workshop methods.

The various follow-up activities in the days after the publication of our magazine bring us to the midpoint of the first quarter I have with my secondary-methods students, a key turning point in my four-hour-per-week, two-quarter class. Addressing the students, I make one of the few presentations I read directly from my notes:

> *While only six weeks into this quarter, we have traveled a long way together. We have shared stories of our own literacy-learning; we have reviewed what we currently know about learning to read and to write, and we have examined conservative assertions about the importance of traditional methods, direct instruction, and teacher authority. And we have experienced, as well as studied, the methods we have examined.*
>
> *But we have spent most of our time with the assumptions and practices of process methods. Using Nancie Atwell as our model of what such methods may look like when practiced in secondary classrooms, we have examined, read about, discussed and practiced this method. Indeed, our study of process methods forms the core and center of this class.*
>
> *This emphasis has been purposeful. The methods popularized by the process movement are widely recommended. Its assumptions—particularly with respect to drafting, revising, student choice, and the power of inductive processes that allow students to acquire literate skills through naturalistic activities modeled on those that "real" writers and readers use—are broadly accepted by people like myself and widely taught in courses such as this one. Schools do not always practice what subject-area experts preach, but process methods—particularly within the teaching of writing—are currently elevated above all others as the "best practice" standard within secondary language arts.*
>
> *Yet consensus can foster excess. Innovations are typically strengthened by critique. And, if Hegel is right, the pursuit of truth is necessarily dialectic, requiring that all theses be met with their antithesis before new and more useful syntheses are reached. We do not yet have such a synthesis within methods of teaching writing and literature, but we do now have important critiques*

of aspects of the process approach. For people like you, preparing to teach
writing and literature in secondary schools, these critiques create important
problems to be solved. For the remainder of the course, this is our work.

IV: Problems with Process

The broader process movement, and particular assumptions within process approaches, have undergone numerous attacks and critiques. Many of these are
chiefly theoretical, rooted in recent debate concerning postmodernism, subjec-
tivity, and social constructivism. Others are chiefly applied. But a few are both,
providing important challenges to the theory and practice of using process
methods to teach writing within secondary schools. These are the critiques I
emphasize.

My use of these critiques is selective and changing, reflecting my own interests and the nature of the problems they pose. In the most recent section of
secondary methods I taught, we followed Atwell with Margaret Finders'
ethnography *Just Girls: Hidden Literacies and Life in Junior High* (1997), a
pair of articles from *Reading Research Quarterly* (Stotsky 1995; Carver and
Leibert 1995), and Lisa Delpit's *Other People's Children* (1995). For the purposes of this article, I'll describe our review of *Just Girls* most closely; in my
methods course each critique is weighted equally.

I introduced *Just Girls* by locating the book within Finders' own experience as a middle school teacher:

> *Margaret Finders was a middle school language arts teacher. In this book,*
> *she returns to a middle school language arts class as an ethnographer. Be-*
> *friending two groups of girls, Finders followed them over the course of a year*
> *in school, hanging out with them in their homes and watching them in class*
> *while also interviewing their teachers and families.*
>
> *The teachers of these girls "cited Nancie Atwell as a key source of their*
> *pedagogy" (Finders 1997, 27). They used the terms "workshop," "student*
> *centered," and "writing process pedagogy" when describing their curricu-*
> *lum. Summarizing, Finders notes that "Gaining fluency by writing in a risk-*
> *free environment and connecting reading and writing to one's personal back-*
> *ground were commonly articulated as the foundation of the language arts*
> *pedagogy." "The unifying theme," she adds, "was a commitment to a teach-*
> *ing style in which students would feel comfortable and safe" (27).*
>
> *In short, this ethnography provides one picture of how students experi-*
> *ence the methods we have been studying.*

Together with other critiques–such as Lad Tobin's *Writing Relationships:*
What Really Happens in the Composition Class (1993)—Finders' study illuminates wide rifts between the theory and practice of process methods. A large segment of the girls Finders befriended felt none of the safety and freedom their
teachers sought to provide, but in this case it was not the teacher who was to

blame but the peer group and the larger, hegemonic context of becoming accul-turated as an adolescent female. Wanting to appear grown up, many of these girls felt forced to resist texts and assignments they later admitted they enjoyed and learned from. Wanting to fit the norms established by their peer groups and the media images they soaked up in teen magazines, they read romances even when they didn't want to and used workshops to write personal narratives that bored them.

In Finders' (1997) portrait this acquiescence is almost excessively Gram-scian. These girls oppress themselves (and one another) so well that overt male oppression proves unnecessary. One student, for instance, repeatedly tells Finders that she wants to write topical and persuasive essays on controversial subjects, yet, while given dozens of opportunities to choose her own forms and topics in writing workshop, she never does. Instead, she writes personal narra-tives and poems. Finders comments: "Each of the teachers articulated the ne-cessity of designing a curriculum built on 'free choice.' Yet, as has been evi-dent throughout this study, there was no free choice" (111).

When asked what changes they would like to see made in school, one girl wished that teachers would assign formal position papers on controversial top-ics. Another, tiring of the consistent praise and support her writing received, said it would be better if teachers responded to student writing with more "input" and direct criticism. Reflecting on these conclusions in our discussions of *Just Girls,* my students invariably point out these practices suggest the very kind of teacher authority that proponents of process methods claim are oppressive and suspect.

We work through other critiques in this fashion, moving in a dialogic fash-ion from the theory and practice of process methods to their criticism. We ex-amine the assertion that students "learn to write by writing and learn to read by reading" by reviewing *Reading Research Quarterly* critiques of these views by Sandra Stotsky (1995) and Carver and Leibert (1995). Stotsky criticizes the "extreme" reliance on personal writing within expressivist pedagogies; Carver and Leibert assert that secondary students do not improve as readers unless pushed to take on material slightly more difficult than they are accustomed to. Most recently, we concluded with *Other People's Children* (1995), a book that grew out of Lisa Delpit's misgivings with the writing project movement and her view that writing process methods may be inappropriate for many African American children.

V: Problem Solving

Whereas academic training extends discernment, encouraging students to ques-tion their biases and to think longer and harder before reaching conclusions, teaching requires clear and rapid decisions. There is a natural chasm between these activities, and I typically find my students need a strong push before they build up enough momentum to leap it. The final project—their answer to the problem of how they will teach writing and literature—provides this.

Surprisingly, my students tend not to take middle-of-the-road positions, striking a balance somewhere between the binary contrasts with which we began. More typically, they align theory and practice with specific tasks. Many recommend student-centered writing workshops for writing directed toward student audiences, for instance, while recommending more teacher-centered processes for more traditional assignments. Some decide to teach with process methods, but to do so in a manner informed by their critiques. Others assert that the kinds of activities Atwell recommends are better employed as a tool than a method. A few remain true believers, their faith in process methods only hardened by the critiques they have examined. Conversely, a student sometimes surprises me by declaring herself (more women than men, so far) a current-traditionalist.

In these ways, the conclusion to the course reflects its origin as students solve the problem of how to teach writing and literature in terms that acknowledge the diversity of experiences and influence suggested by their opening biographies. Grafting this breadth onto the theoretical knowledge and pedagogic expertise they've built and the firm why of what's at stake in school literacy learning with which we began, my students practice the professional stance of subject-area experts. Responsible for determining their own solutions to the problems we review, they reach their conclusions through the very kind of "dialogic exchange" cognitive theorists find at the center of thinking and learning (Paul 1987). The solutions my students pose may be less homogenous than those of graduates from other programs. Yet, inasmuch as the process is more important than the product, they are better positioned to begin careers as language arts specialists. Students of writing deserve no less. "Writing" Kurt Spellmeyer reminds us, "actually proceeds through a deliberate series of problematizations" (1993, 18). Why should teaching writing and writing about teaching writing be any different?

8

Combining History, Theory, and Practice in the Writing Methods Course

Dan Royer and Roger Gilles
Grand Valley State University

Teaching the writing methods course is fraught with tensions that often revolve around theory and practice: Students want practical advice; we want to supply a conceptual framework and let practice take care of itself in the many different classroom contexts in which our students will eventually find themselves. Students think of themselves as prospective teachers of second, or fifth, or eleventh grade, and they want to think about theory and practice as *about* these grade levels; we think of writing on a continuum of literacy development that extends from the symbol weaving practices of kindergarten to the most sophisticated writing practices of adult learners. Students have learned to write in curricula nominally based on "developmental" educational theories and the "process approach," so they carry with them notions of lockstep jumps from "stories" to "reports" to "arguments" and a series of writing "strategies" that lead to surefire "A" papers; we have begun to see semiotic perspectives and genre theory subsume the recursive stage-model approach and place greater emphasis on early symbol-making activity in all genres as a germinal expression of the full range of future literate behavior. Students see writing theory as a static body of knowledge they hope to ingest in fifteen weeks; we, having lived through the last thirty-plus years of reform in writing pedagogy, see the history of writing instruction as an evolving process, perhaps gaining in purpose but still very much open-ended.

Just as there are tensions in the writing methods class, so are there tensions, or at least differences of approach, between compositionists at the university and teachers in the schools. The same, moreover, is true of writing-teacher educators in first-year composition and in English education programs. Whereas compositionists at the university may indulge such notions as "postprocess" theory and debate abolishing first-year college writing instruction, teachers in the schools must continue to generate fresh writing assignments and think of inventive ways to engage students in rhetorical activities. And whereas the first generation of writing theorists thought little of the distinction between "English ed" and "comp/rhet," it seems unusual today for the two to meet. NCTE and CCCC draw different groups of people, though this was not always so.

We—Dan and Roger—feel many of these tensions pulling when we teach the writing methods course. They are not always unhappy tensions, just the gravitation of different subcultures as we make passes in our elliptical orbits around what sometimes seem like the different worlds of English education and composition studies. Those of us more fixed in our orbit about one or the other worlds may not feel this same tidal swing, but it has played a definite role in our particular careers. Dan taught high school for eight years before joining Roger as a comp/rhet specialist at a university where we both have directed the composition program and taught academic, creative, and professional writing courses. Our department began hiring specialists in both English education and composition/rhetoric in the late 1980s and early 1990s and for the most part assumed that both groups would share the teaching of the writing methods courses, but in truth it has been an uneasy alliance. The comp/rhet folks have been perceived by English ed folks as short on practical experience and overly theoretical, whereas English ed folks have been perceived by comp/rhet folks as overly concerned with lesson-plan formats and "what to do on Monday." Our desire to bridge the gap in these perceptions, to somehow get the best of both worlds, led us to develop a new course design that aims to be both theoretical and practical, rooted in both history and current (and future) practice.

Presenting a Living History of Composition

The course we teach is anchored in a historical understanding of composition's recent past. The field has made notable progress in America because of British and Australian scholarship, but it's the Deweyan roots of our own educational culture that have permitted a level of experimentation and change not seen in many other countries. Without having felt these "winds of change"—to dust off Maxine Hairston's (1982) still inspiring rallying cry—students in our methods course are less likely to understand the momentum that continues to power and excite our developing field. We ask students to read Joseph Harris' *A Teaching Subject: Composition Since 1966* (1997), and we've organized a reading list around his five broad rubrics: Growth, Voice, Process, Error, and Community. These five chapters give students a broad historical view of the issues that have dominated discourse about writing for the last forty years. Harris resists the easy, cumulative progression from one idea or approach to another in favor of a history of real people engaged in real tensions surrounding these five key terms of debate.

As a kind of counterbalance to Harris' broad sweep, we ask students to read Nancie Atwell's *In the Middle* (1998), the very situated account of one teacher's attempts to develop a writing workshop in a middle school setting. Atwell's experiences reflect the kind of informed experimentation that Harris observes as having gone on in the field since the early days of Britton, Graves, and Moffett. But Atwell's story is not simply an illustration of a model teacher at work. It is also a contribution to the ongoing debate, and we ask our students to engage it and see how others have engaged it since its initial publication some fifteen years ago. A premise of Harris' book, and of our course, is that reflective teachers continually adopt, defend, and reject viewpoints and approaches, so we are not interested in "handing" our students anything without asking them to give it a serious test. Our general approach is to present students with one approach or theory and then to complicate it with a competing one by asking the students to take a position and defend it within the context of their past experiences as students and their expectations as future teachers. Do they accept one theory over another? Do they want to draw pieces from both? Or do they reject both in favor of something else they have read or heard? The point is to help students develop into reflective practitioners, yes, but also to help them see that theories compete with one another, that theories get changed as they are put into practice, and, of course, that no theory lasts forever.

Thus, even though we use Atwell to counterbalance Harris, we also counter Atwell with a pair of *Language Arts* articles by David and Peg Sudol, "Another Story: Putting Graves, Calkins, and Atwell into Practice and Perspective" (1991), and "Yet Another Story: Writers' Workshop Revisited" (1995), which investigate and problematize the notion of instituting a writers' workshop in school settings less ideal than Atwell's.

With each course unit—Growth, Voice, Process, etc.—we ask our students to contrast received or prevailing notions in the field with other positions that challenge our understanding and to suggest alternative pedagogies. Following the model of Harris' book, each of our students reflects on the writing of a student in the schools with whom they will work through the semester. We ask them to keep an ongoing journal describing their meetings, the students' writing, and the connections they see between the students' work and the readings in our class. For each unit our students then write what Harris calls an "interchapter," an analysis of the general issues located around the theme under consideration, with a sample of student writing as "evidence" at the center of a discussion of their point of view. Working with writing in this way teaches methods students to begin looking at their own students' writing in sophisticated ways. It also helps them develop their own views about these important and complex themes in the field of writing studies.

In this way, students become surveyors of the entire field and participate in the scholarship rather than being consumers of it. Their ideas of "field" expand to include the first-grade classroom their little brother is now experiencing, their memories of tenth-grade English, their experience as a college writing center tutor, and reports from their peers currently engaged in student teaching. Students see in this continuum not separate theoretical worlds of elementary and college writing instruction but rather a world unified by the working out of recurrent themes: growth, voice, process, error, and community.

Counterbalancing Moffett with Newkirk

In order to understand the complexity as well as the practical applications of Harris' five key terms, we also read Moffett's *Teaching the Universe of Discourse* (1968) and its counterstatement, Newkirk's *More than Stories: The Range of Children's Writing* (1989). Moffett has more than survived the last thirty years of research about teaching writing; his work remains a germinal statement about literacy and learning. However, it has not been received as an "accessible" book, and its merits are often overlooked, even by its supporters. The abstract, philosophical bent of Moffett's style sometimes resists the practical promise of the later chapters, such as "Grammar and the Sentence." Many students simply don't ever make it to these chapters, and of course it is the promise of fresh practice that is foremost in our students' minds.

Moffett's (1968) premise is that the movement of student growth is from the center of the self outward—from conversation to publication, from writer based to reader based, from narrative to expository, and from particular to universal. "The detailed forms which this movement takes" he writes, "are various and often paradoxical. In moving outward from himself, the child becomes more himself." With profound insight, Moffett concludes his first sixty pages: "The teacher's art is to move with this movement, a subtle act possible only if he shifts his gaze from the subject to the learner, for the subject is in the learner" (59). The philosophical heart of Moffett's book is in these first sixty pages. There he aligns his notion of growth and abstraction with Piaget's "notion that people decenter from an initial egocentricity as they get older" (1968, 57). Growth, and the corresponding ability to self-consciously play the scale of rhetorical abstraction, takes a lifetime.

A theory like Moffett's—a theory "meant to be utilized, not believed" (Moffett 1968, 15)—is a theory that can sustain a strategic hold on the practical classroom through many years of teaching. This is why, of course, we should want our students to know it. Relative to a theory of language and learning, published standards change like the seasons; lesson plans grow stale in a week. A good theory of discourse like Moffett's is a stable and powerful tool in the hands of an intelligent teacher. Moffett's universe of discourse is not a simple or contrived formula. The theory has limitations, but they are not due to its lack of depth or vision.

This is one theory—and it's a damn good one. Nevertheless, as Moffett himself points out, "to abstract is to obtain a loss of reality for a gain in control" (1968, 23). For Thomas Newkirk, there is just a little too much reality given up here.

Newkirk's main objection to Moffett's theory is that it is simply not adequate to the reality of children's experience in the world of discourse. The danger is that the theory, limited in certain ways, may create the very limitations in child development that it presupposes. Newkirk puts it this way: "Moffett pictures young children as occupying an overly circumscribed world—storyland. If children make narratives do for all, they may be responding to our own limited vision of what is possible" (1989, 24).

In contrast to Moffett, Newkirk stresses the continuities among the most basic signage in our culture (stop signs, for example) and the complexity of a literary essay. Newkirk says, "I believe that Moffett's model of development fails to account for the range of non-narrative writing that children attempt because he does not recognize the influence of environmental print. But as long as children have access to a variety of non-narrative forms, they will adopt them, just as they adopt other forms of adult behavior" (1989, 24). The evidence, Newkirk argues, supports a very different view. Nonnarrative writing, essays of generalization, evaluation, writing for distant audiences—all forms of discourse are present, often in embryonic forms—in much of what children compose. There is just too much evidence that contradicts Moffett's scheme. Newkirk cites a number of studies that point out the limitations and overstatements of Piaget. What Newkirk calls the "Great Divide" separates the "storyland" of elementary school and the "expository" world of high school. Dan's experience as an eleventh-grade high school teacher agrees with Newkirk: students met with novels, essays, speeches, and technical instructions invariably described their reading assignment as a "story."

Well, this is another theory—and unlike Moffett's book—*More than Stories* (Newkirk 1989) offers ample evidence of children's work that illustrates and recommends the semiotic over the developmental perspective.

The Course Plan and Assignments

So then, the methods course presented here ("Teaching Writing: History, Theory, Practice") gets its energy by asking students to investigate competing theories of discourse as possible ways to guide and illuminate their own students' writing.

An illustration of the course plan follows. One can see that the five units organize the readings, which are meant to comment on and complicate the themes. Each unit spawns assignments, but through the course of a semester students need to write at least three essays, each of which explores and explains the complexity and takes a position on the unit's theme. To the extent that students can use one theory of discourse and literacy or the other to guide and illuminate their essay—and most importantly, to explain the sample of student writing they use as exemplar and focal center of their essay—to that extent they do well on the interchapter assignment.

Course Plan

Unit I: Growth

Week	*Activity*	*Assignment*
1	Discuss:	The "process revolution." Our experiences as student writers. Our experiences with developing writers.
2	Read:	Harris: Chapter 1, "Growth." Newkirk: Introduction. Moffett: 1–59.
	Discuss:	Students we know.
3	Read:	Newkirk: Chapters 1–4 (the dilemma of writing development).
	Discuss:	Our writing autobiography. Students we know.
	Write:	Growth interchapter prewriting. Hand out essay assignment #1.
4	Read:	Atwell: Chapters 1 and 2 (learning to teach; adolescent growth).
	Discuss:	Planning versus responding to what happens.
	Revise:	Writing workshop: bring assignment #1 draft to class.
5	Discuss:	The complex notion of "growth." Assignment #1 due. Designing assignments for growing writers.

Unit II: Voice

Week	*Activity*	*Assignment*
6	Read:	Harris: Chapter 2, "Voice." Moffett: Chapter 3, "Drama: What is Happening."
	Discuss:	Spandel and Stiggins (1997) chapter on voice: examples from student writing. Interchapter/discuss. Give essay assignment #2.
7	Discuss:	Students we know.
	Read:	Atwell: Chapter 3, "Getting Ready." Peter Elbow, "Closing My Eyes as I Speak: An Argument for Ignoring Audience" (1987).
	Revise:	Writing workshop: bring assignment #2 draft to class.

Unit III: Process

Week	*Activity*	*Assignment*
8	Read:	Harris: Chapter 3, "Process." Moffett: Chapter 6, "Learning to Write by Writing." Atwell: Chapters 4 and 5, "Responding to Writers and Writing."
9	Read:	Perl, "Understanding Composing" (1980). Sudol/Sudol, "Another Story" (1991) "Yet Another" (1995). Hairston, "The Winds of Change" (1982) (read for midterm). Flower and Hayes, "A Cognitive Process Theory of Writing" (1980).
	Write:	Hand out take-home midterm (first draft in class).

Unit IV: Error

Week	Activity	Assignment
10	Read:	Hillocks, "Grammar and the Manipulation of Syntax" (1986).
		Moffett: Chapter 5, "Grammar and the Sentence."
	Discuss:	Essay assignment #3.
11	Discuss:	Shaughnessy, "Some New Approaches Toward Teaching" (1994).
		Connors/Glenn, "Responding to and Evaluating Essays" (1992).
	Revise:	Writing workshop: bring assignment #3 draft to class.

Unit V: Community

Week	Activity	Assignment
12	Read:	Harris: Chapter 5, "The Idea of Community in the Study of Writing."
13	Observe:	NCTE's *Standards for the Language Arts.*
	Read:	Newkirk: Chapter 6, "Questions, Comments, and Stories."
	Discuss:	Reflecting and writing about our students' communities. Practice responding to student writing.

Unit VI: Conclusion

Week	Activity	Assignment
13	Read:	Newkirk, "Roots of the Writing Process." Faigley, "Competing Theories of Process: A Critique and a Proposal" (1986).
14	Observe:	Portfolios in the classroom.
	Write:	Reflecting on writing instruction: writing an introduction to your course portfolio.

The next selection from the course syllabus presents a detailed version of our "growth" interchapter assignment. Because this assignment occurs early in the term, when students are still locating and getting to know the school-age students they work with for the entire term, and because we wish our students to reflect on their own growth as writers as well as on the growth of others, we give our students the option of writing about themselves or about a student writer.

Growth Interchapter Assignment[1]

Subject: Your own growth as a writer, or the growth of a writer you know or have observed.

Purpose: Reflect on the issue of writing growth through specific incidents and examples.

Speaker: You, as a teacher/student of writing, reflecting back on your own development or on the development of someone you have observed.

Audience: Fellow teachers; the members of our class; readers of Harris, Moffett, Newkirk, and Atwell.

Form: An essay discussion modeled after Harris' interchapters.

Prewriting Activity Schedule

You should write informally about your own growth as a writer, perhaps settling on a particular instance, and you should respond to the theories of growth presented in our readings. Your goal early on should be to reflect on how your own growth as a writer occurred and how one particular instance of growth managed to occur—through teacher intervention, through the subject matter, and so forth.

Observe and Interview a Young Writer

Collect samples of writing and art work from a young person. If you can find examples of early and later work, this might work out even better. If you write about your own experiences, try to find samples of your own earlier writing. Read this collection as you would a literary work, looking for substance and evidence that supports one theory or another.

Criteria for Evaluation

We are all looking to learn about the nature of growth and how we might best help our students grow as writers. Your interchapter essay should combine general, theoretical discussion of writing growth with specific references to the growth of the writer you are studying. The content and development of your interchapter will be the most important criteria for evaluation, followed by structure, clarity, style, and correctness.

Next, we present the essay of one of our students, Leanne Reilly, writing in response to the growth interchapter assignment. In our view, Leanne exemplifies the ways in which students integrate Moffett and Newkirk and their respective theories of literacy into their own learning and thinking about their experience as writers.

Growth Interchapter Example:

My Struggle with Following Directions

Leanne E. Reilly

Looking back at my experience as a writer, I see, in light of this course and the theories presented to me, many interesting characteristics in my early writing. As a youth I enjoyed reading and writing, but for the most part, I was bored by the assignments my teachers gave. My growth at that time, in my opinion, was stifled by the method my teacher had taken toward teaching writing. I found an example of a book report I did in sixth grade which, examined under a theorist's eye, illustrates my boredom or lack of interest with the assignment. I merely repeated the facts of the book. This is my book report:

*I read a book called HALF MAGIC by EDWARD EAGER. It's copyright date
is 1954. It was published by HARCOURT, BRACE, AND CO., and it was il-
lustrated by N. M. BODECKER. The main character in this book is Jane. It
didn't mention her last name, just Jane. Jane has one brother and two sisters,
their names are Katherine, Martha and Mark. Their mother's name is Allison.
She is a newspaper editor. In this story Jane finds a charm that can be wished
upon. Each of the children are allowed to make wishes for themselves. So they
each take a journey forward and back through time. But the charm works differently, it only receives wishes in halves so whenever they make a wish they
must wish twice for it. For instance, their mother was at an annoying relatives
house when she has the charm with her (she didn't know it had powers) and
unknowingly she wished she was home, and the next thing she knew she was
halfway home. This is rather confusing to you but in the book the author made
it sound interesting. I recommend the book to anyone who is adventurous, but
not to anyone who has no imagination. This book's illustrations matched the
book very well. They sort of spoiled the fun of imagining though. This book
took place when there was no T.V. and only a few motor cars, but there were
radios and cinemas and other modern things, but the time didn't seem to matter very much anyway. If I have the chance in the future I will read this book
again and I urge you to read it too. I am sure you would like it.*

Leanne Tonn

After reading this piece over some thirteen years later, I find it interesting
that after I recited the facts, I broke through with what I thought, at the time,
was literary criticism. Newkirk would say that I was experimenting with persuasive writing, although because of the specific requirements of the assignment, I was left little room for expressing my own opinion. Although I received
an A, I was unchallenged by the assignment and followed the directions to
please the teacher.

Strangely, I remember that my teacher, Mrs. Franco, was very innovative in
assigning writing projects. This was not one of her better assignments. My grade
breakdown, which I still have attached to the report, focused primarily on following directions. . . . With older and wiser eyes, I can see this assignment was
only an attempt to see if I could follow directions and spell correctly. It did not
encourage creativity at all, in fact creativity was extra credit. Despite my lack
of enthusiasm in regurgitating the facts, I can see my development by grade six.
I was experiencing rhetorical growth. I was writing to a larger audience and recommending the book to someone else. In this case, I was directing the commentary to my teacher, but the same voice I used in the report could have been
directed to a larger group. If I were to publish this in a magazine which critiques books, it could have been directed toward the general reader. I used my
own voice, but I also directed it toward "you," the reader, about "it," the book.
At a very elementary level, I followed the Moffett model for growth. Without
my teacher's admission I have no way of knowing if Moffett was the model she

drew from, but from my writing it seems that was the progression. At that time, the Moffett model stifled my growth by limiting my progression. An assignment which allowed me to express my opinions to my audience would have expanded my creativity and would have allowed me to feel some ownership for what I had written. I was a master of the organizational devices that my teachers enforced and at the expense of creativity, I followed them. . . .

While this approach may have worked for other students, I was bored or beyond that level of writing. After assessing the theories introduced in this course toward the teaching of writing, I would have to say that Atwell's approach is more appealing. Looking back I can't say that the A grade I received was motivating, in fact it probably made me more lazy or less interested in trying harder to be creative in my writing. After all, if I could receive an A for just following the directions, why should I bother attempting to be creative?

The framework that Atwell constructed within her writing workshops at Boothbay Elementary best suits the way of learning to write that I would like to emulate as a teacher. Frankly, I must say that as a student, her strategies are the way I would have liked to learn. She allows her students freedom to choose their own topics and encourages them by giving them the time to shape their own ideas and concerns and put them down on paper. I agree that responses and revision help the student most during the revising process, as opposed to after, when the student hands in the finished piece. Not only should the teacher see drafts of a work, but also peers who can give insight. Unfortunately, peer input and its value are often underestimated by teachers. . . . In my eyes, despite the way in which I learned, I must say that through workshops, prewriting, drafting, revising and editing, a writer develops a better understanding of his or her own writing, as well as an understanding of how other people write. Once they have experienced this method they can better decide for themselves which path of growth they wish to take.

Conclusion

In the last thirty-five years, professional journals have proliferated in our field, yet the number of "really big ideas" has not. School teachers today, even though Leanne Rielly might not agree, could thrive using Moffett (1968) without modification. Much classroom practice, we submit, would even improve if they did so. Teachers at all grade levels must conceive of writing tasks, put their students to work, and offer some kind of response to students' efforts. Thinking rhetorically about these writing tasks is pure Moffett; nevertheless, moving beyond this point does not require us to repudiate the gains that writing instruction has made by following Moffett's advice to develop student writing across the rhetorical spectrum.

However, with notions like a "socially constructed self" and the idea of community, writing instruction has become more complex, perhaps more interesting, and our students should be familiar with the broad outlines of the latest theory-building taking place in writing studies. At this point in our field's history, we can no longer look at writing as strictly developmental as it traverses this spectrum. The semiotic model and theories of genre that have developed in recent years require that our pedagogies evolve as we see the problems our writing students face in a new light. Our approach in this methods course resists the tendency to compartmentalize the course even further—establishing, say, elementary and secondary sections. Instead, it challenges us to confront all our students, from elementary through college levels, with the same pedagogical problems and to help them to seek solutions with analogues in every writer's experience, young and old, beginner and expert. As these tensions in our working theories play out we test again and again "what works" as we look for fresh ways to engage our students in literate activities. The methods course we have developed encourages students to think of the subject of composition as an evolving history of competing ideas about literacy and learning and not as a catalog of methods and approaches that can be chosen from a bookshelf. Finally, our hope is that our writing methods students begin to shift their gaze, as Moffett says, from the subject to the learner, achieving the pragmatist ideal of teaching students and not subjects.

Note

1. This assignment is based on the "Job Sheet" designed by our colleague Brian White.

9

Teaching Teachers and the Extracurriculum

Douglas Hesse
Illinois State University
Kirsti Sandy
Keene State University

Illinois State University prepares three types of college writing teachers, and the mix directly shapes the program we've developed, although not entirely in ways we planned. Among our seventy or so graduate assistants each year are, first, several for whom teaching writing is the means to a professional future that will never, they imagine, include teaching again. They imagine careers as technical writers, poets, or teachers of literature. Yet for at least two years they will teach our undergraduates, and they need to do it well. In contrast, students in our Master's in Writing with an emphasis in two-year college teaching know that composition will be the major portion of their careers. In addition to various specific electives, they take "Teaching Writing in the Two-Year College," and most complete an off-campus teaching internship not unlike the kind of student teaching that undergraduate English education majors do.

The third group consists of doctoral students. With an emphasis differing significantly from more traditional programs, our Ph.D. in English Studies prepares students explicitly for college-level teaching and requires all candidates, whether concentrating in literature, rhetoric and composition, or linguistics, to complete a teaching internship and an advanced seminar in composition studies. The nature of this Ph.D. is perhaps best understood by knowing that the comprehensive exams, based on reading lists and synthesis statements generated by each student, cover three areas: issues in English studies (integrating literature and literary theory, composition studies, rhetoric, and linguistics); pedagogy in English studies; and a specialty area. All dissertations must have an integral component dealing with teaching, often accomplished through a study of students or classrooms, in concert with more traditional historical, interpretive, and theoretical arguments. But while Illinois State doctoral students are explicitly preparing for teaching careers, and while there is a generalist component to their degrees, not all identify themselves as professional teachers of writing. As a result, there is within the Ph.D. program a form of the master's program split between future writing teachers and others.

These differences complicate writing teacher preparation, since some students are in it for the professional long haul, but others are not. This situation—and Illinois State is hardly unique in it—affects courses in pedagogy. But it also affects the extracurriculum in ways that are sometimes problematic but more often positive. That extracurriculum bears much of the weight for teacher preparation.

Teaching the Newest Teachers

In "Training the Workforce: An Overview of the GTA Education Curricula," Katherine Latterell (1996) identifies four main ways that university writing programs train teaching assistants: through teaching methods courses, apprenticeships, practica, and theory seminars. Illinois State uses a combination of the last three strategies.

Our process begins, as do many university writing programs, a week before the fall term, when all new graduate assistants attend a five-day workshop led by the writing director, assistant director, four doctoral student program assistants, and various members of the writing faculty. The thirty or so newcomers are joined on the fourth and fifth days by experienced teachers, many of whom have central roles in the teacher preparation process. This workshop introduces readings in the theory informing our freshman course: social epistemic rhetoric, emphasizing argument, heavily informed by process pedagogies. But the workshop concentrates mainly on course goals, policies, and classroom practices. The TAs read several freshman portfolios from the previous year and discuss the writing and teaching issues they raise. They practice commenting and responding, and they play roles as undergraduates in model class sessions taught by the workshop leaders. Crucially, they spend time in one of the twelve networked computer classrooms that will host every meeting of every class they teach, learning the technology and, equally important, learning the feel and dynamics of this environment.

Doctoral students are assigned two classes during the ensuing fall. New master's level TAs are not assigned sole responsibility for a class their first semester on assistantship. Instead, each is paired with an experienced teacher in a mentor/apprentice relationship, with the mentor having primary responsibilities for designing the course. Each mentor/apprentice pair is assigned to an intensive section of freshman writing that meets five days a week. Placed into these intensive sections are less-prepared writers, and the extra meetings are designed to offer more in-course tutorial and workshopping time. During the pre-semester workshop, then, mentors and new teachers meet one another and begin planning the course they will eventually teach together.

All first-semester TAs enroll in a one-credit teaching proseminar that meets weekly to discuss issues in teaching writing, from designing assignment sequences to responding to drafts to holding conferences. More substantially, all master's and most doctoral TAs also enroll in a three-credit course, "Introduction to Composition Studies." The aim of the course is theoretical, designed to introduce research in rhetoric and composition. In fact, syllabi over the years frequently have included explicit declarations that the course is not specifically devoted to teaching. Just as frequently, however, students wish the course were more explicitly about teaching, and we analyze that tension further, below.

After their first semesters, TAs are organized into small groups that gather occasionally and informally in meetings led by one of four program assistants, advanced Ph.D. candidates in rhetoric and composition. They also attend teaching colloquia that are usually held once a month and often feature graduate student and faculty presenters. Each spring the department sponsors an all-day Symposium on Teaching, a series of concurrent sessions in a professional conference format; classes are canceled so all TAs can attend. Finally, in their second year in the program and beyond, a majority of TAs themselves become mentors to beginning teachers.

Promises and Problems with the Illinois State Model

No single component of Illinois State's TA preparation program is unique. We expect that several other writing programs prepare new TAs just as extensively as Illinois State does, requiring a combination of preservice workshops, a continuing proseminar, a graduate course in composition theory and research, a teaching apprenticeship, mentoring, and ongoing colloquia and small-group discussions. However, we're less certain that any programs are more intensive—or that even the intensity we've outlined is an ideal one. Following is an analysis of strengths and weaknesses of our model.

The Push for Pedagogical Practicality

As Latterell notes, programs that require a full-fledged graduate course for new teachers tend either to organize the course as "how to teach English 101 at our institution" or as theory and research in writing studies. Several years ago Illinois State chose the latter, with even a further twist: we intentionally minimized attention to pedagogy in the course, focusing more broadly on the nature and status of writers and writing. One reason was practical. In the mid-1980s we developed a new Master's in Writing, and the course "Introduction to the Composing Process" was required for all students in the sequence, from creative and technical writers to would-be teachers, from students who were TAs to students who were not. As one might expect, cognitivist research and rhetorical theory were central aspects of the course, along with things like the *Paris Review* interviews of poets and novelists. The course made the social turn in the late eighties with the rest of the profession, with Barthes, Bakhtin, and Foucault added and Vygotsky resurrected, but we strove to keep its focus on broad theoretical issues.

If one reason was practical, another was philosophical. We believed our composition courses were best served by teachers grounded in research and theory who understood writing as a fascinatingly complex activity. Teachers who early in their careers explored these broad issues would, we thought, be more reflective about their practice. We also thought they might be enough seduced by the intellectual issues surrounding writing that they would reject depictions of composition as drudge work, maybe even pursue additional courses. To a large extent this did happen. But students' practical teaching concerns so "disrupted" the course as we envisioned it that we added teaching issues more explicitly to the mix of theory and research, thus blurring the line we hoped would contain teaching in other parts of the program.

New teachers' concerns about practical matters are perfectly understandable and even admirable as a sign of responsibility toward students. But there is a certain tyranny of pedagogy when writing is viewed through formal teaching, and teaching is prematurely constrained by the status quo. It would be callous entirely to ignore teachers' immediate practical concerns. On the other hand, making them the lens through which writing is solely seen is limiting.

Teachers as Assistants and Mentors

There are obvious benefits to first teaching as an apprentice. Graduate students new to teaching can gradually ease into their new roles, gaining classroom experience without the sole responsibility of creating a syllabus, establishing course policies, and grading. The apprentice is expected at first to learn, then to lead, and this process can allow for a longer period of acclimation and reflection. Since many new teachers enter the classroom nearly as soon as they arrive on campus, a mentor can provide immediate answers to crucial questions and necessary feedback later on. In short, apprenticeship can allow graduate students to remain substantially as *students,* at least during their first semester of graduate school. The benefits of being a mentor can also be far-reaching, and some mentors provide advice and support to apprentices until they complete their degree programs.

Further benefits come from the fact that our apprentice teachers have concurrent duties beyond the classroom. Each also tutors six hours a week in the writing center, with a seventh hour spent in a staff meeting. We developed that tutoring dimension of our training program for two reasons. Tutors are more inclined to be "on the student's side," less constrained by the authoritative role of teacher and grade giver and thus better positioned to share helpful expertise with student writers. That's a stance we wanted to develop for the classroom, too. Also, tutoring offers a grandstand seat for understanding how students deal with challenging—and often problematic—writing assignments or instructor comments, a seat without the complication of the tutor's having made the task or remarks.

The second virtue of tutoring was more base: money. When we proposed taking first-semester TAs out of the classroom but keeping them on assistant-ship, we had to help the university come up with the $90,000 or so a year to pay for doing so. (That's three full-time instructors, plus benefits, for the academic year.) Replacing undergraduate tutors with graduate assistants generated a few thousand dollars. The administrators were mostly persuaded by the better quality of teaching they believed would come from the mentor/apprentice model, but cutting the cost incrementally did help.

Mentor/apprentice relationships are complicated and do not in one semester "solve" the problems new teachers are bound to encounter. Although new teachers in our program face neither isolation nor an overwhelming lack of preparation, they do face the challenge of gradually establishing independence from their mentors and finding a niche within a web of conflicting theories, pedagogies, and relationships. We hope the mentoring relationship accomplishes three goals. First, it should offer the apprentice the opportunity to observe and reflect on the practices of a successful teacher of writing. Second, the collaboration should also permit apprentices gradually to adopt the teachers' roles and to practice leading class sessions, creating assignments, and responding to student work. Finally, mentors and apprentices should learn to negotiate their differences and provide a cohesive set of practices and standards, or, in the words of several mentors and apprentices, "provide a unified front."

Much of what we have just outlined does happen, yet for many mentors and apprentices, the path is neither smooth nor free of conflict. One of us (Kirsti) conducted a two-year qualitative study of mentor/apprentice relationships that generated a number of complex findings. Since the mentors themselves differ in regard to their own academic interests and backgrounds, their approaches to co-teaching vary greatly as well. Some consider the mentor/apprentice relationship a true collaboration, involving the apprentice in all classroom decisions, large or small. Others consider the apprentice a more advanced student and view their own role as that of teacher educator. Less effective mentors tend to enact an employer/employee dynamic, approaching the apprentice as an extra pair of eyes and hands, a personal assistant to help alleviate some of the burdens of teaching.

As the preceding suggests, mentors and apprentices often voice concern over issues of power and authority in the collaboratively taught classroom, with many gauging the success/failure of their own collaborations by the tales they hear of other partnerships in hallways and behind closed office doors. Conflicts that become public often concern a mentor's perceived exploitation of an apprentice and/or an apprentice's alleged incompetence. Managerial issues—

disputes about dividing the workload and office hours—tend to remain at the forefront of many disputes. These struggles are often worded in language appropriate for the workplace: "She is consistently five minutes late" and "He dresses too casually for the classroom." Power struggles over classroom authority and teaching competence are often depicted as the lack of a shared work ethic, which is often compounded by apprentices' fears that their mentor will be called on to recommend them for future teaching assistantships. For many apprentices, the need to be viewed as a "diligent employee" overrides the desire to communicate honestly with their mentors, to question, and, ultimately, to learn.

When conflicts arise that explicitly deal with writing, these are often explained away by mentors and apprentices as clashes of personality. In several instances, mentors and apprentices who disagree about what ought to be taught in a writing classroom overlook the more interesting and complex theoretical issues arising from the debate and, instead, focus on issues of character. For example, in one classroom, a mentor who privileged rigid, formulaic writing chastised an apprentice who was praising students who wrote more reflectively. The difference could have been couched in theoretical terms. Yet the two respectively insisted that the problem was that the mentor was too "rigid" and the apprentice was too "touchy feely."

Apprentices who conflict with mentors often attempt to form supportive relationships with students, often describing themselves as student advocates. They claim to play the role of mediator in the classroom and value their own ability to maintain harmony between both groups. When apprentices' relationships with mentors deteriorate, they often seek program administrators or peers for support, encouragement, and advice. That is, they tend to seek connections with those in authority or in similar mentoring situations to establish independence from the mentor.

Predictably, apprentices of mentors who play central roles in the writing program and whose syllabi and assignment sequences most clearly reflect the program's theoretical orientation tend to express more satisfaction with their roles as co-teachers. These apprentices also seem to better understand and articulate the goals of the program. On the other hand, apprentices of mentors who seem more at odds with the orientation of ISU's Writing Program (or who adopt an approach that they label "unconventional") tend to have more difficulty adapting to their teaching situations. These apprentices often express confusion ("My mentor said to respond to papers this way, but in the proseminar I was told that was not how we evaluate here"), and they have more difficulty integrating the different components of the teacher education program. For these apprentices, much of the work they do as apprentice teachers and as graduate students seems conflicted and segmented.

Although many mentors claim to focus on the *whys* as well as the *hows* of teaching writing, many admit that the day-to-day work of teaching makes it difficult to provide, in the words of one mentor, a "theoretical basis for every assignment." Since doctoral students who act as mentors are often researching, writing dissertations, seeking jobs, and since they are not compensated for the additional work of mentoring, communication between mentors and apprentices is often brief. What was initially planned as a collaborative classroom often turns into a relay race, with one teacher taking over (or attempting to) where the other has left off. Several mentors admit, as well, that the apprentices are not given many opportunities to assist in planning the assignments for the course. Many apprentices confess that a lack of communication with the mentor leaves them feeling as if they are substituting in another teacher's class.

Despite this lack of communication with mentors, however, apprentices are quick to form allegiances with one another. As a group, the apprentices seem to privilege the creation and maintenance of supportive teaching relationships, and they prize the ability to negotiate several complex relationships at once (with mentors and students, for example). What apprentices seem to understand is that writing programs serve several interests and that these interests must be negotiated—even those interests that seem to directly conflict. They are beginning to understand that teaching writing requires understanding a complex rhetorical situation, one meeting the needs of several different audiences and maintaining strong working relationships with each of those audiences, even in the case of disagreements.

Teaching Professional Writing Teachers

Central to any apprenticeship model are the mentors, and the core of this group at Illinois State are the doctoral and master's students preparing for writing teacher careers. Mentoring constitutes a substantial part of their own training.

Four specific courses and one topics course make up the graduate curriculum in writing pedagogy. Most prominent is "Teaching Writing in the Two-Year College," which concentrates on that venue but also generally treats teaching first-year writing. More obviously specialized is "Teaching Technical Writing." "Problems in the Teaching of English" is a doctoral seminar that engages broad issues of pedagogy in English studies, including the teaching of literature and writing. A selection of the readings from the last two offerings of the course suggest the mix: Bloom, Daiker, and White's *Composition in the Twenty-First Century: Crisis & Change* (1997); Graff's *The Labyrinths of Literacy: Reflections on Literacy Past & Present* (1995); Raymond's *English as a Discipline* (1996); Slevin and Young's *Critical Theory and the Teaching of Literature* (1995); Anson's *Scenarios for Teaching Writing* (1993); Karolides' *Reader Response in Secondary and College Classrooms* (2000).

The fourth specific pedagogy course is "Seminar in Composition" required of all doctoral students. Because not all of them have a professional stake in teaching writing, despite knowing that composition is part of most jobs that Illinois State graduates tend to get, the course raises a rarefied version of the tyranny of pedagogical practicality issue we noted earlier. The problem is not that all discussions bend toward teaching—that's the focus of the course. Rather it's that many noncomposition candidates tend to be so pragmatic regarding composition that in this final-semester course they resist further complications of writing pedagogy. "Just tell me what to do" to pass my comps respectably and to teach efficiently as I write my dissertation.

In addition to these courses, teaching writing is the focus almost every semester in one of the department's graduate topics courses. Recent semesters have offered courses in Secondary Writing, Writing Courses and Writing Programs; Technology and Teaching Writing; Writing Assessment; and the Rhetoric of Inquiry. An especially innovative offering of one of these courses in the spring of 1999 was taught by eight visiting scholars, each in residence for two days: Steve North, Jackie Royster, Gesa Kirsch, Robert Connors, Kurt Spellmeyer, George Hillocks, Susan Jarratt, and Peter Mortenson.

The final portion of the formal curriculum for both master's and doctoral candidates in the teaching of writing is a required teaching internship, a capstone course coming in addition to experiences students have gained as TAs. The internship is marked by three main features. First is the teaching site. Over the years we have developed arrangements with several area two- and four-year colleges whereby our graduate students can teach a semester in their writing programs, a program not unlike secondary student teaching but for an adjunct's salary. Since relatively few of our graduates take positions in Ph.D.-granting institutions, experience in other settings is a useful credential as well as a pedagogical challenge. Some students complete their internships in courses taught on campus, but even this site is usually "new," as they teach advanced or specialized courses that graduate assistants aren't routinely assigned.

The second main feature is formal planning and reflection on the internship experience. Two semesters before the internship, students write a brief letter, endorsed by their advisors, to the Director of Graduate Studies describing the course they would like to teach and providing a rationale noting how the internship relates to their dissertation, research, or professional goals. In the semester before the internship is to take place, students submit a five- to ten-page proposal, including a bibliography. Students pursue one of two kinds of internships. The first and relatively less common one uses the internship as a site for gathering data leading to a thesis, dissertation, or formal study. The second kind of internship focuses on pedagogical innovation. Making a case from theory and research, students propose and defend a specific approach to a course. Approval of the proposal constitutes a sort of license to pursue that approach, and the final project consists of a fifteen- to twenty-page essay reflecting on and analyzing the teaching experience.

The last feature is that the student's major advisor is the faculty member of record. This means that mentoring shifts from one's peers and the formal apparatus of the writing program. For Ph.D. students in literature, for whom an internship is also required, this means that for perhaps the first time they formally have a mentor in the teaching of literature. For students in rhetoric and composition, the new relationship marks the continued transition from being a teacher within a well-defined program to being a teacher with some autonomy and collegial responsibility.

The Pedagogy of the Extracurriculum

With several courses and a required internship, Illinois State graduate students preparing for careers as college writing teachers receive formal preparation in pedagogy plus extensive extracurricular responsibilities. Virtually all these students serve as mentors to new teachers for a year or more. Most doctoral students in the area eventually serve as a program assistant, a mentor of mentors, if you will. As they move from new teacher to mentor to program assistant they almost necessarily have to develop deeper understandings of program philosophies and strategies. After all, they're the primary translators of these to their peers.

But something more subtle happens than the program's merely cloning itself via the agar of mentors. Even as they become teachers of teachers, the graduate students are students of composition theory, pedagogy, and research. Through the internship, they are researchers themselves. As a result, they view Illinois State's writing program in relation to composition studies writ large, and they aren't reluctant to critique what they see. On the other hand, as mentors or program assistants they have a kind of access and audience that TAs generally do not. The program director and faculty rely on them not only to "deliver" the curriculum but also to reflect back their peers' efforts and perspectives. Teaching assistants love critiquing the systems in which they teach, but mentors and program assistants can't inhabit the easy world of unfettered complaint. Because of their roles, they view teaching from the broader perspectives of institutional constraints and wider practice.

These broader perspectives are most challenged by the type of teachers we characterized at the outset of this chapter: new master's students who are not professionally interested or invested in the teaching of writing, people for whom a section of English 101 is mainly a tuition waiver, $600 per month, and too many anxious hours a week. These TAs are usually extremely responsible and effective; our point is that they are teaching writing largely by default. As a result, they don't necessarily understand or value the enterprise in the same ways that more "intentional" writing teachers do. They are, in short, much like the faculty colleagues within and beyond English departments with whom rhetoric and composition graduate students will deal after they earn their degrees. Discussing pedagogy in a graduate seminar or among like-minded peers is one thing; doing so with bright but unconverted new teachers is quite another.

Being a teacher while being a student while being a mentor richly parallels the professional worlds in which most college writing teachers live. That's the bright side of Illinois State's program. The darker side is that these graduate students are so busy juggling various roles in a two- or four-year program that there is less room for reflection and analysis than we think is healthy. We suppose that we could gilt-edge this cloud by noting that such is the work life of rhet/comp faculty, but doing so uncomfortably suggests teacher preparation as a form of professional hazing. In the *Rise and Fall of English,* Robert Scholes (1998) imagines a Ph.D. program lasting ten years, with students earning a living wage throughout but alternating their time toward the degree between years spent purely in study and years spent purely in teaching (175). Even barring practical considerations, Scholes' proposal has drawbacks, yet there is something sane about the rhythms it invokes. The pace at Illinois State is somewhat more intense and frenetic. We believe this is mostly exhilarating and effective. We know it is not ideal.

10

False Prophets and True Mentors

Transforming Instructors into Teachers

Melissa E. Whiting
The University of Southern Mississippi

Years ago as an undergraduate student, I experienced what I'm sure is a common situation for many undergraduate students. It was the second week of my Composition II class. By then, I had determined that I had the most pompous, arrogant teacher of all time. "Mr. Lumm" considered himself the master purveyor of the glorious English language. He took great joy in humiliating his students for their writing abilities, or lack thereof. He constantly reminded us that he was working on his Ph.D., specializing in Eighteenth Century British Literature (as if we even cared). He didn't act interested at all in the degrees that we were pursuing (at least he was honest); in fact, he didn't act interested in us, period. He explained that if we wanted to make a good grade in his class, we would have to work like the devil to achieve his own high standard of writing excellence. By Wednesday of that second week, after yet another series of pronouncements, I stood up. In his midpontification, I told him I was excusing myself to go sign up for the CLEP test, since I felt like I was in a foreign language class rather than Composition II. Quickly, I departed the room. As I closed the door behind me I heard a "your loss" tossed out as his final words on the matter. Subsequently, I tested out of Composition II and managed to spend the next year or so avoiding this man in the Liberal Arts Building.

I did learn something valuable from Mr. Lumm, however. I learned that no student should be subjected to abject dictatorial posturing from a teacher. I learned that the classroom is not the place for humiliation and scare tactics. I also learned that not everyone who stands in front of the room in the paid position of authority is truly a teacher.

That the university is not welcoming to all students should come as no surprise, especially those academically underprepared and culturally dislocated students who arrive most in need of an empathetic teacher/mentor. Tradition, ritual, and experience (Applebee 1974) shape the familiar roles both students and teachers act out in the university setting. This social context provides language through which activities and events are perceived and represented in special ways, laden with specialized meanings and values. Furthermore, these culturally constructed "ways" are a learned network of associations growing out of a particular cultural environment, constructed, in part, with the intention of excluding a portion of the population. In short, academia was not set up to welcome all learners into the fold. Wertsch (1993) points out that some entering university students depend on ways of making meaning that are not valued because they do not match the selective, culturally valued tools of the academy and the teachers who work within it.

Thus, many students spend their time making meaning in accordance and in conflict with two different worlds. Each of these worlds can have differing notions of effective language use and of appropriate discourse themes, structures, and styles (Hymes 1980). Although teachers presume to offer what they hope will be relevant and intellectually engaging activities, within the students' worlds these activities may be interpreted in new and diverse ways, infused with unexpected, and even suspect, social and cultural meanings. Anson (1989) asserts that in the college composition classroom teachers respond to meaning, but their perspectives are often limited to narrow linguistic and rhetorical concerns—the logical progression of ideas, the appropriate use of evidence, the presence of a thesis, and the sophisticated use of cohesive ties. In addition, he points out that writing teachers who hope to encourage students' growth in literacy often focus on language to the exclusion of many other dimensions of these students' intellectual development that are informed by other intelligences and represented by other types of tools. Moreover, theorists such as Vygotsky (1986) and Wertsch (1992) argue that making meaning from such linguistic tools as a text is not simply a matter of focusing on the language of the text itself but includes the experiences, beliefs, and cultural backgrounds of the students. However, students are not free to operate within this broad focus unless teachers acknowledge and express an appreciation for what these students bring into the classroom. How can true classroom membership occur if one person holds all the cards and takes great pains to silence genuine input from the rest of its members? For example, in many college composition classes, teachers are concerned mainly with keeping writing in its functional boundaries rather than allowing students to draw on their own cultural tools in different forms of expression (Aronowitz and Giroux 1985). Paulo Freire, in *The Education for Critical Consciousness*, underscores this idea when he states that "Knowledge is not extended from those who consider that they know to those who consider that they do not know. Knowledge is built up in the relations between human beings and the world, relations of transformation" (1973, 109).

Knowledge and Relationships

Thus, it is the relationships between teachers and students, and not simply the methods of instruction, that are the critical, and sometimes the overlooked, element in the education of writing teachers. Sometimes this relationship is potentially strained even before the first class meets or in the first instant when teacher and student view each other. One teacher's syllabus for a Composition I class exemplifies this point. I was working in an athletic writing center and had the opportunity to be the reader of not only many student writings but of many syllabi brought in by the student-athletes. In many cases, these syllabi revealed the instructors' overall attitudes toward their students and were highly predictive of the relationships that developed over the course of a semester. One syllabus particularly stands out in my mind. The introduction in her syllabus went like this:

> Instructor: Kara Hill, B.A., MA, and Ph.D. in progress
>
> Requirements: Students must write two drafts of each paper and turn in ON TIME. They must contribute kinetic energy to all course requirements with special attention to ACADEMIC LANGUAGE. In short, however you talked before—you are now at the university and you are expected to perform AS SUCH. There will be NO TOLERANCE for shoddy work. There will be NO TOLERANCE for any absences. There will be NO TOLERANCE for tardiness, speaking out without instructor's permission, or not communicating through academic discourse. . . .

The students not only had to wade through five pages of this syllabus but then were expected to live within its borders for a whole semester. Predictably, they did not have the slightest clue as to how to achieve this. Kara had obviously misconstrued the idea of what constituted "demanding" to be nothing short of imposing a particularly cruel form of tyranny. For example, her last assignment was a ten-page genealogy essay in which the students were to trace their families' backgrounds. George, one of the student-athletes assigned to me, truly struggled with this assignment, since his father grew up in an orphanage, and his mother was raised in a series of foster homes. His parents lived seven hundred miles away and had no email access. Thus, George was faced with producing an authentic text with no information to fill in the gaps, but he was determined to complete the assignment. He produced eight pages that detailed what his parents could tell him, over the phone, of their own upbringings. He turned the assignment in and received a D for his efforts. His final grade for the class was an F, although he had, through much effort, completed every assignment. He appealed the grade, and finally struck a compromise with Kara, that if he would reattend her Composition I class during the next semester, she would consider a grade change. He attended her class for yet another semester, and she changed his grade to a C. At the same time, he took Composition II from another instructor and received a B. Kara's parting comments on George's final revised essay reflected her unwavering stance for the entire two semesters. She wrote that his communication skills "had grown so much in the past year with (her) guidance and mentorship." She further added that he "appeared to be outgrowing (his) previous illiterate attempts to communicate." She erroneously believed that she had somehow fixed this young man. She had no clue that her own culturally blocked attempts at communication were far more misguided than the efforts of the students she taught and that instead of being a mentor she was sorely in need of one—an idea that never occurred to her. Let me present another example.

Mutuality by Demonstration

When Charlie walked into Bill's Composition I class on the first day, Bill immediately disliked him. Bill passed out the syllabus to his twenty-five students and then paired the students up to make initial introductions of one another to the rest of the class. Bill reveals that

> One student, named Wilson, stood out in class, not only because he was the only African American in the room but also because he was wearing the all-black techno gear common to the urban, dance-club, cyberpunk scene. His partner introduced him by saying that he made his own clothing, so I asked him if he had made anything he was wearing that day. He said that he hadn't because he usually made his clothing from rubber, leather, and items found at Radio Shack. At this point, Charlie shook his head violently and let out an extended, disgusted "ugh."

This event stood out in Bill's mind because it confirmed many of his prejudices. Bill continued by revealing that he had been living in the rural western state for only about a month before the class started, and

> wasn't liking what I had seen. To me, [this] was a backwater, hick state, full of pickup-driving, losers. I am not usually prone to making such hateful generalizations, but I was trying to figure this state out. I moved here from St. Louis with a much more urban progressive culture. Even though this town offered some of the amenities I was used to, the rest of the state seemed to be a vast cultural wasteland. I didn't even see the ethnic and racial mix I expected. The community college where I had taught in St. Louis had a fairly large number of African-American students. By contrast, on that day in my classroom, I saw a lone black face surrounded by two-dozen white ones.

Bill continued by observing that

> Even before his outburst, I had pegged Charlie Smith as a typical farm-boy. He was, most obviously, a big man, an athlete, about 6'6". This combined with his clothes made him seem like the ultimate redneck. He was also unreserved about expressing his opinions. He was loud and obnoxious, and his response

to the other student's lifestyle seemed to me to be yet another example of a big ole, loud-mouthed country boy trying to suppress someone whom he saw as weird.

Charlie's writing ability was equally unimpressive. The first assignment was a personal narrative about a significant remembered event in the student's life. Charlie could not think of a topic, so Bill, a bit sarcastically by his own admittance, suggested that he write about his first day in class. Charlie took him up on it much to Bill's dismay. As Bill recalls

> because the event he was "remembering" had happened only recently, I sensed he was being lazy and also lacked any type of imagination. He obviously had not taken any time to pick out a topic that was truly significant. His response to Wilson in class and the way he described him in this paper seemed to be unduly judgmental and hostile.

Charlie's First Draft

On my first day here at _____, I encountered many different people. I met my roommate again for the fifth or six hundredth time. See I am a football player from a small town of about two thousand plus. I graduated with thirty-four kids. Well actually only thirty, four of those did not get diplomas.

Now what I am about to tell you is about the first day of my college career. It was a very interesting day to say the least. It all started about seven-thirty that morning when my alarm went off. Not having the slightest idea of what I was about to get into, I headed off to my first class of the day. English 11:13 was the place of my first adventure of the day. Professor Bill White was the first college teacher to see my face in a classroom, and boy will he regret that some day.

The one event that took place that made me realize that this place is a nut house, had to be the interview done on this student in my class. See our teacher, being the kind hearted man that he is, wanted us to get to know the people of our class. We split up into groups of two and conducted our interviews.

What shocked me was when I looked at him I figured he made the stuff. Because I figured know body in there right mind would buy the stuff that he had on, out of a store. But he likes to use rubber, and plastic, and other things you buy at Radio Shack. Now that's when I knew I had stepped in a world that was completely different from what I was used to. In fact I made the statement that I will never get used to this place. What I should have said was the people is what I will never get used to. I guess my small town background makes me think of the people up here as being nuts. But I guess everyone is entitled to have their own hobbies . . . I figure that if a man enjoys making clothes. Than he must be a few sandwiches short of a picnic. But you watch in five years when I graduate I still won't understand them. And that's even after I had already been around them for five years.

Bill's Reaction

What Bill initially saw in this paper was a student who had no tools that would allow him into the academic world. Nothing in this essay indicated that Charlie had any clue about the conventions associated with academic writing, much less grasped those elusive "standards" associated with academic principles. Although it was Bill himself who had suggested Charlie's topic, Bill's frustration also stemmed from Charlie's inability to understand what the requirements demanded. Bill observed that

> He didn't even try to make himself understood. He was always just so very obvious. He seemed dumbfounded when I told him I didn't understand what he was trying to say. I didn't think he had any chance. Not only would he fail my class, but if he couldn't capitalize on the given chances to revise the paper, since I had been working with him on it, then there was no way he was going to write anything for any instructor ever that would make any sense.

My reaction, once I read Charlie's essay, was a bit different. What I saw in Charlie's essay was a bewildered eighteen-year-old who, like many other student-athletes signed up to spend time in our writing center, had moved completely out of his culturally familiar element. Given Bill's concern and Charlie's written work, we immediately signed Charlie up for tutoring in our writing center, where I worked with Charlie on his essays. But working with Charlie on his essays was only one part of this particular scenario. I also was working with Bill with the intent of culturally refocusing Bill's viewpoint of Charlie. The only way that my intervention could be successful would be with Bill's willingness to change his own initial beliefs about Charlie and, in this case, students from rural cultures. I won't belabor this point, but when Bill was encouraged to make the conscious decision to explore his own prejudices about some of the students he taught, his willingness to be part of the "change" that took place was the true encouragement that Charlie needed to propel himself within reach of the academic community.

Through class sessions and writing conferences, Bill eventually discovered that his initial impressions about this student were misleading. Once he began not only to talk with Charlie but to actually listen to him, Bill found out that

> There was a lot more going on that first day of class than first indicated by Charlie in his essay. That day was a very significant moment in his life. See, he told me that he was from a very small town, and [this place] seemed unbelievably huge to him. I realized from our conversation that Charlie, until that moment, had never encountered anyone like Wilson. Wilson's extreme urban counter-culture presence was about as far from Charlie's life as anything could be. His response came from being overwhelmed by newness and difference rather than from obnoxiousness and cruelty. He just didn't seem to be able to articulate all of this and was just overwhelmed by the university and everything that surrounded him. Academia was not his arena—the football

field was, and he had no place in the academic community. So, if I didn't try to understand him, he would fail to find an acceptable place in the academic arena.

The common narrative of a student's gaining admittance to the academy is a story that centers normally around that student's carving out or finding a place by making radical changes in order to fit into the system. But, Bill, and I, as agents of the academy, also had to recognize our roles in this process and work together to help the academy make an entry point for Charlie. Our willing intervention also meant disrupting the academy's alienating image and showing Charlie that he could, in fact, make sense and meaning in the academic world.

Bill's mentoring of Charlie went much further than recognizing Charlie's cultural adjustments to the university. Bill went one extra step and allowed Charlie's background knowledge and expertise to work for him in the classroom. Rather than dominating the acceptable topics for writing assignments, Bill opened up the types of topics for each essay; thus, his students had the opportunity to present themselves as authorities on subjects that actually mattered to them. Charlie and the other students in the class were able to make meaning in the composition classroom because the assignments allowed them to establish positions of authority and expertise from which they could write. The remembered-event essay allowed for Charlie's authority because he was writing about his own domain, his own memory. The second assignment, the explanation of a concept, allowed Charlie to call on his expertise as a football player as he explained the duties of a defensive lineman. In this case, Charlie was definitely writing to an audience who had less expertise in the subject matter than he. Bill's willingness to allow for this type of assignment gave Charlie a chance to engage an academic audience on his own terms and the necessary authority to turn out an essay meaningful not only for Bill, but also for himself.

Making Sense of the Questionable

By giving up, or at least sharing, some of our authority in the classroom and honestly allowing our students' voices to be heard, we will work to create communities of teachers and learners that have respected places in this academic world. This is an essential component of the very idea of writing "methods," and a central priority for all of us who mentor beginning teachers. It is fine and necessary to teach the pedagogical approaches needed in order for beginning teachers to instruct students in how to write effectively; however, beginning teachers also must learn that human beings come in all sorts of funny packages and voices. And wonderful gifts often emerge from those packages who initially might seem so strange and out of place.

11

Personal and Distant Mentors

William Broz
University of Northern Iowa

I have a very cool photo from about 1982. It is a picture of Cleo Martin and Donald Murray talking at a conference. Martin, then Professor of Rhetoric at the University of Iowa, was and is my most important, personal mentor for my practice as a writing teacher. Murray, though we have exchanged only a sentence or two once or twice, is my most important distant mentor as a writing teacher. As luck would have it, in 1992, Bonnie Sunstein came to the Iowa English education program from the University of New Hampshire, became my dissertation chair, and became a personal mentor as a teacher of writing teachers. Donald Murray, professor emeritus at the University of New Hampshire, was and is one of her personal mentors. Though I was already steeped in Murray's writings, Bonnie was the person who eventually introduced me to *The Craft of Revision* (1995), the Murray book that is the subject of this chapter. When I graduated I gave her a copy of the Martin/Murray picture, a photo of the meeting of our two important mentors.

My writing methods students need such mentors, the personal kind and the distant kind (Vera John-Steiner calls them "distant teachers" (1997, 61)) to guide and support their developing teaching practices. When the students come to me they bring the basis of a teaching practice inherited from the secondary and college writing teachers (informal mentors) in whose classrooms they happened to have found themselves. From the practices of those teachers have come the methods students' first ideas about teaching writing—which could also end up to be their last—unless they are willing to examine and reassess their student writing experiences (including the experiences they have with me). From that examination will come their loyalty to personal mentors. Similarly, from their reflective engagement with the professional literature will come their acceptance of some collection of professional figures like Bonnie Sunstein, Cleo Martin, and Donald Murray as distant mentors.

Writing Process Pedagogy

I am a writing teacher who believes in writing process pedagogy. The path my practice takes through this broad territory is essentially and necessarily individualized and collaborative, an instruction in which the teacher/reader/responder assists student writers in making personally engaging meaning while the student writers maintain as much control over the content and form of the writing as is developmentally possible. I have always enacted this practice as a writing workshop. When I set up and operate a writing classroom like this, which I have done in many contexts for twenty-five years, I believe I am enacting fundamental language learning theory. When my students struggle to use language to explain their experiences, and I anticipate the direction of their struggles and supportively collaborate with them toward the next level of understanding, the student and I are as close to Vygotsky's (1986) "zone of proximal development" as we are likely to get. As legitimate as the critiques of process pedagogy are, especially those coming from social constructionists (for example, see Finders 1997), as far as I know, process pedagogy, generally construed, and adjusted as much as possible to accommodate individual student difference, is still the best model for promoting "fluency, clarity, and correctness" (Knoblauch and Brannon 1984) in writing, and the best way for my students and me to avoid the "dummy runs" that James Britton (1970) warns us about.

I did not like the dummy run, drill and skill, five-paragraph theme, formal writing instruction I was given in grades K–12, though the writing instruction I experienced in college was much more broadly construed and satisfying. Because college writing promoted a range of genres—poetry, fiction, real essays—I became captivated and set my course toward teaching writing. However, as a novice high school teacher I had difficulty trying to enact the writing workshop classes I had experienced as an undergraduate. It was almost as though I had not paid close enough attention to what my college writing teachers were doing when I had those experiences that made me a writer and made me want to become a writing teacher. Here was my dilemma: I had a clear idea of the traditional practice *I did not* want to enact but lacked an articulated understanding of how to enact the practices I believed in. Then, in the summer after my sixth year of teaching high school writing I enrolled in a summer institute of the Iowa Writing Project, which offered me two kinds of experience for which I was as primed as anyone could be.

First of all, the writing workshop leader, Cleo Martin, enacted with me and for me a writing process pedagogy in which she took pains to make explicit the means–ends relationships of her teaching practices. I wrote as a student writer while thinking as a writing teacher and then accepted the invitation to step behind the curtain to learn how she was pulling the levers. This experience amounted to a new "apprenticeship of observation" giving me the experiential "teacher knowledge" (Grossman 1990) to enact a writing process pedagogy myself. I saw that for some of my fellow workshop participants who did not mind traditional practices one bit, Martin's writing process workshop offered an experience so different as to "overcorrect" for their initial beliefs. Those participants acquired new beliefs in writing process pedagogy and "knowledge of instructional strategies"(Grossman 1990). I acquired that knowledge, had my beliefs strengthened, and adopted Cleo Martin as a personal mentor.

Second, from Jim Davis, Iowa Writing Project Director and the leader of our fifteen three-hour morning seminars on teaching writing, I got an immersion into the literature of writing process pedagogy. I learned, for example, that Peter Elbow's catalog of kinds of response to student writing, "pointing, summarizing, telling and questioning" (1973), articulated the peer-and-instructor response I was experiencing in the institute. As his words became integrated into my experience Peter Elbow became a distant mentor for my teaching writing practice of almost equal importance to Cleo Martin.

At the time of my first writing project experience, I had not encountered the theories of "teacher knowledge," but later when I studied a writing project summer institute as a graduate student I immediately understood how concepts like "knowledge of student understanding" and "apprenticeships of observation" (Grossman 1990) articulated the writing project experience for some participants—the ones who actually wrote and had new experiences as student writers. During that study I also came to value Michael Fullan's (1991) idea that there are three criteria necessary for teachers to adopt new practice. Fullan's criteria are that teachers must *believe* the new practice will meet student needs (*congruence*), teachers must understand how to enact the practice in their own teaching contexts (*instrumentality*), and teachers must *believe* that enacting the practice is worth the *cost* of making the change. What I got from the summer institute was mostly "know how" (instrumentality), because I already had the belief in congruence and cost. Many participants got *belief* and know how (Broz 1996).

Further, as many writing teacher educators have pointed out (see, for example, Schrofel 1991), our preservice students come to us with beliefs in certain teaching practices. They believe they know how to teach writing, and they will try to enact those beliefs unless they are encouraged to challenge and examine them. In this respect the challenge of educating preservice teachers is nearly the same as that of educating experienced teachers. Through my experience as a writing teacher and teacher of writing teachers, I have come to believe two things—that new experiences as writers can allow preservice and inservice writing teachers to develop new beliefs about teaching writing, and that writing process/writing workshop experiences can inspire new beliefs.

To make sure students in my writing methods classes have had at least one strong writing process/workshop classroom experience, I use an assignment that I call the "Murray Paper." Students, first independently and then with peer support, write an essay following the prototype for writing process instruction Donald Murray delivers in *The Craft of Revision* (1995). The composing experience, the sharing of the resulting essays for peer response, and the reflection

on the whole phenomenon seem to give my students a dramatic and meaningful entrée into the world of contemporary writing instruction. Additionally, students meet this "Murray," ubiquitously referred to in the professional literature,
and from whose pen, lore has it, came the term "writing process." For some
Murray will become their first distant mentor.

My primary goal as a teacher of writing teachers is to do for my students
what Cleo Martin (and others) did for me, to help them develop an articulated
belief system for teaching writing, a personal/professional philosophy that can
support their developing teaching practices well beyond their brief time with
me. Therefore, the culmination of my writing methods class is not a teaching
unit or a session of microteaching to peers but a "tentative position statement"
on teaching writing they can carry with them when they leave my classroom
for their own.

Making Metacognitive Thinking Overt

To pursue the goal of offering students a "new apprenticeship of observation"
in which the means–ends relationships of my teaching strategies are clear, I do
not allow more than five minutes of the first class period of my writing methods
course to expire before I insist that students take note that I am enacting with
them and modeling for them the same teaching strategies I use with students in
my first-year college writing class, practices very similar to those I used with
eleventh-grade students for twenty-one years. Sharing with students my ongoing teaching practice and my past secondary school teaching experiences in-
vites class members to "talk shop" as future writing teachers while they also
experience my practice as student writers. To begin, we arrange the chairs in a
circle so we can talk with one another and set up the "get to know you" activities to learn each other's names and develop a little shared background. I participate in all these activities right along with the students so that I start to become less of a stranger to people who are going to share their writing with me.
Learning about one another makes us a better audience for our writing, builds
the trust necessary for sharing drafts-in-progress, and allows us as writers to
tailor our writing to a real audience. Time spent constructing a classroom atmosphere begins to pay dividends almost immediately as students contemplate
the prospect of returning to class next week with writing to share with their new
peers. Even as they begin to "think like teachers," the community building still
works for them in their roles as student writers.

One way to describe metacognitive thinking might be to call it the articulation of experience into more generalized and abstract concepts. The concepts
that result from the students' articulations of their writing experiences become
the building blocks of their philosophies of teaching writing. As a doctoral student I assisted Bonnie Sunstein in writing methods classes. Her method of inspiring metacognitive thinking was to periodically ask students to "think on the
ceiling," to look down from the ceiling on themselves as students and on her as
their writing teacher in order to analyze and reflect on their educational expe-

rience and on the enacted pedagogy. In her study, Grossman's (1990) methods teacher tells his students: "I want you to switch heads now (117)." Tom Romano references Nancie Atwell in saying that he "tak[es] off the top of [his] head" as a writing teacher to show his methods students his teaching writing practice. Although I have not as yet developed any code word for this process, I do rely on the theories of Donald Schon to inform my thinking about this issue (1987). As I enact my teaching writing practice in methods classes I talk about what I am doing and why. In Schon's terms I am "thinking in action," "reflecting in action," and "reflecting on action" both as a means to further develop my own practice and as a way to share my practice with students who are apprentice writing teachers. Using his construct improves the quality of the apprenticeship by making sure the means–ends relationships of the practices are overt and clear to students.

The Murray Paper: Cornerstone of a Writing Methods Course

The First Class: The Murray Paper Assignment

What I tell students at the end of the first three-hour, once-per-week night session is: "Go home and read the first two chapters of Murray's *The Craft of Revision* (1995), and do what it says. Try to write a first draft of a paper using his instruction. Come back next week with a draft of that paper to share for peer response in small groups."

The Second Class Session

The peer response during the second class period takes two forms. The first is "say back," in which pairs of students read their papers aloud to each other. The reader reads with pen in hand and license to stop reading to make any necessary notes on the draft. The listener is charged to listen closely to the meaning and say back to the reader as many of the important points of the content as she remembers from the reading. From that icebreaking and very structured (thereby safe) response activity, writers take their papers into groups of four to six students who are instructed (at least during the first class periods) to listen closely to each person read his or her paper and to confine responses to "pointing to strengths" (Martin 1988, Daiker 1989, Probst 1989, Lyons 1981), identifying and praising specific aspects of the papers that are interesting, worthy of notice, or that catch the eye and ear of the listener in a positive way. Even though Donald Murray makes some statements lobbying against "positive response," in the first edition of *The Craft of Revision* (1991), he states, "I do not depend on enemy readers. I learn the most from friendly readers who support me but make suggestions that cause me to write better (81)."

At the end of the second class I charge students to "Go home, read the rest of Murray's book, and try some of the revision strategies he suggests. Then

come back to the third class meeting with copies of your Murray Paper, ready
to share with the whole class by reading it aloud for supportive peer response."

Here, a couple of excerpts from *The Craft of Revision* (1995) illustrate how
Murray leads the methods students through topic generation and early drafting
of their Murray Papers.

> Take a piece of paper—or an empty computer screen—and brainstorm, writ-
> ing down whatever passes through your mind. . . . Write fast to catch the
> thoughts, memories, ideals, specific details, you didn't know were in your
> mind. . . . Stop and read the list, circling what surprised you and connecting
> with line and arrow those items that are related. (7)
> [later]
> Test what I have been telling you by taking a topic from your brainstormed
> list and writing as fast as you can: so fast your hand writing almost skids off
> the page. . . . Read what you have written aloud to hear a potential voice rise
> from the page; read to discover . . . a clue of what you should be saying and
> how you may be able to say it. (12)

Writing methods teachers who decide to try the Murray Paper in their methods classes should be warned to keep their office door, phone, and email open
to students after the first and second classes, because at least some students will
need reassurance that the assignment is really broad enough to allow for the
topic they have generated and broad enough to allow for the form in which they
are writing. Many students will have never experienced this much control over
"school writing" and will feel sure that what they have generated is not acceptable. This is also your opportunity to prove to students that you believe in
student control of writing processes by accepting their topics and forms.

The Third Class Period: Publishing Murray Papers

As I write this it is the middle of the third week of the spring semester, and
tonight is the first session of sharing Murray Papers. It will take parts of three
class sessions to get all twenty-three three- to five-page double-spaced essays
"shared" aloud in class. We start the class tonight with a one-page student response to Hunt's (1987) article on responding to student writing, "Could You Put
in Lots of Holes? Modes of Response to Writing," and a discussion of response
to student writing that focuses on publishing and celebrating final drafts by responding to strengths. Then, eight student writers in a row read their essays to
the class for large-group peer response. I coach the class to have pens in hand
and mark on their copies of the essays the strengths they want to talk about. For
some of the readings, I assign half of the class to give verbal response while the
other half writes quarter-sheet notes to be passed to the writer. Tonight we start
with Tom's piece about being a high school swimming champ and trying and
failing to relive that experience in college. We move on to Lisa's researchy love
affair with Mountain Dew, complete with a reference section of seven websites

dedicated to her favorite drink. Ninety minutes later we finish with Matt's account of finding true love that begins and ends with reading in the bathroom. It is a lively mix of form and content demonstrating the eclectic ingenuity of eight different student writers bent on making meaning and communicating that meaning to a waiting and increasingly familiar audience of their peers.

Before class is over we are back to discussing the professional literature when another student passes out copies of her "one-pager" response to the Daigon (1982) chapter in *To Compose* (Newkirk 1990), the collected edition from which half of the course's short professional readings come. (The one-pager is also a gift from Donald Murray, which I inherited from Bonnie Sunstein, who inherited it from Murray.) Based on the Daigon one-pager we discuss "assignments, prewriting, drafting, revising, publishing, and evaluating" for the first of many times. Students are quick to note that what we have been doing with the Murray Papers tonight is a kind of publication. I explain the moves I made tonight to orchestrate this sharing performance—such as making sure that we ended on an upbeat piece and planning to guarantee enough time for response to the final piece shared. In the same vein, students discuss my questions: "How would the response have gone if all of the papers had been written to fulfill the same narrowly constructed assignment? Who would want to be the eighth person to share his or her paper? In a writing workshop, why is it essential for students to have a large measure of control over the form and content of their writing?" And in this discussion I see the layering I hope for and try to make happen: new experiences as student writers, reinforced by professional literature; reflections on past student writing experiences articulated and scrutinized through the lens of professional literature, articulated and scrutinized through current experiences as student writers. For some class members Donald Murray nearly takes on flesh as he becomes a distant mentor.

Student Reflection on the Murray Paper Experience

Here is most of Sarah's "writing process paper," her second paper for the course. In it she compares her former student writing experiences with her current, Murray Paper, experiences as she describes, analyzes, and comments on her own writing process. It is important to note that the assignment for her writing process paper does not suggest that she write about Murray or the Murray Paper, nor does it even suggest that her writing process might be changing.

Sarah Wallace: Writing Process Paper—
Draft 4. Title: From Thinker to Writer

Think, think, think, . . . think some more. Whoops, out of time! Better start writing now. Write, then edit. Whew! Finished just in time! Yes, I was a "thinking-writer." But fortunately for me (and probably for my teachers, too), I have discovered this isn't the best way to go about writing.

Prewriting activities were almost nonexistent in my world of thinking-writing. In fact, until this semester, I had not heard a word about prewriting

activities since the seventh grade. . . . Besides, my high school teachers usually gave us a topic to write about, *so why would I need to brainstorm ideas
anyway? . . .*

When I finally started writing, the first thing I did was create an outline
[and] thesis statement. . . . Then I would compose the rest of my paper, using
a pencil to write so that I could erase and correct mistakes as I went along. . . .
If the teachers wanted to see a rough draft along with the final product? *Well,
I would just write a fake one. The teacher would never know!*

My style of thinking-writing didn't allow much room for self-discovery
or self-involvement in my compositions. . . . For instance, I wrote an essay in
a high school class about divorce. When I finished the essay, I realized that I
didn't like it. I didn't even agree with most of it. Even worse, I managed to
make a personal topic sound uncaring, mechanical, and boring. Maybe if I
had tried "free writing" to allow myself to come to a conclusion instead of
creating a fake one, then my essay would've turned out entirely differently—
more honest and more personal.

However, now I find that my writing habits are changing. I am becoming
a "writing-writer." For the first time since seventh grade, I brainstormed ideas
before writing the Murray Paper. I put a pen to the paper and let the ideas appear—without any thinking or planning. It wasn't easy, since I am out of practice, but it did improve some aspects of my writing. . . . Because I allowed myself to work through my ideas instead of creating a conclusion first, I became
more involved in my writing. . . .

Sarah's Murray Paper was remarkable because the first half of the paper, in
which she describes her two jobs and her twenty-one semester hours, is written
in a very "rushed and hectic" style. Just reading it wore me out. But the second
half, in which she identifies her reasons for rushing (so she can spend calm,
quality time with her boyfriend, her nieces, and her family), is written in a style
that feels like a Sunday stroll by the lake—a creative use of form and style and
a great departure from the expository prose she describes as her "thinking-
writer" process above.

About experiments with style in her Murray Paper she says:

I was trying to make the reader feel the difference in my life between school
life (rushing) and home life (relaxation). I must have done it somewhat effectively, because a fellow student pointed out that she liked that aspect of my paper. . . . [W]ith the help of some of Murray's ideas . . . I think I am more aware
that form can add to the meaning in a piece of writing. I contrasted the first
and second halves of my essay in order to add to the meaning—a contrast in
the two aspects of my life. The Murray book talked about form in that we
should choose the best form for our ideas (ie. [*sic*] we would choose an essay
over poetry when writing about how to build a tree house), but I think my interpretation of his idea works, too.

Here, Sarah is beginning to understand the most essential element of the
limiting grip current-traditional practice has on student writers, the belief that
the form of the writing is set and unavailable to the student as a tool for making meaning. Furthermore, these last comments clearly show Sarah's engaged,
meaningful interpretation of the words of a new distant mentor.

A Look at the Rest of My Course *

Excerpts from Syllabus

Required Texts: *The Craft of Revision* (Murray 1995); *To Compose* (Newkirk
1990); *Getting the Knack* (Dunning and Stafford 1992); *Writing Relationships*
(Tobin 1993); *Portfolio Portraits* (Graves and Sunstein 1992); "The Great
Grammar Debate (Again)" (1996) *English Journal* 85 (November): 7; "Teaching Writing in the Twenty-First Century" (2000) *English Journal* 90 (September): 1; *Teaching Composition: A Position Statement* (NCTE 1985).

Course Requirements

- Attendance and active participation
- A course response journal that comments on the readings and connects to
  class discussions
- Five short papers (double-spaced—turn in all drafts with best draft on top)
  - Paper 1: Murray Paper [3–5 pages] plus one-page commentary
  - Paper 2: Description and Analysis of Your Own Writing Process [3–5
    pages]
  - Paper 3: Sketch of a Writing Teacher You Have Known [3–5 pages]
    & commentary
  - Paper 4: Tentative Position Statement, synthesizing theory and prac-
    tice [4–6 pages]
  - Paper 5: Portfolio of Yourself as a Writer plus commentary on port-
    folio-making [3–5 pages]
- Two one-page responses (*One-Pagers*) duplicated for everyone in the class
- Two poems written from the exercises in *Getting the Knack*
- Eight hours of classroom observation and brief oral report to class
- Writing portfolio as described in Paper 5

Excerpt from a Tentative Position Statement

In their Tentative Position Statements, students combine references to past student writing experiences, references to new writing experiences in my class,
and references to the wisdom of their new distant mentors, taken from the

*I inherited several components of this syllabus from Bonnie Sunstein, James Marshall, and Cleo
Martin.

professional literature, to begin articulating their beliefs for practice. Inclusions in these statements run the gamut from formulations of "writing processes" citing Perl (1980) on "recursiveness" and "the felt sense," to grappling with evaluation, assessment, and grading referencing Elbow (1993, 1983). The students also do some referring to and citing of Bill Broz, always prefacing their comments with statements like, "Now, I'm no brown-noser. . . . "

The following excerpt from Brian's Tentative Position Statement references another Murray article and Elbow's (1973) *Writing Without Teachers* (sometimes I even assign such sacred texts) in addressing the same issues of form and content and traditional practice that Sarah addressed in her comments on her Murray Paper.

> "Genre is a powerful but dangerous lens. It both clarifies and limits. The writer and the student must be careful not to see life merely in the stereotype form with which he or she is most familiar but to look at life with all of the possibilities of the genre in mind and to attempt to look at life through different genres" (Murray 1990, 38). Oh, if only my former teachers could have sat and talked with Murray! Veteran soldiers of the old school, my former teachers served the Five-Paragraph Essay Empire with undying loyalty. Although some teachers tried to give choice in topics or even complete freedom to write what we wanted, the form was always a constant: essay. Ironically, the form my teachers labeled as "essay" was, in fact, not even what the literary world defines as an essay. Rather, this was a form which one could not alter, or stray or deviate from—like a sonnet or villanelle: introduction, thesis, topic sentence, supporting paragraphs, conclusion. If ever we hoped to show our students the joys of writing and its infinite possibilities, we must rise up in revolt against the tyranny of form, the oppression of the "Essay Empire." "Allow your writing to fall into poetry and then back into prose; from informal to formal; from personal to impersonal; first-person to third-person; fiction, nonfiction; empirical, *a priori*" (Elbow 1973, 54.) Allowing and encouraging students to experiment with language and genre in any writing assignment not only gives a feeling of liberation, but also shows students that there are many vehicles in writing for expressing ideas. In turn, students will write with more passion, depth, and perception, creating, in effect, better writing. . . .

This young prospective teacher is ready to articulate, enact, and, importantly in our current climate, defend his developing teaching writing practice. He has experiential and professional knowledge to call on, as well as his personal and distant mentors at the ready.

Concluding Stance

And that is my goal—an articulated (though developing) position statement grounded in examined apprenticeships of observation and in the professional literature of writing process pedagogy. This approach seems to give some of my students the necessary teacher knowledge and the motivation to begin a contemporary teaching practice. Am I doing my students a disservice by offering them only writing process pedagogy and writing process mentors? I think not.

First, some students come to me ready to five-paragraph theme and grammar their future students to death. Sarah might have been one of those. These students need a startling, "overcorrecting" experience to steer them away from current-traditional practice. Second, students in my methods class have plenty of experiential knowledge on which to base a current-traditional practice, should they choose to enact one. Both Sarah's and Brian's accounts of traditional practice prove that. Third, as a writing teacher who also educates writing teachers, sharing my practice with preservice and inservice teachers is one of the resources I must use. That practice consists of a fairly narrow and extreme collection of writing process/workshop practices.

The state of affairs in English education regarding writing pedagogy *as it is actually practiced in the field,* although probably not unique to our teaching discipline, is frustrating and unfortunate. Writing process pedagogy has been the recommended practice of the profession for nearly thirty years (see, for example, NCTE's *Teaching Composition: A Position Statement* referenced in the syllabus excerpt), yet many practitioners have never developed belief in these practices or learned how to enact any version of them. That is a situation to which I am not willing to contribute.

"The winds of change" (Hairston 1982) that brought us writing process pedagogy, though currently variable and turbulent, have not yet shifted. When the paradigm does shift, spurred by current critique or critique yet to come, some components of writing process will be part of the new model. And my students at least will know where the wind shifted from and upon what past the new pedagogy is built. They will also know at an experiential level who the people are who created, promoted, and believed in writing process pedagogy, and what they believe in.

12

Mapping a Writing/Teaching Life

Gregory W. Hamilton
Teachers College, Columbia University

On the first night of our teaching of writing class I ask a group of graduate pre-service English teachers to write down and then share out loud what they think they need to know to become confident and prepared teachers of writing. Their responses to this writing prompt vary.

> Christine: If I'm going to become a confident teacher of writing then I need a bent, a system—I need to have some idea about what writing is—or do I?
>
> Tammi: A good writing teacher is manipulative.
>
> Tori: A good writing teacher should be able to define and recognize good writing.
>
> Dennis: She should be in the game of writing with kids.
>
> Melissa: A good writing teacher needs to learn how to evaluate writing.
>
> Dominique: . . . models her own struggles.
>
> Brenda: All I can think about right now is that I've forgotten the basics of grammar. How am I going to teach writing?

These soon-to-be English teachers are proficient writers. The strategies they have learned and the processes they have used to generate essays, short stories, and research papers are imbedded in their writing habits and practices. Yet their successes with writing don't necessarily translate into confidence about their abilities to teach writing. They have been given a variety of commands to write but have never torn apart what it means to be a writer. As students of writing they have rarely been asked to step back and deconstruct *how* writing instruction has influenced what they think they know about writing. This question, plus issues of pedagogy, and concerns about writing and writing instruction are the focus of a weekly four-hour time block student teachers in our graduate education program are required to take (concurrently with student teaching) to complete a master's degree and fulfill state requirements for a secondary teaching certificate in English. The four-hour time block gives us time to focus both on our development as writers and on our visions of ourselves as teachers of writing. The challenge is organizing and ordering activities that help students see the relationships between knowing oneself as a writer and becoming a writing teacher.

In this chapter I look at how a writing activity I introduce at the beginning of the course helps us reveal assumptions and beliefs about writing and teaching writing. Through discussion, the examination of these assumptions and beliefs helps us generate principles for writing and teaching writing that emphasize a symbiotic relationship between one's role as a learner and one's role as a teacher.

Mapping a Writing/Teaching of Writing Course

There are two components to the writing course our graduate students take to complete a master's degree in English Education and fulfill state requirements for a secondary teaching certificate in English. First, students participate in activities and complete assignments that ask them to live as writers, generating pieces of writing through series of writing prompts, drafts, peer responses and critiques, revisions and edits, and finally celebrating a finished product. Second, students are asked to live as beginning writing teachers. They examine teaching strategies; raise and explore pedagogical issues, dilemmas, and concerns related to writing instruction; and design lesson plans and curriculum they can implement in the classrooms where they student-teach in preparation for their first year of teaching. The following syllabus reflects one way to organize a writing course in a way that addresses both of these components.*

Required Texts:

Atwell (1998), *In the Middle: New Understandings About Writing, Reading, and Learning;* Fletcher (1993), *What A Writer Needs;* Kirby, Liner, and Vinz (1988), *Inside Out: Developmental Strategies for Teaching Writing;* Romano (1987a), *Clearing the Way: Working with Teenage Writers.*

Additional Reading

Read two books by a writer on writing, including one of the following: Fletcher (1996), *Breathing In, Breathing Out: Keeping a Writer's Notebook;* Heard (1995), *Writing Towards Home: Tales and Lessons to Find Your Way;* Lamott (1994), *Bird by Bird: Some Instructions on Writing and Life.*

---

*This syllabus also reflects the collaborative efforts of Randi Dickinson, David Schaafsma, Ruth Vinz, and other instructors in our program who continue to share ideas, texts, and activities across the courses we teach.

Course Schedule

Class session 1: "Getting to know ourselves and each other as writers."

- Play name games.
- Map a history of your life as a writer.
- Share maps in small groups.
- Discuss in large group, "What can we learn from these maps?"
- Use the maps to respond to the following questions in writing and then discuss as a large group.

You as a writer: What kind of writing are you most comfortable with? Successful with? What are your own weaknesses as a writer? When do you write? Where do you write? What inspires you to write? What kind of structures do you need in place to help guide your writing? How do you follow through with your writing? How do you develop a piece of writing, and are your strategies different for different types of writing? Are there any texts that have helped you become a better writer? Are you comfortable sharing your writing? What kind of support do you like to get from other writers?

Becoming a teacher of writing. What are writing teachers supposed to do? How should a writing class for middle school children be structured? For high school students? What kind of support do young writers need? What might a typical writing class in a middle school/high school look like? What disciplines would you connect with teaching writing? What do you need to know to become a confident and prepared teacher of writing for middle school/high school? What have you seen other writing teachers do that you want to model? What habits do you want to avoid?

Class session 2: "Beliefs and assumptions:
What do we know about writing?"

- Weekly writing prompt: conversations with yourself (Heard 1995, 27)
- Revisit last classes' discussions on writing history maps, beliefs, and assumptions about writing
- Partner interviews: get to know each other as writers
- Review syllabus
- Introduce Nancie Atwell, Tom Romano, Ralph Fletcher, and Kirby, Liner, Vinz: Approaches to the teaching of writing

Class session 3: "Mapping a favorite place:
Creating flexible boundaries"

- Weekly writing prompt: "rent-a-parent"
- Discuss Atwell (Chapters 1, 3, 4, 5, and 6), Romano (Chapters 1–6), and Kirby, Liner, Vinz (Chapters 1–5)

- Memory maps

[The following class sessions are presented by title only.]

***Class session 4: "Conferencing with each other:
Establishing writing group rituals"***

Class session 5: "Responding to student writing"

***Class session 6: "Conferencing with our students:
listening, learning, and talking it through"***

Class session 7: "What is good writing?"

Class session 8: "Centering on the needs of the writer"

***Class session 9: "Lesson and unit planning:
Sustaining flexible boundaries"***

Class session 10: "The reading/writing connection"

***Class session 11: "Revisiting our goals and objectives
as writers and teachers of writing"***

Class session 12: "Assessment: Generating rubrics together"

***Class session 13: Center School teachers share writer's workshop
unit outlines, assignments, and resources (handout packet)***

***Class session 14: "Revisiting: Reading/writing connection;
portfolio assessment"***

Class session 15: "Celebrating the work"

Ongoing Assignments

Writers on writing. Select a book to read by a writer on writing. Draft a two-
to five-page response/presentation.

    Keeping a journal. If you don't already, begin a notebook/journal and
write every day. Ralph Fletcher writes, "Keeping a notebook is the single best
way I know to survive as a writer. It encourages you to pay attention to your
world, inside and out. It serves as a container to keep together all the seeds you
gather until you're ready to plant them. It gives you a quiet place to catch your
breath and begin to write" (1996, 1).

    Making media matter. Each week read *The New Yorker.* Skim each issue;
read one piece in each issue carefully. Respond weekly in your notebook/jour-
nal to one particular piece, e.g., likes, noticings, wonderings, inspirations, or

criticisms. Bring your issue and your response to class each week. Also read the *New York Times* as often as you can. Try to read a variety of sections. Read the "magazine" on Sunday. Read a sports columnist on Monday. Read a piece from the "Science Times" on Tuesday. Read the op-ed page, the editorials, the news summaries, and so forth. Keep a folder of the pieces that you like personally or that you might find useful in your classroom. Inside the cover of the folder jot down ideas for each use as they occur to you.

Observing, analyzing, and evaluating. Take notes on how writing is being taught in the school where you are student teaching or working. If possible, visit another classroom where a teacher is working with writing.

Requirements

Class participation. Actively participate during discussions. This includes active listening. Try not to monopolize airtime. I encourage everyone to help monitor this and will model my own way of opening up and keeping a discussion going.

Assessment. Your grade for the course will be based on your participation and the portfolio you turn in at the end of the semester. We will design a rubric for assessing the portfolio together. Your portfolio will include the following:

- One "finished" piece of writing, including drafts and revisions, self- and peer responses to drafts, and my responses as well.
- A stamped envelope addressed to an appropriate place where you are going to send a piece of writing in hopes of seeing it published.
- Five lesson plans and/or a miniunit developed for a middle school and/or high school classroom. We will spend class time discussing lesson and unit planning, including goals, objectives, do-nows, activities, assignments, and assessment options. This assignment will reflect classroom management strategies and a philosophy of teaching. You may work on this project individually or in a small group (two to three members). All members must submit a copy of the project in their portfolio.
- Five photocopied entries from your journal/notebook representing the different kinds of journal entries you made and a reflection statement on your experience using the journal.
- Your *New York Times* folder and responses to *The New Yorker.*
- A two- to three-page introduction to your portfolio, synthesizing your thoughts on being a writer and becoming a teacher of writing.

Mapping the History of a Writer

On the first night of our writing class I like to use the metaphor of mapping to encourage preservice teachers to explore the experiences they have had as writers. Their histories as writers and writing students can literally be laid out on paper and mapped, creating an opportunity to trace the different beliefs and assumptions about writing that they have come to hold. Mapping and sharing these experiences in a writing class challenges preservice teachers to examine and reexamine their beliefs and assumptions about writing and at the same time supports the move to make my own writing instruction transparent. It helps them become more conscious and critical of what is going on in the classrooms where they are student teaching. It also encourages them to think more carefully about how they will map their own writing instruction when planning for their first full year in a junior high or high school English classroom.

After spending our first hour together getting to know one anothers' names I introduce the first mapping activity—mapping the histories students have had as writers—using the chalkboard to begin mapping my own experiences as a writer. I start with my earliest writing memories, "scribbles and symbols," writing these words in a bubble on the lower left side of the chalkboard. My mother saved many of the drawings I made when I was two and three years old on various sizes of construction paper. I include these scribbles in my experience as a writer because I believe they represent my first attempts to document on paper my responses to the world around me. From this bubble a path leads to other bubbles: "elementary school;" "The Story of Mike," written in first grade; the name of my fourth-grade language arts teacher, Mrs. Dyer, who taught me the parts of speech; and another story title, "I Lost My Mother," written in fifth grade.

As I generate bubbles I share my thinking out loud. I let students know that they might begin their own maps at different points in time and may even use categories other than "grade levels" to trigger their own memories of pieces of writing, writing teachers, and events that led to a piece of writing or a learned skill.

Before beginning my own map on the chalkboard I have already handed out several large pieces of newsprint to everyone in the class along with colored pencils and markers. As I talk some students begin their own maps while others watch and wait for me to say, "Let's get started." I move from the chalkboard to my own piece of newsprint once all questions have been asked and answered, taking time to complete my own map and move around the room to coach and notice how each map in the room is evolving.

Mapping is not a new idea. Students will encounter various presentations of how mapping might be used in a writing course in the required texts we will read and discuss during the semester and in other classes they take in our program. Each author's version of mapping defines and illuminates many of the important reasons for using a map as a starting point in a course about writing. Tom Romano, in *Clearing the Way,* defines mapping as a "discovery process" (1987a, 61). Dan Kirby, Tom Liner, and Ruth Vinz, in *Inside Out,* encourage writers to think of a map of one's life as a place to "illustrate the hills and valleys, the thrills and conflicts" (1988, 33). And Lucy Calkins, in *The Art of Teaching Writing,* believes mapmaking involves a process of "finding—and making—plot lines in our lives" (1994, 412).

During our first night of class, once students have mapped their writing lives and before they have encountered in their readings different rationales for making maps, it is important to let them voice their own responses to the mapping activity. Mapping activity encourages the process of getting to know one another and also triggers self-reflection and becomes a holding place for memories they can begin to tear apart and analyze together. After spending half an hour or so making their maps, students begin to identify for each other:

- Connections between reading and writing
- Contrasting images of writing teachers
- Various "physical" activities involved in writing
- Moments of inspiration related to people and events in their lives
- Important places where writing took place
- The range of writing projects they have been exposed to
- Contradictions in their need for structure and need for freedom
- Contradictions in definitions of what counts as writing

Discussion of the maps and what we notice about writing lays important groundwork for the activity that follows: responding in writing to two overarching questions: *Who are you as a writer?* and *What does a writing teacher do?* As the quotes at the beginning of the chapter reveal, responses to this series of questions generate a great range of beliefs about writing and writing instruction. As students share their written responses and go back to their maps to clarify and search for relationships among events, categories, and so forth, they begin to identify a range of beliefs and needs related to writing and writing instruction. They become able to identify some of their beliefs and needs surrounding how to work and live as a writer, too. For example, as a writer, Christine emphasized the importance of small classes, her idea of a "safe environment" for self-disclosure. Tammi recognized "when and what I'm learning when I write" and equated writing with being both inspired and feeling compelled to get everything down on paper. Tori attributed her ability to write to the teachers who made writing the central activity in the English classroom. Dennis realized he relied on "baby steps" to get a piece of writing out, "re-writing, refining ideas, and playing with the sounds of words." Dominique told everyone she had never admitted to herself before how often she froze when given a creative writing assignment, which was similar in some ways to Brenda's love for creative writing conditioned by her ability to "define [her] own parameters."

Students also begin to notice where their beliefs about what they need to know as writing teachers come from. For example, Christine could point to the writing teacher she learned the most from, believing it was this teacher's "bent" or "system" that made what she needed to know about writing explicit. Dominique remembered the teacher she had in middle school who modeled her own struggles. And of course there was the grammar expert Brenda could never forget, even though the elements of grammar emphasized in this teacher's instructional approach had slipped from Brenda's memory. Each teacher's approach emphasized a different focus for teaching writing, a different way of describing what writing is and how to define a teaching/writing life.

By the end of the first night's class students end up having looked pretty carefully at their experiences as students of writing instruction and having recalled the teachers whose varying approaches to writing instruction have influenced their own moves to become writing teachers. They are positioned to begin tackling the task of designing lesson plans and writing units—their own instructional maps—that will influence the writing lives of their own middle and high school students.

Our conversations on the first evening, then, could be described as working across these three tiers of reflection and learning: self as writer, the influence of writing teachers, and working toward becoming a writing teacher.

The Influence of Writing Teachers

It is always a sobering moment when I look at a student's map of his or her writing history and read the label "Teachers College, 2001" or "Professor Hamilton's *Teaching of Writing* class, 2001." My reaction is a response to the fact that a student might see me as his or her last writing teacher. It is also a reminder that as one of a student's many writing teachers I might have a significant effect shaping how a student maps his or her life as a writer. Because the graduate students I work with are student teaching in classrooms where their own students identify them as *the* writing teacher, I look for opportunities and/or moments in the curriculum of our writing class when I can help students examine how *I* am defining myself as a particular type of writing teacher. In short, I want to make transparent for students those moments when I question or evaluate my own teacherly thinking as a way to encourage students to take time to step back and consider how their actions are playing out in their own classrooms. Also—I hope—sharing aspects of my writing life—the good and the bad—helps challenge the notion that writing teachers occupy the magical position of expert and know-it-all. I want students to feel comfortable "not knowing," "unknowing," or "guessing," "playing," and "experimenting" with language and the rules that govern language when they struggle with the decisions they must make for their own practices.

Implications for Teacher Education

Know Your Students

The first rule I would stress for teacher educators who want to help beginning teachers map their writing/teaching lives is to stress the importance of getting to know each writer you work with, or if numbers and time create roadblocks, then learn to structure class time in a way that allows each writer to share his relationships and experiences with writing with someone else.

Make Time for Writing

Time is always a very real consideration. How often and for how long a teaching writing class meets depends on the individual program and college schedule. The four-hour once-a-week time block we have created allows students to work in small and large groups, break for minilessons, start an assignment in class, or take thirty minutes over a cup of coffee in the cafeteria to try something I have introduced and then come back for questions and more reflection. Four hours gives us time to do a variety of things in one evening, emphasizing the interconnectedness of activities and the different ways a piece of writing or a lesson plan for teaching writing can get worked. The key here is to try out, tear apart, and interrogate different writing habits, what it means to be a writer, and the strategies and processes we use to generate essays, short stories, and research papers.

Learn from Many Teachers

Invite students to locate and interrogate the sources of their habits and beliefs about writing, as well as how they've come to know particular strategies and processes. We can realize the influence our own teachers have had on how we've come to feel about ourselves as writers and at the same time broaden our notions of what constitutes a writing teacher. Sometimes a newspaper story or hearing a group of peers laugh at something we have written can change our perceptions of ourselves as writers or even teach us something about craft, form, or audience we may have never realized before.

Emphasize a Teaching/Learning Construct

Helping our students grow as writers and teachers means inviting them to see a relationship between teaching and learning. Teacher educators need to address the awkward and confusing location beginning teachers are speaking from when they voice concerns like, "I'm somewhere in between being a student and being a teacher and so I don't really know who I am." When students hide behind or blatantly reject the tenets they have learned from their own teachers or rely on a reified system, they often lose sight of or shortchange their abilities to problem-solve, challenge their own assumptions, and develop strategies that are flexible or adaptable to different situations. Mapping our past and looking at our own maps alongside others, interrogating what is both concealed and revealed, can open up new spaces and places from where we can continue to map our writing/teaching lives.

13

Mailing It In

Taking Writing Teacher Education on the Road

Michelle Tremmel
Iowa State University

The Problem That Became 392 . . .

In 1989, when my colleague Bob joined the English education program at Iowa State, he taught a relatively new course called English 493, "Composition and Rhetoric for Teachers." This was the first of two methods courses that students took in sequence just prior to student teaching. One obvious problem with this arrangement was that throughout their entire experience as undergraduates, Bob's students had only late and sometimes minimal contact with the English education faculty who taught the methods courses and supervised student teaching. An even more serious problem was that these students had no official field work or even contact with secondary classrooms and students until they were practically finished, certified, graduated, and out the door. The result was hermetically sealed, low-impact, too-little-too-late teacher education that seriously disserved those students who arrived in schools to student teach only to discover they did not necessarily enjoy working with adolescents and had invested four years' worth of time and money in a profession they suddenly disliked.

Obviously, such a system was far below the standard for good English education programs and, in fact, bordered on professional malpractice. The first step in working with this problem was to rearrange the program of study so that students began working with the English education faculty earlier in the professional course sequence. This was accomplished by replacing 493 with a new course, English 392: "Practice and Theory of Teaching Writing in the Secondary School."

Currently, English 392 opens with a five-week commitment to "daily writing." Solidly entrenched in expressivism and process pedagogy, this part of the course occurs at the same time that the class studies Nancie Atwell's *In the Middle*. Daily writing begins at the first meeting when students are asked to informally compose their "writing autobiographies," a reflective piece they share with one another in small groups during the second class meeting, thereby introducing themselves as well as beginning to think concretely about how writers are educated and become—or fail to become—writers. After this autobiography, students, as much as possible, construct for themselves a disciplined daily writing practice in which they try to make contact with the experience of writers responsible for running their own writing lives. The purpose is for them not only to get a small taste of what it is like for writers to be on their own but also to acquaint—or reacquaint—themselves with their own composing processes in a context free from the teacher's agenda or someone else's narrow sense of process. Class sessions during the daily writing segment of the course try out various workshopping and peer-response techniques and lead eventually to a series of revisions of one piece that each of the participants, teacher included, polishes and publishes in a class anthology.

For the second third of the semester, 392 focuses on a range of theoretical and practical frameworks, issues, and methods for the teaching of writing, using the text *Language and Reflection* (Gere et al. 1992), which, in addition to expressivism, considers current-traditional, cognitivist, and social constructionist rhetorics and pedagogies. Class sessions in this part of the course operate more like conventional college classes than the beginning workshops, with students discussing and arguing about the readings. There are also lectures that extend the theory discussions by focusing on the history of the discipline; the rise and decline of process research and pedagogy; the roles that teachers and scholars from James Britton to James Berlin, Peter Elbow to Paulo Freire have played; and various other issues of interest and import to writing teachers.

Even though the first two parts of 392 are constantly changing, the final third has received and continues to receive the most overhauling. During the first few years it was taught, the final challenge for students was a three-week writing unit complete with full-blown lesson plans and an academic commentary. Later, the unit requirement was replaced with an assignment to compose and explain a tight sequence of writing tasks (Dowst 1980, Harris 1997, Krupa 1982). Most recently, students have completed English 392 by writing a multigenre paper in the manner elaborated by Tom Romano in *Writing with Passion* (1995b) and *Blending Genre, Altering Style* (2000).

. . . and the Problem That 392 Became

As I mentioned previously, one of the problems 392 was designed to solve was the lack of early field work in the English education program. Accordingly, the initial design for 392 included a concurrent fifty-hour practicum administered by the College of Education. The goal was to provide time and space in 392 for students to make presentations about their field experiences; to discuss what they saw, heard, and did there; and to make connections with the theoretical, practical, social, and cultural contexts that were emerging in their class work.

The initial problem, though, was that after 392 came on-line it required an additional couple of years to make the necessary administrative adjustments to initiate the practicum. Unless Bob was willing to postpone doing what needed to be done, which he was not, he needed some inexpensive, easy-to-implement, yet effective way to put students in contact with the schools and let them begin learning about their future students. Fortunately, about the time 392 was revealing its problematic nature, Bob met me, a middle and high school teacher in mid-Michigan, at an NCTE convention.

Exchange: How Twenty-Three Seventh Graders Solved the Problem

As we talked at the convention I was shocked to learn that Bob's students' only contact with secondary English students consisted of a meager four weeks observing at the beginning of their student teaching semester. I offered an interim solution: my class of twenty-three seventh graders. These students, new to junior high, faced, in me, someone who asked them to think of themselves as writers and didn't use worksheets; who challenged them to choose compelling topics and demanded that they write more than one "sloppy copy;" and who believed, as they did not, that revising meant more than correcting errors. My idea was that working with my students not only would benefit these soon-to-be teachers but would also support my campaign to teach my students that writing is a complex but rewarding process. Thus, from our dual need sprang the beginning of our students' collaborative conversation, "Friends Across Two Waters," which lasted for three semesters and involved approximately seventy-five middle school and forty-five methods students.

In an approach that tied my students' writing workshop to the daily writing component of Bob's course, I could introduce the seventh graders to the idea of workshopping by showing them that "real" people—adults—in other places actually write and struggle with writing, and Bob could give his students close professional contact with "real" middle school students. Also, the exchange could provide my seventh graders another audience, more knowledgeable than their classmates but less judgmental than the teacher/grader, while offering the methods students practice in giving students feedback on their writing, something they would soon be required to do in their own classrooms. Finally, since getting mail and writing letters would be perfect for my note-passing-addicted students and fun for college students too, a mail exchange seemed ideal for demonstrating to Bob's and my students that writing in school, especially to a real audience, can be personally engaging and educational.

During each semester of our partnership we sent packets of materials three times, first exchanging the ISU students' writing autobiographies and my students' literacy statements, reflective writings in which they created a thorough

picture of their experiences as readers and writers from kindergarten through
sixth grade. In this beginning activity I not only wanted to introduce the basic
aspects of writing processes but I also wanted my students to see that one of the
many roles they had assumed in their lives so far (along with basketball player,
dancer, or musician, etc.) was the role of reader and writer, a role for which they
had already amassed quite a history.

After various prewriting activities the seventh graders next wrote a free-
form first draft of their literacy statements, and we practiced a simple three-part
response to get them ready to interact with their ISU partners. This approach to
responding, which Bob borrowed from Iowa writing teachers Cleo Martin and
Bill Lyons (1981), and I learned from reading Atwell, has students (1) Praise
or note at least one positive aspect of the writing, (2) ask one Question, and
(3) make a suggestion for Polishing—or PQP. As a model, I responded orally
to each piece as students listened and took notes. Then they worked on beginnings and endings and paragraphing, responded in small groups to this second
version of their pieces, wrote a third draft, and finally proofread and edited, getting help from peers, family, and teacher. After all this, they were ready with a
polished draft to share with their friends at ISU.

In a letter, the form that some students chose for this initial piece, seventh
grader Emily introduced herself to her college partner:

> Dear Faith,
>
> Hi! I am writing this letter to tell you my reading and writing experi-
> ences. It all started in kindergarten. I learned how to read and write in Al-
> abama, in kindergarten. When I was in first grade I lived in Indiana. Their
> reading and writing skills were new and different. We had a phonics station
> we went to every day. It was supposed to help you with sounding out letters.
> It worked pretty well. There was also a handwriting station. We had to write
> words and letters over and over.
>
> Every year, from first to fifth grade, we would have a Young Author's
> Competition. Everyone in the school, from kindergarten to fifth grade, had to
> write and illustrate a story . . . I didn't really like writing stories for this be-
> cause I had to read them in front of people. I always thought my stories were
> stupid and no good until the fifth grade when I won. That was fun. My story
> was the true story of Little Red Riding Hood . . .

While Emily and her classmates worked on literacy statements, Bob's students followed a similar but more informal pattern in workshopping one anothers' writing autobiographies, with his teaching directed toward helping his
students think about the responding and workshopping processes from the perspective of "teacher" and "seventh grader." Here the methods students did what
I think all good writing teachers must do: participate in the experience of student
writers by trying out their own assignments in order to see students' struggles
from the inside out. In an excerpt from methods student Gina's autobiography,
one can see how these older student writers explored some of the same pleasures and struggles related to writing as did seventh graders like Emily:

I have an old cardboard box. It is brown and stained but inside it holds all of my "special Gina things," keepsakes and mementos. One of the things I have in this box is a spiral notebook containing the first writing I ever did and the first writing that was ever important to me. The spiral is a result of Mrs. Mc-Cattie's second grade class. Every morning after our announcements we would have personal writing time. I remember enjoying that time because I got to write in my blue spiral notebook and I got to use my favorite blue pen. My favorite color was and still is blue. I was encouraged to create my own story, complete with illustrations, and I thought it was a mini-masterpiece.

My special story was about a ghost named Mr. Bones. He was originally supposed to be a skeleton, but I found drawing all the bones a bit too difficult. Ghosts were easy to draw and manipulate. Mr. Bones was a fun ghost who enjoyed solving mysteries. By the end of the school year I had a full notebook and a sense that I had found something that I was good at. I also had found something that could be fun and entertaining. . . .

Beginning pieces like Gina's and Emily's allowed our two sets of students to get to know one another, creating a comfort zone for subsequent responding. Also, this initial sharing showed the seventh graders that despite differences in age and place, writing is a way for people to connect, and it allowed the methods students a glimpse into typical reading and writing backgrounds of secondary students.

To continue the conversations begun with these autobiographical writings, we settled on the "Things to Do" poem activity as a way for our students to see what each could do with the same creative prompt. This exercise, based on Gary Snyder's poem "Things to Do Around a Lookout," which Bob has done many times as a poet and visiting artist in the schools, goes like this: First, he tells students a little bit about Snyder, focusing on his early career as a poet, student, and fire lookout for the U.S. Forest Service. Next, he reads the poem and discusses it with students, trying to help them note especially Snyder's use of precise, straightforward, concrete language and listing. Finally, he asks students to write their own poems based on "things to do" around some place they know well. In our exchange, both groups did this writing and sent it to their partners.

Here things got interesting for some of the methods students who found themselves challenged to think as teachers rather than merely older peer responders. This shift can be seen in an exchange between middle schooler Hope and her university partner Julie, a postal worker, in connection with Julie's "Things to Do" poem:

Things To Do Around the Post Office

Freeze your fanny off because the air conditioner is on
   inside when the weather outside requires long johns!
Bitch and moan about your inflexible work hours
Gossip like old hens with your co-workers about your miserable
   job

Ignore the person next to you who thinks she is singing Barry
    Manilow under her breath
Pay no attention to the person next to you who is breathing
    like she is on the top of a mountain
Listen to love stories on audio books that leave you feeling
    breathless–maybe that is why the person next to you is
    breathing hard!
Request time off knowing that it will not be granted to you
Go into training for the fiftieth time when you run out of mail
    to process
Read the postcards of people who are dumb enough to spill
    their guts out on them
Pray to the Gods that your 8-hour shift does not seem like 24 hours
Send the bills of people you know to Europe
Heck, send your own bills to Europe! Bon Voyage!
Stare at the time clock hoping it will change to the time you go home
    with just a blink of your eyes
Walk, no RUN, out the door as fast as your limbs will take you
    before they ask you to stay.

When Hope read Julie's poem, an interesting dialogue occurred because she felt uneasy about Julie's use of *bitch* in the first draft, which she later changed to *groan* in the second. In the "Questions" part of her response, Hope asked Julie, "Do they usually let you swear when you write poems?" and then made the following suggestion for revision: "If you can't swear, then you probably shouldn't put swear words down." In her next letter to Hope, Julie responded, addressing Hope's concerns about diction and audience while considering the effect of her language choices as not only a writer but a teacher. In a "P.S." she told Hope, "By the way, in response to your response about cussing, yes I can cuss. I am an adult. However, I try very hard not to! When I used the word 'b–ch,' it was being used as a synonym for the word 'complain.' Therefore, it really wasn't a "cuss" word, just a poor choice of words! Thank goodness for REVI-SION!!" In ways like this our exchange allowed natural (and reciprocal) teaching moments and a look inside junior high heads for the methods students.

For our third exchange, students shared a piece of their own choosing, one, in the case of Bob's students, pulled from daily writings, and one, for my students, taken from some short workshop pieces. In this part of the correspondence the methods students got to see the variety of topics and forms typical for seventh graders and the kinds of revision suggestions they can give. By this point in the exchange the methods students had "taught" the middle schoolers about what helpful response to writing means through their own sincere and interested responses. Though Bob's students were learning about seventh graders' writing, they were also teaching their partners about the worth of their writing, which caused my students, uncharacteristically, to take the process of responding and revising very seriously.

One can see the kind of sophistication students were developing in a set of responses to Faith's piece "Gratuity" by seventh graders Emily and Karen, a particularly interesting pair because their academic abilities were quite different. One was bright, proficient in writing, and academically successful, whereas the other was hardworking but had below-average reading and writing abilities. Despite these differences, though, both their responses show how their exchange with Faith taught them to give the kind of thoughtful, specific feedback that pointed to what worked in a piece and helped the writer consider further revision. By looking at Faith's opening and Emily's and Karen's responses, one can easily see the competence of these students, who until two months earlier had never done such intense responding to others' writing. Faith begins:

> I've learned a lot about people in the last four years as a server at the Paradise Cafe, a restaurant that specializes in fine dining. One of the most important things I've learned is that people are generally stupid. I suppose stupid isn't the right word because most of the people who patronize the Paradise Cafe are very well educated. Too educated in my opinion. I'd say eighty percent of our weekday crowd is made up of professors and university administrators who are obviously very well educated. However, it seems to me that common sense was abandoned somewhere down the line to make room for useless knowledge.
>
> The intellectuals that I have come in contact with are usually very interested in highly intellectual conversation. This isn't a bad thing in itself. I've managed to learn quite a bit about quantum physics when I've chosen to eavesdrop. The problem with this type of behavior is that they tend to get so wrapped up in their conversations that they easily forget all about the server. . . .
>
> "What do you mean we have to *tell* you what we want, can't you see that we're having a highly intelligent conversation here? I'll take the fish." With that, the fuzzy faced, spectacled and balding man returns to his conversation concerning the macrosocioeconomic effects of cappuccino on the blah blah blah. . . .

Emily approached the "What I Like" part of her response by mentioning a specific passage and a general quality she thought were effective: "I liked a lot about this piece but limited it down to two; I liked how you said that people are generally stupid. That was funny. I also like some of the detail." Karen's approach was to copy out her favorite sentence (the beginning of paragraph three). In addition, both girls asked questions about detail and the opening of the piece. Emily asked, "What kind of restaurant is the Paradise Cafe?" And Karen wanted to know, "Why did you start with a long beginning?" For a revision suggestion, Karen said, "You should put more action in it," and Emily advised, "I suggest you describe the Paradise Cafe more."

What these excerpts illustrate is the indirect, but powerful, teaching and learning our exchange made possible for both seventh graders and methods students. Perhaps the strongest lesson the seventh graders learned was that writing development is a continuous process with many struggles that all writers—including English teachers—go through. As my student Emily put it, "The most surprising thing I learned is they're just like us. They need help improving their stories as much as we do." Nicki agreed, "They make errors too. Even though they're in college they're not perfect. We all make simple or maybe even big mistakes."

Of course, the college students, because of their broader experience, were not surprised that writers make mistakes and that writing can always use work. They did learn, however, about not only the limitations of middle schoolers' writing but also the latent abilities just waiting for a teacher to nurture—as well as the pleasures and challenges that are part of that nurturing. Bob particularly noticed the curiosity and enthusiasm his students showed toward the exchange and their partners. On days when the methods students were expecting a new batch of writings, there was a palpable air of excitement in class (and if the mail was delayed, a lot of "groaning" and moaning about Julie's employer, the U.S. Postal Service). As soon as Bob handed out the packets of letters and writings from my students, they were eagerly opened and perhaps shared with classmates or tucked carefully away in a notebook. For many of Bob's students, this was their first introduction to students like those whom they would soon teach, and they were well aware of the value of the experience.

As we came to the end of each semester's exchange we compiled self-selected writings in a joint anthology, pairing one piece from each student with his or her partner's piece, and the seventh graders created a cover. We also exchanged final letters, and a number of students shared home and/or email addresses to continue the relationship they had forged through writing. Commenting on the experience, most said they were sad to see the project end and regretted that they could not have exchanged more letters and pieces of writing.

The students' comments also brought up a larger issue of design Bob and I had wondered about when we first configured the exchange: the use of surface mail as opposed to what has become, perhaps, the more common email format for similar school–university or secondary–elementary exchanges. Surprisingly, we discovered from those of Bob's students who had experienced email exchanges in other education courses that surface mail seemed more valuable than email for them as future writing teachers. For example, although Gina liked the frequency of email exchanges she had experienced in other university courses, she preferred exchanging the more tangible letters, pictures, and writings. Julie added that "a weakness was that [the email exchange] didn't discuss writing; it was more like the conversation you'd have with a pen pal. Through the regular mail is better because you get full sets of drafts and revisions, and having an up-close look at real secondary students' writing is an important benefit."

Also, because not all the random pairings went off without a hitch, the methods students experienced firsthand something beyond middle school writing: resistant middle school behavior. And one student even had an opportunity to test how she might handle such resistance. From the first sentence of one seventh grader's initial letter, Clare could see he was less than thrilled with our project. He announced he hated writing letters and then "introduced" himself through details about violent activities he and his friends did for "fun." Clare was immediately concerned about these disturbing revelations but used them as an unique opportunity to practice how to respond to what she described as "unpredictable and 'touchy' situations" in teaching students who may try to "get attention by shocking." In the controlled setting of the exchange, this methods student took on the role of a teacher not only of *writing* but of *students* and worked sensitively and subtly through the problem.

How did Clare's indirect method work? Pretty well. It allowed me to talk with my student about considering his audience when choosing details to include in a piece of writing, and in his return letter, he admitted he had written to Clare as he would a friend and, being bored, had fabricated most of the letter to have some "fun." From here, Clare and her partner's exchange proceeded smoothly for the rest of the semester, and even this problem provided learning beyond how to teach writing for this preservice teacher.

"Friends Across Two Waters" filled a temporary void in English 392 and, though simple, "It was actual practice; it was the real thing," as one of the methods students said. This pairing of students in the "real thing" allowed Bob and me to be mentors to the methods students as they tried on the role of "teacher," which enabled them to mentor the seventh graders in developing their roles as readers and writers. And, most of all, the seventh graders taught the would-be teachers and retaught us veterans much about the power of writing to make contact with others and bridge various gaps, like distance and age. Truly, in our simple, inexpensive exchange, teaching became learning became teaching, but such an exchange is only one creative way to do what I believe is a fundamental, nonnegotiable bottom line for writing teacher education—all teacher education for that matter—and that is to provide opportunities for beginning teachers to learn firsthand who their students will be—academically, culturally, concretely—before day one.

No matter what the venue, there is never a valid excuse for not meeting this bottom line. In both English education and first-year composition, practica and supervised observation are always desirable, but cheap and useful exchanges are just as easy to accomplish for preservice TAs as they are for preservice secondary teachers. The only administrative requirements are ingenuity and the determination to succeed.

Let me close by describing an ingenious plan devised by Richard Bullock (1999). He designed a preservice "student teaching component" for new TAs based on a four-morning workshop to orient incoming English 101 composition students. The selling point to students was that by attending the workshop they would "become better prepared for their fall quarter writing classes, [would] get accustomed to being on campus and so avoid first-year student confusion, and [would] do better in their classes than students who [didn't participate]" (11). The workshop was set up so that beginning TAs worked with experienced TA mentors in leading small groups of first-year students through various writing activities and helping them produce an anthology of writing. Since the TAs were already under contract for the week during which the workshop ran, Bullock needed no additional funds for staffing. In addition, each first-year student who attended paid a $25 fee that could be applied to scholarships or student loans. In return they received not only the direct benefits of the workshop but "Introduction to College Writing" T-shirts. However, the main benefit of the program was that the new TAs were able to teach, with a mentor in the room, "the equivalent of a half a quarter of normal teaching" (12) before taking over a classroom of their own. Bullock is justifiably enthusiastic about a program in which everyone is a winner:

> The new TAs start their first quarter far more self-assured and calm, with a much clearer understanding of the rhythm of teaching and their roles in the classroom than they had before. They also develop contacts and friendships with experienced teachers that last throughout their careers—and lead them to volunteer to return early the next fall to mentor the next year's group of new TAs. Most important, they are far more consistently successful in their classrooms than before, with higher student evaluations to show it. The effects on those [first-year] students—higher grade point averages and greater retention rates than those of students with virtually identical records who did not attend the workshop—are a bonus that has generated good publicity for the program within the university administration; and the money the workshop generates—about $12.00 per student, after the shirts, publication, and conference fees for doing the paperwork—gives the writing program a small pot of money to use for books, periodicals, and travel for graduate students who want to attend conferences (13).

The Ripple-Effect of Mentoring

Extending the Layers Outward

Sally Barr Ebest
University of Missouri–St. Louis

In the spring semester of 1998 I received a research grant from the University of Missouri–St. Louis that funded site visits to nine universities whose graduate composition/rhetoric programs excelled in the preparation of their students either to teach, to conduct research, or to administer a writing program. One of my site visits was the writing program at Texas Christian University because of its use of mentoring and service-learning to develop graduate students as teachers and Writing Program Administrators (WPAs). This was a three-layered, increasingly complex mentoring program: the faculty mentored new TAs, the WPA mentored her associate directors, and these directors designed a second-year composition course that taught TCU second-year students to mentor public school elementary students.

This mentoring program was a direct result of the English department's collaborative efforts to "re-invent itself." In her first year at TCU, then WPA Rebecca Howard developed a composition advisory committee comprised of all the rhetoric faculty, a literature faculty member, a graduate student, an adjunct, and a representative from the Writing Center. Together, they revamped first- and second-year composition and created a general template of policies, procedures, expectations, and requirements. Department chair Alan Shepard explained that the intent was to take the program in new directions while capitalizing on its strengths. One result of this process was a program that began on the TCU campus and extended into the Ft. Worth community.

Layer 1: Faculty Mentoring TAs

At TCU, English department TAs teach one course per semester, either first- or second-year composition courses or lower-division literature courses. During their first year, though, TAs always teach freshman composition, which focuses on analytic, academic writing. Throughout that semester, new TAs and adjuncts are partnered with mentors from among the regular faculty members, who receive one course release a year in compensation. The purpose of these mentoring groups is twofold: mentors provide a forum for advice and discussion, and they observe their mentees' teaching. Department chair Shepard felt that involving the faculty as mentors contributed to a sense that everyone shared a collective responsibility for their graduate students' pedagogical skills—not just teaching per se but also designing and evaluating assignments, selecting textbooks, and developing a viable curriculum.

Since the department was comprised of twenty full-time faculty and twenty TAs, the context was ideal for one-to-one relationships, which in turn meant that if a student needed a great deal of mentoring (such as weekly class visits), the mentor would have the time to do so. In addition to "official" mentoring, the small size of the department made it possible for additional layers of informal mentoring—e.g., discussing a successful class or seeking advice on grading a problematic paper—due to the proximity of TAs' offices to one another and to those of the faculty. All this interaction and support naturally boosted the TAs' morale and self-confidence. Although at the time of my site visit the program was only in its infancy, already the faculty were impressed with how much TAs could learn through this one-to-one relationship; consequently, there was strong support for the program's continuation.

The graduate students I spoke with also appreciated this relationship. One TA admitted she had never heard of writing pedagogy before beginning her coursework at TCU; however, as a result of the mentoring, she had become interested in teaching writing and had gained an understanding of composition pedagogy. Another said she had been informally mentored by two different faculty members. Because of the size of the department, such relationships were fairly easy to establish. In her case, these experiences had been very productive: she was given the opportunity to present papers at conferences and to publish, both of which impacted her writing process professionally. "Trying to do these things on your own, just as a graduate student coming in with a BA, it's like a mountain when you first view it," she said. "But when you have someone saying 'why don't you think about this?' writing becomes so much easier and less stressful." As a result, she tried to establish a mentoring relationship with her undergraduate students, and she intended to mentor her own graduate students when she began her professional career.

Layer 2: The WPA Mentoring Associate Directors

Throughout 1998–99, to help with the overhaul of the writing program, four experienced TAs worked half time as associate WPAs, two in the fall and two in the spring. The first two TAs were assigned administrative duties in the fall (in lieu of teaching) and taught in the spring, when the new associate directors began their duties. To ensure continuity, all four associate directors participated in WPA staff meetings throughout the year. WPA Howard viewed the position as an important element in the graduate students' professional development, providing them not only with credentials but also with hands-on experience regarding the decisions, resistance, delays, and compromises that must be made when developing and running a writing program. Because of this, Howard tried to devote a portion of each staff meeting to discussing the principles underlying writing program administration.

In the meeting I observed, five to ten percent of the time was devoted to writing program theory, with the rest of the time focused on more pragmatic issues. TA participation was only in its second year, as was the newly established curriculum; consequently, a good deal of the discussion centered on how to develop guidelines for the new procedures. Throughout this discussion I was struck by the fact that each of the associate directors had a voice equal to Howard's. Howard listened to all their suggestions and then synthesized them into a plan for action, with each person assigned a task.

Because of the climate of curricular change, these graduate students' duties and responsibilities had been considerably greater than the average associate WPA. During their two-year tenure, they had:

- worked on program assessment and designed an evaluation instrument
- observed the writing courses, each visiting four or five sections per semester
- participated in end-of-year assessment that served as a stepping stone to the development of a more integrated writing program
- developed (successful) arguments for the reduction of class sizes
- surveyed other writing programs to determine TAs' duties and remuneration, and surveyed TCU's TAs to ascertain their needs
- helped develop the TA education program
- researched professional development programs for adjunct faculty
- redesigned the freshman and sophomore composition courses
- wrote grants to fund faculty development and curricular change

Needless to say, these responsibilities taught the associate directors valuable lessons. The first one I spoke with told me he particularly valued participating in peer observations, for it helped broaden his perspectives on teaching and his understanding of pedagogical scholarship. Through these visits he became aware of the need for a single, driving vision to make a writing program coherent within the English department and relevant within the university. As a result, he planned to apply for administrative positions at smaller universities so he could balance his teaching, administrative duties, and scholarship. Another associate director, who came to the position with a considerable amount of teaching experience, said administrative work helped her unite pedagogical theory with practice and ignited her interest in administration. Like her fellow associate WPAs, she believed that writing program administration offered dynamic opportunities to accomplish change—if WPAs began with clear-cut goals. She would leave the program with insider knowledge about program development. This knowledge, coupled with her dissertation on the evolution of writing program administration, had already opened the door to a number of positions; however, her work at TCU had shown her what she wanted: to teach first and then become a WPA. She did not want immediate administrative responsibilities, nor did she want a position that lacked the possibility of administration. She wanted a position that married teaching and administration, theory and practice.

A third assistant said that her administrative experiences had taught her how to make connections between assignments and assessment, textbooks, and syllabi, so that her teaching had become more structured and organized. Because of her involvement in the process of curricular revision, she had learned how to coordinate large-scale changes by developing committees to aid in the process. In so doing, she had become aware of the university infrastructure and come to understand the necessity of background work, which she described as understanding the "rhetorical context necessary for change." Because her primary goal in attending TCU had been to learn about teaching on all levels, her (self-assigned) role in curricular change had been to observe first-year TAs' teaching, to develop a teacher's manual, and to write grants to help fund the changes. Participating in this process had been the most valuable element of her graduate career, for she had gained both political and pedagogical knowledge. "Administration," she said, "has so much to do with what goes on in the classroom that [becoming a WPA] is a major goal for me." Her advice to other TAs was to take advantage of similar opportunities, not only because administrative experience is necessary for a career in composition/rhetoric but also because the knowledge it engenders could prevent disastrous career choices. Working as an associate WPA, she said, was a very supportive way to learn about administration.

The fourth associate director initially came to TCU because she wanted to become more involved in education and to study how language works. While learning about rhetoric she grew interested in working as an associate WPA because she wanted to help people realize their vocation through education and community involvement. As she came to understand the role of the WPA she felt that in this position she could accomplish her goals. Working as an associate director had shown her that written communication could be used as an inroad to problem solving at the community level. Indeed, she felt that this experience was the only way a graduate student could have the opportunity to see how important critical writing skills—and writing program administration—could be to populations inside and outside the university. TAs and undergraduates need to move beyond the ivory tower of the university, she said, and become involved with the community in which they are living. The TAs in the English department at TCU could do so by teaching writing in a relevant context. Such a combination could help both the university and the community.

Layer 3: Undergraduates Mentoring Third-Graders

The central area of the curricular change at TCU was the redefinition of second-year composition into a genre course that emphasized collaborative writing. Entitled "Writing in Communities," its structure allowed TAs to decide which community their students would be writing in, choosing between an academic community or selecting a service-learning issue and writing for, with, and to that cohort. In conjunction with this course, TCU's associate directors of composition developed and incorporated their own nonprofit organization, Write to Succeed. This program was designed to connect Ft. Worth elementary students with TCU's second-year undergraduates through mentoring, writing, and exposing the children to different aspects of college life.

Each semester, the second-year writing courses involved in Write to Succeed focused on a different element of TCU life. During one recent semester, for example, the focus was on an exhibit at the modern art museum, and the goal was to produce different types of writing about it. Mentoring included personal letter writing between the college and elementary students and workshops on campus so that the younger students gained some exposure to a college writing workshop. This approach benefited both sides: the elementary students left the workshops with developed pieces of writing, and the college students had the experience of serving as writing consultants, which helped them internalize the skills they were learning and teaching.

These goals were evident in "Community Writing in Multiple Media," (Write to Succeed 1999) the syllabus designed by the fourth associate director. Laid out like a newsletter with graphics, a campus map, and boxed information, the four-page syllabus explained the twofold purpose of the course that semester: (a) to "establish and maintain working relationships with a wide range of people; [and] (b) collaborate with those people to achieve important goals." The writing assignments were to be done "with people within and beyond our writing classroom, representing a broad range of communities (including a modern art museum, a local elementary school class, and a virtual community of college writers)" (Write to Succeed 1999, 1). Students were required to develop a media literacy portfolio, a correspondence portfolio, a memoir about a significant place, a writing partners publication, and a public document (2). Each of these was aimed at a different audience and was worth twenty percent of the final grade; among them, the correspondence portfolio best illustrates the connection between service-learning and mentoring.

During the semester, the undergraduates were to write letters and emails to their classmates and to their third-grade writing partner, ultimately amassing approximately twenty to twenty-five pages of writing. Other assignments, such as the personal memoir, were to consider the third-graders as part of the reading audience and to appeal to their interests not only through language but also through the use of appropriate graphics. Such communication would help develop a relationship while also illustrating the interests of college students and the demands of university work; in the process, it might demystify higher education and make that goal interesting and attainable to these mostly inner-city children.

This project was the first of its kind on the TCU campus. Because of their commitment to service-learning pedagogy, the TAs serving as associate directors of the writing program had "invented it on their own." One of their goals was to experiment with it as much as possible through their positions as graduate instructors in order to strengthen the infrastructure for service-learning at TCU. Recognizing that they would not always be there to run the program, the TAs were collaborating with various organizations on writing a grant to further fund and develop it, in the hope that they would ultimately make a difference in the campus attitude and environment. Such cross-institutional and community outreach goals are rare. That's what makes TCU's program a model to be emulated.

Summary

The graduate composition/rhetoric program at TCU is a work in progress, but unlike some renovations, it is building on a solid foundation, for its placement rate among graduate students in composition/rhetoric is already almost one hundred percent. Since the site visit for this case study, a new WPA has been hired, the role (and number) of her administrative assistants has been revised, and the mentoring program has been reconfigured. Support remains for administrative preparation, but not at the expense of teaching and research skills. In the midst of these changes, the second-year composition course, "Community Writing in Multiple Media," remains a part of the undergraduate curriculum. Hopefully, it will continue to remain there, for its goals and practices provide TCU's graduate students with the opportunity to continue the ripple effect of mentoring.

Methods for Building Bridges

Margaret Tomlinson Rustick
California State University/Hayward

Until I met Bob Tremmel at the Conference on College Composition and Communication in March 2001, it had not occurred to me that my experience teaching a composition theory and methods course to a combined audience of prospective secondary and postsecondary teachers was unusual. However, as I heard a number of conference speakers talk about the need to improve communication across institutional boundaries, I was reminded of the decision several years ago to separate the course I was teaching into two different courses, one for future secondary teachers and one for those who had set their sights on higher education. At the time I objected to that change for reasons that were echoed at the 2001 conference: teachers at various levels need to speak to one another, they need to understand one another's instructional goals and methods, and they need to see one another as colleagues and resources committed to the common goal of improving student writing. To better understand some of the factors that may affect efforts to increase communication between secondary and university writing teachers, I offer the following personal account, which describes the fate of the methods course that I taught from 1990 to 1995.

I first learned of "Introduction to Composition Theory and Methods" when I enrolled in the course myself in 1982, a year after I had received my secondary teaching credential. When I did my preparation for the credential, no subject-specific methods courses were required. However, as a beginning high school English teacher, I quickly realized how little I knew about teaching composition. My search for better ways to teach writing eventually led to a master's degree in 1990. At that time, the professor who had been teaching the methods course left, and she recommended that I take over the class. When I interviewed for the job, the chair asked me how I would handle potential conflicts between the two different levels of teaching, secondary and postsecondary, as this had been an issue in the past. Given my experience as both a high school teacher and a TA,

I was able to respond intelligibly about intersections between the two, and I was hired to teach the class.

In the years since I earned my credential, the university had made the composition pedagogy course a requirement for all prospective secondary English teachers, and about half of my students were preservice or credentialed secondary teachers. Some of those practicing teachers had been in the classroom longer than I had, a situation that was a bit intimidating at first, but that became a tremendous asset when they could explain how their "real world" experience was reflected in the theories and methods we explored. The remaining students were usually prospective teaching assistants, and the range of student backgrounds was further complicated by the fact that the course could be taken for either graduate or undergraduate credit.

I continued to teach this combined methods course until 1994, a year after the department in which I taught separated from the literature folks and a new Department of Rhetoric and Writing Studies was established. There were only three full-time faculty in the new department, plus one whose appointment was split with linguistics. As a result, the pedagogy courses, which by then numbered four or five per term, were taught by adjuncts, including another instructor and me. Nor was the new department entirely free of its connections with the literature department. There was no masters degree in Rhetoric and Writing Studies, so we educated and employed TAs from literature and creative writing, as well as serving a continual flow of practicing and preservice secondary teachers.

Shortly after the Department of Rhetoric was formed, efforts began to strengthen its graduate program. An outside consultant was brought in, and another full-time faculty member was hired on a temporary contract, which became permanent the next year. During that process, students in the methods course were segregated according to their intended level of teaching, either secondary or postsecondary. The new faculty member was given the postsecondary section, whereas the two of us who had been teaching the course were assigned to the secondary sections, which felt in some way as if, as adjuncts, we weren't good enough to work with "serious" graduate students.

Before the pedagogy courses were separated, I argued against that move. One of the challenges in teaching a methods course is always keeping the conversation from devolving into a what-do-you-do-when discussion. For the secondary teachers, those questions often centered on things like behavior problems, parent complaints, legal requirements, and restrictive grading policies. On the other hand, many postsecondary people had a tendency to be a bit too engrossed in deep theory and to hold somewhat naïve ideas about how they would right the injustices of the repressive educational system. So long as both groups were together, they were able to balance one another's interests in positive ways. I was convinced that, in terms of the total educational picture, communication between the two levels was critical. Being together in the combined course, the students were able to focus on shared theories and methods for teaching composition. Regardless of their intended level of teaching, all the preservice teachers were novices together, equal in their lack of knowledge and their anxiety about what they were about to undertake, and both levels developed great respect for the experienced high school teachers who took the class. At the same time, the experienced teachers were energized by the opportunity to see their instruction through a new lens, through the eyes of prospective teachers who still believed anything was possible. Despite some inevitable frustrations, it was good to have all those teachers together for that one semester, and I'm still saddened by what was lost when they were separated.

The only justification I ever heard for that decision was that it guaranteed all TAs had the same training and it allowed them to better prepare for their upcoming teaching assignments at the university. However, that course was never described and offered as a pure TA preparation course. Furthermore, it was possible students in that class would never become TAs but would teach in community colleges or other four-year institutions. It was also quite possible that people like me, who started out in secondary education, would switch and take on that TA role. Thus, I have difficulty believing that the decision to offer separate sections of the pedagogy course was driven solely by a concern for the preparation of the TAs. If that was the reason, it still suggests a greater emphasis on TA preparation than on educating secondary teachers, for no one ever mentioned how the separation would positively affect them. Coming as it did, at a time when the department was trying to build a reputation, I am inclined to believe the decision to separate secondary and postsecondary teachers had more to do with the perceived need for a more *rigorous* graduate program than it did with equitable and effective teacher education.

As with most things in the teaching of writing, there are no simple answers. I realize the irony of my own history. As a secondary teacher in a combined methods course I was at first frustrated, and I came to understand and value composition studies only when I was later engaged in advanced coursework alongside other graduate students. I do believe, however, we are more likely to see the commonalties in our teaching and to understand and respect one another more if secondary and postsecondary teachers have opportunities to explore composition pedagogy together, and the methods course still strikes me as the ideal place for that interaction to occur.

References

Anson, Chris. 1998. "Stories for reflective teaching: Using cases in faculty development." In *Dilemmas in teaching: Cases for collaborative faculty reflection,* edited
by Chris Anson, Lesley Cafarelli, Carol Rutz, and Michelle Weis. Madison, WI:
Mendota.

———. 1994. "Portfolios for teachers: Writing our way to reflective practice." In
New directions in portfolio assessment, edited by Laurel Black, Donald Daiker,
Jeffrey Sommers and Gail Stygall. Portsmouth, NH: Heinemann.

———. 1989. "Introduction: Response to writing and the paradox of uncertainty."
In *Writing and response,* edited by Chris Anson. Urbana, IL: NCTE.

Anson, Chris, Joan Graham, David Jollife, Nancy Shapiro, and Carolyn Smith. 1993.
Scenarios for teaching writing: Contexts for discussion and reflective practice.
Urbana, IL: NCTE.

Anson, Chris, David Jolliffe, and Nancy Shapiro. 1995. "Stories to teach by: Using
narrative cases in TA and faculty development." *WPA: Writing Program Administration* 19: 25–38.

Applebee, Arthur. 1974. *Tradition and reform in the teaching of English: A history.*
Urbana, IL: NCTE.

Aronowitz, Stanley, and Henry Giroux. 1985. *Education under siege: The conserva-
tive, liberal and radical debate over schooling.* South Hadley, MA: Bergin &
Garvey.

Atwell, Nancie. 1998. *In the middle: New understandings about writing, reading, and
learning.* 2d ed. Portsmouth, NH: Boynton/Cook.

———. 1987a. "Building a dining room table: Dialogue journals about reading."
In *The journal book,* edited by Toby Fulwiler. Portsmouth, NH: Boynton/Cook,
Heinemann.

———. 1987b. *In the Middle: Writing, reading and learning with adolescents.*
Portsmouth, NH: Boynton/Cook.

Axelrod, Joseph. 1959. *Graduate study for future college teachers.* Washington, DC:
American Council on Education, 95. Quoted in Janet Marting, "A retrospective
on training teaching assistants," *WPA: Writing Program Administration* 11 (fall
1987): 39.

Ball, Arnetha. 1992. "Cultural preference and the expository writing of African-
American adolescents." *Written Communication* 9.4 (October): 501–32.

Bartholomae, David. 1994. "Writing with teachers: A conversation with Peter Elbow."
College Composition and Communication 46.1 (February): 62–71.

Bartholomae, David, and Tony Petroskey. 1999. *Ways of reading*. 5th ed. Boston/New York: Bedford/St. Martin's.

Bawarshi, Anis. 2000. "The genre function." *College English* 62.3 (January): 335–60.

Beach, Richard, and Margaret Finders. 1999. "Students as ethnographers: Guiding alternative research projects." *English Journal* 89.1 (September): 82–90.

Beach, Richard, and James Marshall. 1991. *Teaching literature in the secondary school*. Fort Worth: Harcourt Brace College Publishers.

Belanoff, Pat. 1994. "Portfolios and literacy: Why?" In *New directions in portfolio assessment,* edited by Laurel Johnson Black, Donald Daiker, Jeffrey Sommers, and Gail Stygall. Portsmouth, NH: Boynton/Cook, Heinemann.

Bennett, William. 1987. "Address to the 29th annual convention of the California Association of Teachers of English." Washington, DC: U.S. Department of Education.

Berkenkotter, Carol, and Thomas Huckin. 1995. *Genre knowledge in disciplinary communication: Cognition/culture/power*. Hillsdale, NJ: Erlbaum.

Berlin, James. 1996. "Social-epistemic rhetoric, ideology, and English studies." In *Rhetorics, poetics, and cultures: Refiguring college English studies*. Urbana, IL: NCTE.

———. 1987. *Rhetoric and reality: Writing instruction in American colleges, 1900–1985*. Carbondale and Edwardsville, IL: Southern Illinois University Press.

Bloom, Lynn, Donald Daiker, and Edward White. 1997. *Composition in the twenty-first century: Crisis & change*. Carbondale, IL: Southern Illinois University Press.

Bomer, Randy. 2000. "Writing to think critically: The seeds of social action." *English Journal: Trends and Issues in Secondary Education* 6.4 (May): 109–20.

Boreen, Jean, Mary Johnson, Donna Niday, and Joe Potts. 2000. *Mentoring beginning teachers: Guiding, reflecting, coaching*. York, ME: Stenhouse Publishers.

Bolin, Bill, Beth Burmester, Brenton Faber, and Peter Vandenburg, eds. 1995. *A forum on composition studies. Composition Studies* 23.2: entire issue.

Boose, Sara. 1999. "Will I 'Run loose'?" *Voices from the Middle* 6.3 (March): 18–22.

Britton, James. 1970. *Language and learning*. London: Penguin Books.

Brodkey, Linda. 1989. "On the subjects of race and class in the 'The Literacy Letter.'" *College English* 51.2 (February): 125–41.

Brookfield, Stephen. 1995. *Becoming a critically reflective teacher*. San Francisco: Jossey-Bass.

Brown, Stuart, Paul Meyer, and Theresa Enos. 1994. "Doctoral programs in rhetoric and composition." *Rhetoric Review* 12.2 (spring): 235–389.

Broz, William. 1996. "Growing reflective practitioners: Metaphor, symbol and ritual— knowledge for teacher change in a summer writing project." Ph.D. diss., University of Iowa.

Brueggemann, Brenda, Patricia Dun, Barbara Heifferon, and Johnson Cheu. 2001. "Becoming visible: Lessons in disability." *College Composition and Communication* 52.3 (February): 368–98.

Bruffee, Kenneth. 1985. "Introduction." In *A short course in writing.* 3d ed. Boston: Little, Brown.

Bruner, Jerome. 1986. *Actual minds, possible worlds.* Cambridge, MA: Harvard University Press.

Bullock, Richard. 1999. "In pursuit of competence: Preparing new graduate teaching assistants of the classroom." In *Administrative problem-solving for writing programs and writing centers: Scenarios in effective program management,* edited by Linda Meyers-Breslin. Urbana, IL: NCTE.

Burniske, R. W. 1994. "Creating dialogue: Teacher response to journal writing." *English Journal* 83.4 (April): 84–87.

Camp, Roberta, and Denis Levine. 1991. "Portfolios evolving: Background and variation in sixth- through twelfth-grade classrooms." In *Portfolios: Process and product,* edited by Pat Belanoff and Marcia Dickson. Portsmouth, NH: Boynton/Cook, Heinemann.

Calkins, Lucy. 1994. *The art of teaching writing.* Portsmouth, NH: Heinemann.

Carver, Ronald, and Robert Leibert. 1995. "The effect of reading library books at different levels of difficulty upon gain in reading ability." *Reading Research Quarterly* 30: 26–48.

Cherry, Charles. 1973. "One approach to a course in the methods of teaching composition." *English Education* 4: 133–39.

Clarke, Shirley (producer). 1967. *A lover's quarrel with the world.* (Robert Frost documentary film). Pyramid, distributor.

Cleary, Linda Miller. 1991. *From the other side of the desk: Students speak out about writing.* Portsmouth, NH: Heinemann.

Coles, William. 1978. *The plural I.* New York: Holt.

———. 1974. *Teaching composing.* Rochelle Park, NJ: Hayden.

Coles, William, and James Vopat. 1985. *What makes writing good: A multiperspective.* Lexington, MA: Heath.

Commission on Composition, National Council of Teachers of English. 1985. *Teaching composition: A position statement.* Urbana, IL: NCTE.

Comprone, Joseph. 1974. "Preparing the new composition teacher." *College Composition and Communication* 25: 49–51.

Cone, Joan Kernan. 1992. "Untracking advanced placement English: Creating opportunity is not enough." *Phi Delta Kappan* 73.9 (May): 712.

Connors, Robert. 1991. "Rhetoric in the modern university: The creation of an underclass." In *The politics of writing instruction: Postsecondary,* edited by Richard Bullock and John Trimbur. Portsmouth, NH: Boynton/Cook, Heinemann.

———. 1986. "Textbooks and the evolution of the discipline." *College Composition and Communication* 37: 178–94.

Connors, Robert, and Cheryl Glenn. 1992. "Responding to and evaluating student essays." In *The St. Martin's Guide to teaching writing,* 2d ed. New York: St. Martin's.

Connors, Robert, and Andrea Lunsford. 1993. "Teachers' rhetorical comments on student papers." *College Composition and Communication* 44.2 (May): 200–233.

176   References

Crowley, Sharon. 1998a. *Composition in the university: Historical and polemical essays.* Pittsburgh: University of Pittsburgh Press.

———. 1998b. "The emergence of process pedagogy." In *Composition in the university: Historical and polemical essays.* Pittsburgh, PA: University of Pittsburgh Press.

Csikszentmihalyi, Mihaly. 1990. *Flow: The psychology of optimal experience.* New York: Harper & Row.

Cuban, Larry. 1993. *How teachers taught: Constancy and change in American classrooms, 1880–1990.* 2d ed. New York: Teachers College Press.

Daigon, Arthur. 1982. "Toward writing right." *Phi Delta Kappan* 64.4 (December): 242–46.

Daiker, Donald. 1989. "Learning to praise." In *Writing and response: Theory, practice, and research,* edited by Chris Anson. Urbana, IL: NCTE.

Daniels, Harvey. 1994. *Literature circles: Voice and choice in the student-centered classroom.* York, ME: Stenhouse Publishers.

Davis, Robert, and Mark Shadl. 2000. "'Building a mystery': Alternative research writing and the academic act of seeking." *College Composition and Communication* 51.3: 417–46.

Delpit, Lisa. 1988. "The silenced dialogue: Power and pedagogy in educating other people's children." *Harvard Educational Review* 58.3 (August): 290–98.

———. 1995. *Other people's children: Cultural conflict in the classroom.* New York: The New Press.

DeStigter, Todd. 2001. "Structured exclusion." In *Reflections of a citizen teacher: Literacy, democracy, and the forgotten students of Addison High.* Urbana, IL: NCTE.

Dowst, Kenneth. 1980. "The epistemic approach: Writing, knowing, and learning." In *Eight approaches to teaching composition,* edited by Timothy Donovan and Ben McClelland. Urbana, IL: NCTE.

Dunn, Patricia. 1995. *Learning re-abled: The learning disability controversy and composition studies.* Portsmouth, NH: Boynton/Cook, Heinemann.

Dunning, Stephen, and William Stafford, eds., 1992. *Getting the knack: 20 poetry writing exercises.* Urbana, IL: NCTE.

Ebest, Sally Barr. 2002. "Mentoring: Past, present, and future." In *Preparing college teachers of writing: Histories, theories, programs, and practices*, edited by Sarah Liggett and Betty Pytlik. New York: Oxford University Press.

Elbow, Peter. 1995. "Being a writer vs. being an academic: A conflict in goals." *College Composition and Communication* 46.1 (February): 72–83.

———. 1993. "Ranking, evaluating, and linking: Sorting out three forms of judgment." In *The Allyn and Bacon sourcebook for college writing teachers (second edition),* edited by James McDonald (Boston: Allyn and Bacon). Originally published in *College English* 55.2 (February 1993): 187–206.

———. 1987. "Closing my eyes as I speak: An argument for ignoring audience." *College English* 49 (January): 50–69.

——— 1983. Embracing contraries in the teaching process. *College English* 45 (April): 327–39.

ing process.*
New York: Oxford University Press.

———. 1973. *Writing Without Teachers.* 2d ed. New York: Oxford University Press.

Elliott, Peggy. 1978. A new way of teaching teachers to teach writing. *Teacher Educator* 14 (fall): 35–36.

Faigley, Lester. 1986. "Competing theories of process: A critique and a proposal." *College English* 48 (October): 527–42.

Finders, Margaret. 1997. *Just girls: Hidden literacies and life in junior high.* New York: Teachers College Press.

Finders, Margaret, and Shirley Rose. 1999. "'If I were the teacher': Situated performances as pedagogical tools for teacher preparation." *English Education* 31.3 (April): 205–22.

Fletcher, Ralph. 1996. *Breathing in, breathing out: Keeping a writer's notebook.* Portsmouth, NH: Heinemann.

———. 1993. *What a writer needs.* Portsmouth, NH: Heinemann.

Flower, Linda, and John Hayes. 1980. "A cognitive process theory of writing." *College Composition and Communication* 31 (February): 21–22.

Fox, Dana. 1993. *Reinventing a composition course in secondary English education.* ERIC Document 366 000. Microfiche.

Freedman, Aviva, and Ian Pringle. 1984. "Why students can't write arguments." *English in Education* 18: 73–84.

Freire, Paulo. 1973. *The education for critical consciousness.* New York: Seabury Press.

Fullan, Michael. 1991. *The new meaning of educational change.* New York: Teachers College Press.

Gebhardt, Richard. 1981. "Balancing theory with practice in the training of writing teachers." In *The writing teacher's sourcebook*, edited by Gary Tate and Edward P. J. Corbett (New York: Oxford University Press). Originally published in *College Composition and Communication* 28 (1977): 134–40.

Gere, Ann Ruggles, Colleen Fairbanks, Alan Howes, Laura Roop, and David Schaafsma. 1992. *Language and reflection: An integrated approach to teaching English.* New York: Macmillan.

Gibson, Walker. 1974. *Seeing and writing: Fifteen exercises in composing experience.* 2d ed. New York: McKay.

Giltrow, Janet. 1994. "Genre and the pragmatic concept of background knowledge." In *Genre knowledge and the new rhetoric,* edited by Aviva Freedman and Peter Medway. London: Taylor and Francis.

Graff, Harvey. 1995. *The labyrinths of literacy: Reflections on literacy past & present.* Pittsburgh: University of Pittsburgh Press.

Graham, Peg, Sally Hudson-Ross, Chandra Adkins, Patti McWhorter, and Jennifer Stewart, eds. 1999. *Teacher/mentor: A dialogue for collaborative learning.* New York: Teachers College Press and Urbana, IL: NCTE.

Graham, Peg, Sally Hudson-Ross, and Patti McWhorter. 1997. "Building nets: Evolution of a collaborative inquiry community within a high school English teacher education program." *English Education* 29: 91–129.

Graves, Donald. 1979. "What children show us about revision." *Language Arts* 56.3 (March): 312–19.

Graves, Donald, and Bonnie Sunstein, eds. 1992. *Portfolio portraits.* Portsmouth, NH: Heinemann.

Grierson, Sirpa. 1999. "Circling through text: Teaching research through multigenre writing." *English Journal* 89.1 (September): 51–55.

Grossman, Pamela. 1990. *The making of a teacher: Teacher knowledge & teacher education.* New York: Teachers College Press.

Gundlach, Robert. 1982. "Children as writers: The beginnings of learning to write." In *What writers know,* edited by Martin Nystrand. New York: Academic Press.

Hairston, Maxine. 1982. "The winds of change: Thomas Kuhn and the revolution in the teaching of writing." *College Composition and Communication* 33: (February) 76–88.

———. 1974. "Training teaching assistants in English." *College Composition and Communication* 25: 52–55.

Haring-Smith, Tori. 1985. "The importance of theory in the training of teaching assistants." *ADE Bulletin* 82 (winter): 33–39.

Harris, Joseph. 2000. "Meet the new boss, same as the old boss: Class consciousness in composition." *College Composition and Communication* 52: 43–68.

———. 1997. *A teaching subject: Composition since 1966.* Upper Saddle River, NJ: Prentice Hall.

———. 1989. "The idea of community in the study of writing." *College Composition and Communication* 40.1 (February): 11–22.

Hartwell, Patrick. 1985. "Grammar, grammars, and the teaching of grammar." *College English* 47.2 (February): 105–27.

Heard, Georgia. 1995. *Writing towards home.* Portsmouth, NH: Heinemann.

Hillocks, George Jr. 1999. *Ways of thinking, ways of teaching.* New York: Teachers College Press.

———. 1986. "Grammar and the manipulation of syntax." In *Research on written composition.* Urbana, IL: NCTE

Hirsch, E. D. Jr. 1987. *Cultural literacy: What every American needs to know.* Boston: Houghton Mifflin Co.

———. 1977. *The philosophy of composition.* Chicago: University of Chicago Press.

Hunt, Russel. 1987. "Could you put in lots of holes? Modes of response to writing." *Language Arts* 64: 299–332.

Hymes, Dell. 1980. *Language in education.* Washington, DC: Center for Applied Linguistics.

Irby, Janet. 1993. "Empowering the disempowered: Publishing student voices." *English Journal* 82.7 (November): 50–54.

Jacobs, Suzanne. 1985. "The development of children's writing." *Written Communication* 2: 414–33.

Jamieson, Sandra. 1997. "Composition readers and the construction of identity." In *Writing in multicultural settings,* edited by Johnnella Butler, Juan Guerra, and Carol Severino. New York: MLA.

Jenseth, Richard, and Edward Lotto. 1996. *Constructing nature: Readings from the American experience.* Upper Saddle River, NJ: Prentice Hall.

Johnson, Nancy, and Jean Mandler. 1980. "A tale of two structures: Underlying and surface forms in stories." *Poetics* 9: 51–86.

John-Steiner, Vera. 1997. *Notebooks of the mind.* Rev. ed. New York: Oxford University Press.

Kansas State University Undergraduate Catalog 1998–2000.

Karolides, Nicholas. 2000. *Reader response in secondary and college classrooms.* Mahwah, NJ: Erlbaum.

Kennedy, Mary. 1998. *Learning to teach writing: Does teacher education make a difference?* New York: Teachers College.

Kinneavy, James. 1971. *A theory of discourse.* New York: Norton.

Kirby, Dan, Tom Liner, and Ruth Vinz. 1988. *Inside out: Developmental strategies for teaching writing.* Portsmouth, NH: Heinemann.

Klaus, Carl. 1999. Interviewed by Robert Tremmel and William Broz, tape recording. Iowa City, IA, 3 December.

Knoblauch, C.H., and Lil Brannon. 1984. *Rhetorical traditions and the teaching of writing.* Upper Montclair, NJ: Boynton Cook.

Kolln, Martha. 1996. *Rhetorical grammar: Grammatical choices, rhetorical effects.* 2d ed. Boston: Allyn and Bacon.

Krupa, Gene. 1982. *Situational writing.* Belmont, CA: Wadsworth.

Kutz, Eleanor. 1986. "Between students' language and academic discourse: Interlanguage as middle ground." *College English* 48.4 (April): 385–96.

Labov, William. 1972. *Language in the inner city: Studies in the black English vernacular.* Philadelphia: University of Pennsylvania Press.

Lamott, Anne. 1994. *Bird by bird.* New York: Random House.

Lang, Bob. 1982. "ERIC/RCS report. Preparing English teachers in writing: New waves in the Tempest." *English Education* 14: 103–8.

———. 1979. "ERIC/RCS report. Writing instruction for writing teachers." *English Education* 11: 121–26.

Larson, Richard. 1969. "A special course in advanced composition for prospective teachers." *Journal of Teacher Education* 20: 168–74.

Latterell, Catherine. 1996. "Training the workforce: An overview of GTA education curricula." *WPA: Writing Program Administration* 19.3 (spring): 7–23.

Leverenz, Carrie Shively, and Amy Goodburn. 1998. "Professionalizing TA training: Commitment to teaching or rhetorical response to market crisis." *WPA: Writing Program Administration* 22 (fall/winter): 9–32.

Lindemann, Erika. 1995. *A rhetoric for writing teachers.* 3d ed. New York: Oxford University Press.

Lloyd-Jones, Richard. 2000. Interviewed by Robert Tremmel and William Broz, tape recording. Iowa City, IA, 11 January.

Loban, Walter. 1976. *Language development: Kindergarten through age twelve.* Urbana, IL: NCTE.

Long, Elizabeth. 1992. "Textual interpretation as collective action." In *The ethnography of reading,* edited by Jonathan Boyarin. Berkeley, CA: University of California Press.

Lyons, Bill. 1981. "The PQP method of responding to writing." *English Journal* 70.3: 42–43.

Martin, Cleo. 1988. "Responding to student writing." In *Ways of knowing: Research and practice in the teaching of writing,* edited by James Davis and James Marshall. Iowa City, IA: Iowa Council of Teachers of English.

Marting, Janet. 1987. "A retrospective on training teaching assistants." *Writing Program Administration* 11 (fall): 35–44.

McMackin, Mary, and Judith Boccia. 1998. "Gone but not forgotten: University-based support for beginning teachers." In *Great beginnings: Reflections and advice for new English language arts teachers and the people who mentor them,* edited by Ira Hayes. Urbana, IL: NCTE.

Meyer, Jim. 1999. "'It's a lot of hectic in middle school': Student-teaching in an urban classroom." *English Journal* 88.5 (May): 45–51.

Milanés, Cecilia Rodríguez. 1998. "Color and Class." In *Coming to class: Pedagogy and the social class of teachers,* edited by Alan Shepard, John McMillan, and Gary Tate. Portsmouth, NH: Boynton/Cook, Heinemann.

Miller, Carolyn. 1984. "Genre as social action." *Quarterly Journal of Speech* 70: 151–67.

Miller, Richard. 1998. *As if learning mattered: Reforming higher education.* Ithaca, NY: Cornell University Press.

———. 1994. "Fault lines in the contact zone." *College English* 56.4 (April): 389–408.

Miller, Thomas. 1997. "The expansion of the reading public, the standardization of educated taste and usage, and the essay as blurred genre." In *The formation of college English.* Pittsburgh, PA: University of Pittsburgh Press.

Mirtz, Ruth. 1995. "LAE 5370: Teaching English in college." *Composition Studies* 23 (2): 20–26.

Moffett, James. 1968. *Teaching the universe of discourse.* Boston: Houghton Mifflin.

———. 1983. *Teaching the universe of discourse.* Portsmouth, NH: Boynton/Cook.

Murphy, Michael. 2000. "New faculty for a new university: Toward a full-time teaching intensive faculty track in composition." *College Composition and Communication* 52: 14–42.

Murray, Donald. 1995. *The craft of revision,* 2d ed. Fort Worth, TX: Harcourt Brace College Publishers.

———1991. *The craft of revision.* Fort Worth, TX: Harcourt Brace College Publishers.

————. 1990. "Write before writing." In *To compose: Teaching writing in high school and college,* 2d ed., edited by T. Newkirk (Portsmouth, NH: Heinemann). Originally published in *College Composition and Communication* 29.4 (December 1978): 375–81.

Myers, Greg. 1986. "Reality, consensus, and reform in the rhetoric of composition teaching." *College English* 48.2 (February): 154–73.

Nemanich, Donald. 1974. "Preparing the composition teacher." *College Composition and Communication* 25: 46–48.

Newkirk, Thomas., ed. 1990. *To compose: Teaching writing in high school and college.* 2d ed. Portsmouth, NH: Heinemann.

————. 1989. *More than stories: The range of children's writing.* Portsmouth, NH: Heinemann.

Newkirk, Thomas, and Nancie Atwell. 1985. "The competence of young writers." In *Perspectives on research and scholarship in composition,* edited by Ben McClellend and Timothy Donovan. New York: MLA.

North, Stephen. 2000. *Refiguring the Ph.D. in English studies: Writing, doctoral education, and the fusion based curriculum.* Urbana, IL: NCTE.

Ojala, William. 1970. "The English methods course: One course or three?" *English Education* 2: 31–34.

Ondaatje, Michael. 1996. *The collected works of Billy the Kid.* New York: Vintage Books, 1970. Reprint, Toronto: House of Anansi Press.

Paul, Richard. 1987. "Dialogic thinking: Critical thought essential to the acquisition of rational knowledge and passions." In *Teaching thinking skills: Theory and practice,* edited by J. B. Baron and R. J. Sternberg. New York: Freeman.

Perl, Sondra. 1980. "Understanding composing." *College Composition and Communication* 31 (December): 363–69.

Peterson, Carole, and Allyssa McCabe. 1983. Developmental psycholinguistics: *Three ways of looking at a child's narrative.* New York: Plenum.

Probst, Robert. 1989. "Transactional theory and response to student writing." In *Writing and response: Theory, practice, and research,* edited by Chris Anson. Urbana, IL: NCTE.

Pytlik, Betty. 1993. *Teaching the teacher of writing: Whence and whither?* ERIC Document 355 542. Microfiche.

————. 1992. *A short history of graduate preparation of writing teachers.* ERIC Document 355 546. Microfiche.

————. 1991. "Teaching the teacher of composition: Evolving theories." *The Writing Instructor* (fall): 36–50.

Ravitch, Diane, and Chester Finn Jr. 1988. *What do our 17-year-olds know? A report on the first National Assessment of History and Literature.* New York: Harper and Row.

Raymond, James. 1996. *English as a discipline: Is there a plot in this play?* Tuscaloosa, AL: University of Alabama Press.

Recchio, Thomas. 1995. "English 300: Theory and teaching of writing." *Composition Studies* 23.2: 10–15.

Romano, Tom. 2000. *Blending genre, altering style: Writing multigenre papers.* Portsmouth, NH: Boynton/Cook.

———. 1995a. "The multigenre research paper: Melding fact, interpretation, and imagination." In *Writing with passion: Life stories, multiple genres.* Portsmouth, NH: Boynton/Cook, Heinemann.

———. 1995b. *Writing with passion: Life stories, multiple genres.* Portsmouth, NH: Boynton/Cook, Heinemann.

———. 1987a. *Clearing the way: Working with teenage writers.* Portsmouth, NH: Heinemann.

———. 1987b. "Literary warnings." In *Clearing the way: Working with teenage writers.* Portsmouth, NH: Heinemann.

———. 1987c. "Writing process in one high-school classroom," In *Clearing the way: Working with teenage writers.* Portsmouth, NH: Heinemann.

Ronald, Kate, Joy Ritchie, and Robert Brooke. 1995. "English 957: Composition theory and practice." *Composition Studies* 23 (2): 59–67.

Rose, Shirley, and Margaret Finders. 1998. "Learning from experience: Using situated performanaces in writing teacher development." *WPA: Writing Program Administration* 22.1–2 (fall/winter): 33–52.

Rumelhart, David. 1975. "Notes on a schema for stories." In *Representation and understanding studies in cognitive science,* edited by D. G. Bobrow and A. Collins. New York: Academic Press.

Sale, Roger. 1970. *On writing.* New York: Random.

Sandy, Kirsti. 1999. "Learning by co-teaching: Mentors and apprentices in an intensive introductory writing class." Ph.D. diss., Illinois State University. Abstract in *Dissertation Abstracts International* 61:01A (1999).

Scholes, Robert. 1998. *The rise and fall of English.* New Haven, NJ: Yale University Press.

Schon, Donald. 1987. *Educating the reflective practitioner.* San Francisco: Jossey-Bass.

———. 1983. *The reflective practitioner: How professionals think in action.* New York: Basic Books.

Schutz, Alfred, George Walsh, and Fredrick Lehnert. 1967. *The Phenomenology of the social world.* Evanston, IL: Northwestern University Press.

Scott, Fred Newton. 1908. "The teacher and his training." In *The teaching of English in the elementary and secondary school,* authored by George Carpenter, Franklin Baker, and Fred Newton Scott. New York: Longman's Green, and Co.

Seattle Public Schools. 2000 Reports. Garfield High School. Rainier Beach High School. Roosevelt High School.

Seidman, Irving. 1998. *Interviewing as qualitative research.* New York: Teachers College Press.

Shaughnessy, Mina. 1994. "Some new approaches toward teaching." *Journal of Basic Writing* 13 (spring): 103–16.

Shrofel, Salina. 1991. "Developing writing teachers." *English Education* 23: 160–77.

Slevin, James, and Art Young. 1995. *Critical theory and the teaching of literature: Politics, curriculum, pedagogy.* Urbana, IL: NCTE.

Smagorinsky, Peter, and Melissa Whiting. 1995. *How English teachers get taught: Methods of teaching the methods class.* Urbana, IL: NCTE.

Small, R. C. Jr., and the NCTE Standing Committee on Teacher Preparation and Certification. 1996. *Guidelines for the preparation of teachers of English language arts.* Urbana, IL: NCTE.

Smith, Frank. 1994. "Reading, writing, and thinking." In *Understanding reading.* 5th ed. Hillsdale, NJ: Erlbaum. 167–82.

Smith, William. 1984. "Using a college writing workshop in training future English teachers." *English Education* 16: 76–82.

Sowers, Susan. 1979. "A six-year-old's writing process: The first half of first grade." *Language Arts* 56: 829–35.

Spandel, Vicki, and Richard Stiggins. 1997. *Creating writers: Linking writing assessment and instruction.* New York: Longman.

Spellmeyer, Kurt. 1993. "Being philosophical about composition: Hermeneutics and the teaching of writing". In *Into the Field: Sites of composition studies,* edited by Ann Ruggles Gere. NewYork: MLA.

Stafford, William. 1986. *You must revise your life.* Ann Arbor, MI: The University of Michigan Press.

Stewart, Donald. 1985. "Fred Newton Scott." In *Traditions of Inquiry,* edited by John Brereton. New York: Oxford University Press.

———. 1982. "Two models and the Harvardization of English departments." In *The rhetorical tradition and the teaching of writing,* edited by James Murphy. New York: MLA.

Stotsky, Sandra. 1995. "The uses and limitations of personal or personalized writing in writing theory, research, and instruction." *Reading Research Quarterly* 30: 758–76.

Stygall, Gail. 1998. "Women and language in the collaborative classroom." In *Feminism and composition: In other words.* New York: MLA.

———. 1994. "Resisting privilege: Basic writers and Foucault's author function." *College Composition and Communication* 45.3 (October): 320–41.

Sudol, David, and Peg Sudol. 1995. "Yet another story: Writers' workshop revisited," *Language Arts* 72 (March): 171–87.

———. 1991. "Another Story: Putting Graves, Calkins, and Atwell into practice and perspective." *Language Arts* 68 (April): 292–300.

Sullivan, Patricia. 1991. "Writing in the graduate curriculum: Literary criticism as composition." *Journal of Advanced Composition* 11.2 (fall): 283–99.

Taylor, Denny, and Catherine Dorsey-Gaines. 1988. *Growing up literate: Learning from inner-city families.* Portsmouth, NH: Heinemann.

Taylor, Marcy. 1998. "Telling tales (in and out) of school: Ethnographies of schooling and the preparation of English teachers." *English Education* 30: 101–20.

Tobin, Lad. 1993. *Writing relationships: What really happens in the composition class*. Portsmouth, NH: Boynton/Cook.

Tremmel, Robert. 2000. "Still loading pig-iron after all these years: English education in the global contact zone." *English Education* 32: 194–225.

Vinz, Ruth. 1996. *Composing a teaching life*. Portsmouth, NH: Boynton/Cook, Heinemann.

Vopat, James. 1989. "The politics of advanced placement English." In *Advanced placement English: Theory, politics, and pedagogy,* edited by Gary Olson, Elizabeth Metzger, and Evelyn Ashton-Jones. Portsmouth, NH: Boynton/Cook, Heinemann.

Vygotsky, Lev. 1986. *Thought and language*. Cambridge: MIT Press.

Weiser, Irwin. Forthcoming. "When teaching assistants teach teaching assistants to teach: An historical view of a teacher preparation program." In *Preparing college teachers of writing: Histories, theories, programs, and practices,* edited by Sarah Liggett and Betty Pytlik. New York: Oxford University Press.

Wells, Susan. 1996. "Giving an ordered history: Narrative in the discourse of the classroom." In *Sweet reason: Rhetoric and the discourse of modernity*. Chicago: University Chicago Press.

Wertsch, James. 1993. *Voices of the mind: A sociocultural approach to mediated action*. Cambridge: Harvard University Press.

———. 1992. "The voice of rationality." In *Vygotsky and education: Instructional implications and applications of socio-historical psychology,* edited by Luis Moll. New York: University of Cambridge Press.

Wilbers, Stephen. 1980. *The Iowa Writers Workshop: Origins, emergence, and growth*. Iowa City: University of Iowa Press.

Wiley, Mark. 2000. "Teaching writing, professing comp: A review essay." *Journal of Teaching Writing* 16.2: 333–52.

Wilhoit, Stephen. 2000. "Re-defining graduate teacher training: Preparing TAs as classroom instructors." Paper presented at the Conference on College Composition and Communication. Minneapolis, MN. 13 April.

Wolcott, Willa, with Sue Legg. 1998. *An overview of writing assessment: Theory, research, and practice*. Urbana, IL: NCTE.

Wollam, Jean. 1981. *Current trends: Writing methods courses for prospective English teachers*. ERIC Document 240 611. Microfiche.

Write to Succeed. 1999. *Community writing in multiple media: Syllabus for intermediate composition, English* 2803/046 (spring). Texas Christian University, Ft. Worth, TX.